Brakhage's Childhood

Brakhage's Childhood

by JANE (BRAKHAGE) WODENING

Introduction by P. ADAMS SITNEY
Afterword by TONY PIPOLO

GRANARY BOOKS • NEW YORK CITY 2015

ISBN 9781887123839

Printed in the United States of America
Book and cover design by Diane Bertolo
of Lotus + Pixel
Photograph of Jane (Brakhage) Wodening
by Steve Clay

Granary Books, Inc.
168 Mercer St. Suite 2
New York, NY 10012
www.granarybooks.com

Distributed to the trade by
D.A.P./Distributed Art Publishers
155 Avenue of the Americas, Second Floor
New York, NY 10013-1507
Orders (800) 338-BOOK
Tel. (212) 627-1999 Fax (212) 627-9484
www.artbook.com

Also available from
Small Press Distribution
1341 Seventh Street
Berkeley, CA 94710
Orders (800) 869-7553
www.spdbooks.org

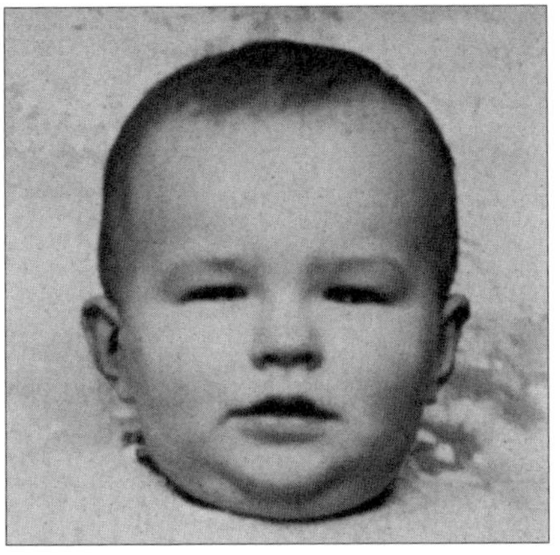

FOR PRECOCIOUS KIDS EVERYWHERE

First they ignore you,
then they laugh at you,
then they fight you,
then you win.
— Mahatma Gandhi

Contents

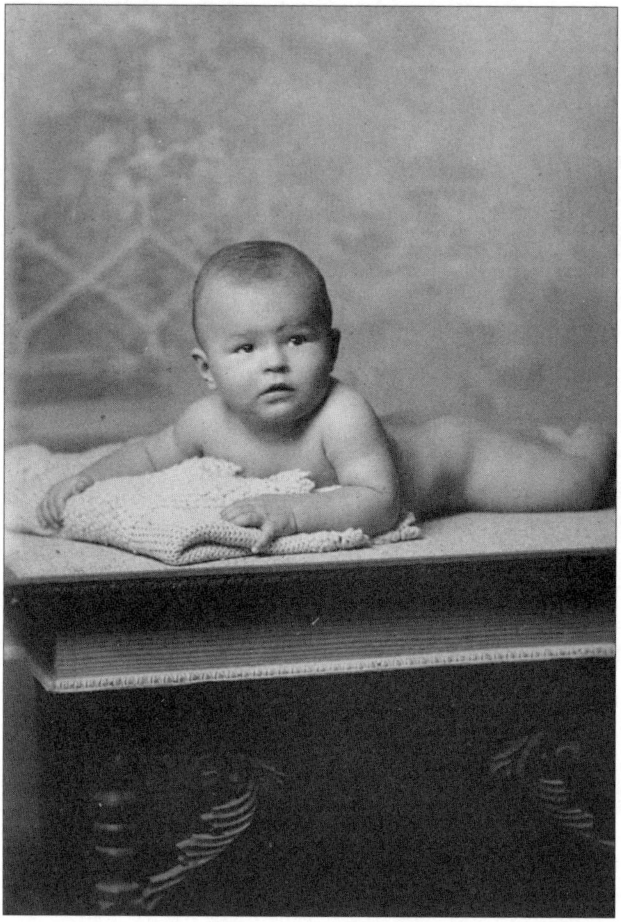

Introduction

BY P. ADAMS SITNEY

NOT ONLY WAS STAN BRAKHAGE an astonishingly original and prolific filmmaker, he was a charismatic raconteur. I was enchanted by his talk even before I fell in love with his films. We met in a luncheonette near the Chelsea Hotel in 1961. I was taking advantage of one of his rare visits to New York to try to set up a screening of his films for my film society in New Haven. At seventeen I had never heard an artist speak the way he did, with such intensity and with so many utterly unfamiliar slants on things I thought I knew. He went on for several hours and I was hooked. Over the next two years I became one of his most ardent disciples, reading his favorite poets, arranging lecture engagements for him, writing on his films, even lecturing myself on them. He sent me everything he wrote and I published what I could; first in my mimeographed journal, *Filmwise*, later in Jonas Mekas's *Film Culture*.

For the small band of disciples, his wife, Jane Collom Brakhage (now Wodening), was a mythic figure. She was so strikingly beautiful that forty years later the celebrated Princeton gynecologist, Dr. David Rose, who delivered her first child at the start of his career, confessed to me that he had never had a more gorgeous patient. The images Stan took of her in his films of the early 1960s haunted the erotic imaginations of our adolescences much as he would later claim that the poetry Kenneth Rexroth wrote of his wives had overwhelmed his.

He told us stories of Jane's magical rapport with animals, her brilliant insights into literature and cinema; he repeated her adages so often we knew them by heart. Brakhage was a tireless repeater. After a few failed attempts to get his talk on tape for a publishable interview, I tried asking him to tell me about Jane's influence and how she worked with him. That was it! He was off and talking for a couple of hours. We both knew we had recorded something remarkable that afternoon. When I transcribed it, we decided immediately it should be the introduction to his first book of film theory, *Metaphors on Vision,* which he had invited me to edit.

So, I first met Jane herself in 1963 when I hitchhiked to Colorado to finish the editing task. That was when I first glimpsed Brakhage as a bully. For about two weeks I stayed in the house in Denver — a suburban dwelling with a theater in the basement — where they were living gratis with their three children in sometimes cheerful poverty. I was so young and innocent of the ways of marriage that I did not perceive the dark side of Jane's total devotion to the Master Artist nor how Stan engineered and fostered that devotion.

That must have been when I first read a manuscript of Jane's writing. "The Birth Film" was a charming and exuberant account of Myrrena's birth and the making of *Window Water Baby Moving*. It was written in the style of Stan's favorite author, Gertrude Stein. I included it in *Film Culture 29* and reprinted it in *The Film Culture Reader*. I'd like to think I was the first to publish her because I hope to plead it as one of my few good works when I stand before the Throne of St. Peter.

My friendship with Stan lasted through most of the Sixties. When his bullying and rages became unbearable, I told him I would never see him again. Perhaps it was because I kept to that and never allowed myself to be vulnerable to his charm and violence, that I was able to continue to see and write enthusiastically about his films for the thirty-five years that remained of his life. The cost of breaking with Brakhage was that I lost contact with Jane and with his children whom I liked as well. I often felt anxious for them as I saw them growing up in his films, for one of the most troubling facets of Brakhage's obsessive discourse was his claim to superior parenting and his attacks on the way so many others that he knew were raising children.

From the time that our relations ended until the early 1980s he made some of his greatest and most mysterious films in autobiographical series: *Scenes from Under Childhood, Sincerity,* and *Duplicity*. Those and a number of individual films were to be included in what he was calling *The Book of the Film* (one of several titles hinting at his self-identification as the Johann Sebastian Bach of the cinema). Later he used that title for his more abstract works and included the autobiographies in *The Book of the Family*. It ends with *Tortured Dust,* a painful evocation of his anxiety and even sexual jealousy of his two teenage sons. Initially, the autobiographical project began with the fiction of a dual focus, on his childhood and Jane's. But as that waned and the film became progressively darker and more solipsistic, Jane took up writing again, inspired this time by Stein's *The Autobiography of Alice B. Toklas.* She would write *The Autobiography of Stan Brakhage.* Yet unlike her model, her book was not a disguised account of herself. It would end long before the subject met her.

As she produced chapters of the book, she circulated them among a few friends. That was how my late wife, Marjorie Keller, read it and began to publish chapters serially in her short-lived journal, *Motion Picture.* During the time that those chapters were appearing, Brakhage started to talk publicly and even showed a film about his adulteries (first called *Love Sacrifice,* later *Confession*). The termination of the marriage that the filmmaker had made a cornerstone of his public myth was protracted but inevitable.

In 2011 the film department of the University of Colorado at Boulder invited me to give a summer course. I looked up Jane. It was a joyous reunion but she was still so traumatized by her divorce and the accumulation of decades of strenuous efforts to sustain the ideal of devotion Stan required, that she did not want to talk of him. *The Autobiography of Stan Brakhage* was a dead issue. He was and had always been utterly untrustworthy: "If he had ham and eggs for breakfast, he would lie saying it was pancakes," she told me.

Risking the taboo, I told her she should meet Tony Pipolo who was coming to Boulder to examine the Stan Brakhage Papers/Archive at the University for material on *Tortured Dust*. Jane didn't even remember which film that was, but she reluctantly permitted me to give her contact information to Pipolo, who is both a film historian and a psychoanalyst. He had been considering a long piece on *Tortured Dust* since he first saw it in 1984. Now Tony and his wife Carole (who was accompanying him) are the sweetest and most generous people I know. I was sure Jane would love them. I was right, but I underestimated their charm even then. Pipolo's work on *Tortured Dust* (*Artforum* March 2014) was so insightful that Jane was astonished at how much he saw in the film and how true it was to the last years of her marriage. She sent copies to all five of her children. More so, she was inspired to take up *The Autobiography of Stan Brakhage* again. She asked him to write an introduction to it, but as the project developed they both thought it would be better as an Afterword. That is how I come to be at the front of this remarkable book, resurrected. Now listen to the tales Brakhage wove about his childhood, keeping in mind Jane Wodening's exquisite ear and her deft narrative skill, then read what Tony Pipolo makes of it all.

Preface

JANE (BRAKHAGE) WODENING

I WOULD LIKE TO TALK ABOUT how this book came into being and what part it played in our lives. It was an important stimulus for tremendous changes in the lives of both Stan and me.

At one point in the fall of 1975, our three adolescent daughters persuaded me that I was hovering over them too much. Our two sons, in junior high, seemed to be doing fine. I was 39.

Backing off from my daughters left a big gap in my day — in my mind — and I remember one quiet moment when I was mulling it over — which way should I go? — Raising kids is a creative act and it seemed that my choices lay between jumping much more deeply into working with Stan in his films or ... what? Oh, writing! I had always dreamed of writing. I knew how to work with Stan in his filmmaking; we worked together well. But Stan's constant womanizing kept me in a depressed state and I felt bitter and unfulfilled. Writing would be much more expansive, would give me a chance to think about things.

So it was, on that occasion, staring out the window, that I decided. And that, as Robert Frost once said, "has made all the difference."

When my friend Barbara Gamov was dying, we went to visit her. She and I had each told the other that we would write some day and it was now clearly too late for her. That night, I leaped out of sleep, finally realizing that my life too was finite. That was my first real story.

For several years, I wrote about things that happened, my numerous animals, about encounters with people, interviewed the neighbors for stories of the mining days, wrote and wrote, thus told stories I had always wanted to think through and tell right, as writing allows one to do. And I found that in telling the story, if I explored an occasion, writing it down would make it come clear. I wasn't interested in making up stories. I found I was writing to understand the world, to understand what was happening in my life. I had some years before (also staring out the window) realized that what I wanted to accomplish in my life was to understand everything. Whatever that means.

My stories began emerging in little magazines and our friends began talking about what I had done. Many disapproved. "There can be only one artist in a family," said a poet who was one of our oldest friends. I wrote only when I wasn't busy raising our five children, minding the house, helping Stan with his films and handling the film business. Writing was my hobby. Stan was the pro. Stan was usually a pleasure to converse with, to think with, although sometimes he'd talk in circles out of nerves, just talking. He wanted respect, always, so sometimes there were days when I did nothing from dawn to dusk but listen to Stan talking. I would drop in a relevant comment here and there.

A case could be made that he was a natural magician, always distracting his audience from what he was actually up to with hypnotic or otherwise irresistible imagery, telling one thing, or many things, keeping the actual thought hidden. "Facts are nothing! Feelings are nothing! It's the light, the light!" he would propound, early in our marriage. "It's the red and green and blue balls and falling water and shooting stars that I work with!" It was a way of being on top; fooling people makes them all fools, right? Also, by the same token, I realized from the start that these stories he gave me from his childhood had grown and developed across a lifetime, as stories do. He was not alone in any of this. I accepted the stories as he gave them to me and I stand by them as such.

He tried to tell about his way of thinking in his films *Sincerity* and *Duplicity*. But two is as easy to juggle as one. What if he had made the leap and called the series *Deviousness*? But he was trying to make a case that there was sincerity in his deviousness. It was just the way he did things.

By 1983 I was feeling on the one hand as though I had done some writing, had become a writer, but at the same time, I was running out of stories in my life, stories that people told me, and of animal stories too. Stan's childhood stories as he dropped them into conversation, sometimes, were so charming as well as exotic to me that I asked him if I could write them up, all of them, as a narrative.

He had the most amazing memory I had ever encountered. He said I could, but that he had little time for it and so I found myself feeling out his tone for weeks at a time before I could interview him again. I think partly this was because he wanted to pull together the next chapter in his mind so that he could tell me the tales uninterrupted while I sat in a low chair taking notes. Each session was a chapter and usually, each chapter was a place. I would take my notes then, and before I forgot the details, I'd organize them, write them up, edit them, and in a few days, would read them back to Stan. The changes I made in the stories were minimal but the bitterness and hatred he had for his mother I left out. And I changed the tone of the book from that of a highly articulate but resentful fifty-year-old man to the dependent submissive tone of a child. When I read the chapter to him after a few days, he would listen rapt, a rare treat for me. He was always pleased to hear it, found no corrections, was, or so it seemed to me, still amazed that I was able to write. Then it would be a matter of a few weeks before he would consent to do it again, say a month each time. This seemed a strange rhythm but it worked all right. I could do other stories in between.

And so, in fact, two years passed and in the book we had made it to the next year after the end of World War II and Stan was twelve or thirteen years old. Twenty-three chapters, a hundred thousand words. *Motion Picture Magazine* in New York City was serializing it. In the next chapter, he was going to leap from being a sickly, bullied and bespectacled child to being Head Boy in his class, loved and admired by everyone in the school. Interestingly, and sadly, this tremendous transformation seemed, in the book and in the character I had been writing of, unjustifiable, impossible to follow in the story I had been writing. I asked for backup, some thread I could put into previous chapters to make it work. It was as though, remembering so very much of his childhood, he was keeping secret the thread of power that caused him to burst into blossom in junior high.

But he had nothing to suggest. At that moment, I remember feeling him leap away from me irrevocably and slam the door, as though I had tried to enter Bluebeard's secret room. It seemed that the thought of answering — or even entertaining — my request never entered his mind.

Many years later, mulling it over, trying to understand, I believe that the "thread of power" was in his thoughts, in his self-image. He had the self-centered arrogance of a lonely and spoiled child who would rage to get his way. He told me no stories of himself raging as a child, but he raged often in adulthood. Rage by itself wouldn't bring power, but rage with theatrical manipulative thought behind it could develop that rage and use it as a tool. He always had a lot of respect for his rages. With that premise, I could imagine this precocious kid, struggling always for the spotlight, clumsily raised in a home with little love in it, raging, as some do, from birth, and his mother, Clara, obeying it, her predictably hysterical responses encouraging him. Then, as he grew older, thinking, working to develop his power, finding a kid like Jon Stark whom he wanted to impress, he would, like a growing nation, see the value of diplomacy, making allies, etc. "Follow your feelings," he said, often, but he didn't mean emotion or ideals, he meant to feel out the situation, make it your stage, and grab that spotlight. "All that is is light," he liked to quote from Duns Scotus Eriugena. When he raged at me, very often much of what he said was garbled and meaningless, full of insults and threats, his hands gripping my throat, his face contorted into a monstrous snarl. But, raging in public, he felt as though he was inspired. He called it his "Holy Rage." To my knowledge, he never outgrew that notion. If the preacher in Winfield, Kansas, could hold the audience in the palm of his hand by shouting, so by the same token could Stan. If he had allowed himself to go back through and tell me this aspect of his life, who got which part in what drama, his inner-child mind, the life of Stan's response as a child, could be superimposed over these stories in this book to show what he made of each occasion in his mind, in his self-image, in the drama that his life was. If I had had those stories from inside, I could have seen how he suddenly became editor of a newspaper in the seventh grade and Head Boy in the eighth grade, then went on to be the kid that the high school was most proud of, even (or so he said) eclipsing the athletes for those years.

However, I have not done this, have left the stories intact as he told them to me. My text remains only the stories that he told me. It could be that this book is the "red and green and blue balls and falling water and shooting stars" of his childhood doing their job as always to protect the inner thoughts, the responses and, most particularly, the motives.

Nonetheless, I believe that the telling of his childhood had a strong effect on Stan. He was remembering and exploring, month after month, all the pains, fears, resentments, frustrations, etc. of his dra-

matically insecure childhood. It may have been that was a sizable part of the reason he needed to wait a month or so each time before telling me another chapter of his life.

I wonder if going on with the book would have helped him to resolve these emotional problems, but Stan had found a woman in Boulder that he wanted to live with and I realized that in proposing to write this book, I had brought the very thing that had separated me from his work into my work, his womanizing bringing me to depression in the very activity that had brought me out of it. We stopped the interviews right there and for a few weeks or months, he continued to live at home most of the time, but soon he moved to town to be with his girlfriend and again we hesitated, having been married nearly thirty years, about getting a divorce, selling the house, dividing up what we had. But eventually it all happened across the next couple of years.

For decades since then, I considered this a flawed book. But I realize now that the great transformation that happened to the boy Stan with the Hultman family and also the Abstract Company job during the period of the end of this book would have to begin another book, a totally different book. It would have to be a book of adolescent energy leaping blindly and decisively one way, then another, as teachers, peers, neighbors, books, movies, and family would throw out tantalizing routes to follow. It would certainly be an interesting book, the study of a kid flailing to grasp his identities and his future, I hope someone writes it soon, from the viewpoint of the adolescent himself.

This is a biography of a child, taken from the memory of that child grown up. I can only assume that we stopped the interviews, stopped the book, stopped the marriage, at exactly the right moment. Stan and I worked together a lot in his medium; this time, we worked together in my medium. If you like, consider this book to be a reply to Stan's film series, *Scenes From Under Childhood*. This, in writing, is a study of his childhood. And I'm glad I wrote it. When Stan moved to town, I told that same poet who had said "only one artist per household" that I wanted to be glad it all happened as it did, and, although it took time, I truly am.

Jane Wodening
May 8, 2014

1

Birth

MY MOTHER'S NAME WAS MIRABELL. Mirabell Sanders. At least so I've been told. Some people say she was a nurse at The Willows and others say she worked for a lawyer in Kansas City, Kansas up until the eighth month. Anyway, she had me at The Willows, which was a place for unwed mothers, on January 14, 1933 in Kansas City, Missouri. I went to The Willows a few years ago. It was a vacant lot part way down a pretty steep hill with a lot of steps going up, a lot of wide steps leading up to a cement foundation with a couple of elm trees, no willows, some rotten old junk and a lot of weeds. I found some oilcloth with pictures of teddy bears on it in rows and brought home a piece of it. Not that I felt that my mother might have touched it or anything like that but it was a connection to the place of my birth. It was sort of the teddy bear that my mother never gave me. I don't know where it is now.

I've always felt bad that my real mother and father deserted me but at the same time I have that as a fantasy to fall back on. I could be a prince. I always dreamed about what I might be. This was a great solace to me all through my childhood, a solace that other children didn't have. That's why I liked Moses so much. And *The*

Ugly Duckling. I used to fantasize a lot about being The Prince and how they'd come for me someday and then everone would know who I am at last.

My high school teacher Harold Keebles thought I was the son of Thomas Wolfe because of my writing style. One time he and an old professor at CU talked about it. They both agreed that I was most probably Wolfe's son. The professor remembered Wolfe from when he was at CU for a residency. He got all excited looking at me, talking with me, reading my writings because he said that my style was like Wolfe's too. They talked a lot about Wolfe and about the editing job that Maxwell Perkins did on him, how Wolfe would send in mountains of manuscript and then Perkins would cut out all the description and make it into a simple narrative story and then it'd sell like hot cakes. But Wolfe would write hundreds of pages of description, for instance describing someone who went to the store to buy ice cream and on the way home stopped by to visit some people, and then Wolfe would slowly, in infinite detail, develop the people visited, their front porch with the squeaking porch swing, the slow sweep of expressions across their faces, the kitchen, the teapot and the sugar bowl, the dirty teacup with a spot of tea dried on the side, the cat stretching on the windowsill, the long cracker barrel conversation about everything from the neighbors' roses to infinity, pages and pages, hundreds of pages maybe, exquisite stuff,

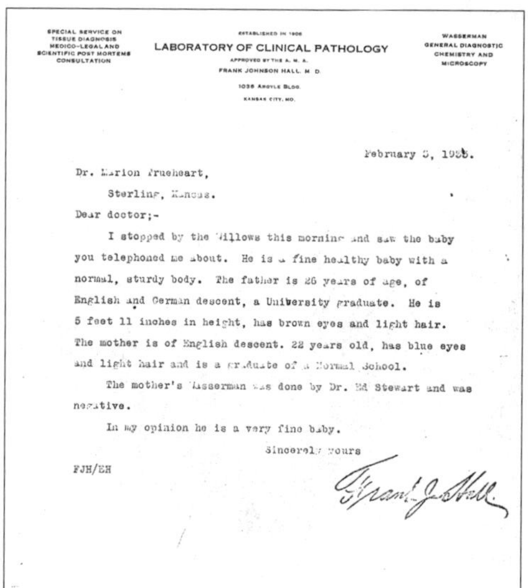

SPECIAL SERVICE ON TISSUE DIAGNOSIS MEDICO-LEGAL AND SCIENTIFIC POST MORTEMS CONSULTATION

ESTABLISHED IN 1906

LABORATORY OF CLINICAL PATHOLOGY

APPROVED BY THE A. M. A.

FRANK JOHNSON HALL, M. D.

1036 ARGYLE BLDG.

KANSAS CITY, MO.

WASSERMAN GENERAL DIAGNOSTIC CHEMISTRY AND MICROSCOPY

February 5, 1933.

Dr. Marion Trueheart,

Sterling, Kansas.

Dear doctor;-

I stopped by the Willows this morning and saw the baby you telephoned me about. He is a fine healthy baby with a normal, sturdy body. The father is 26 years of age, of English and German descent, a University graduate. He is 5 feet 11 inches in height, has brown eyes and light hair. The mother is of English descent. 22 years old, has blue eyes and light hair and is a graduate of a Normal School.

The mother's Wasserman was done by Dr. Ed Stewart and was negative.

In my opinion he is a very fine baby.

Sincerely yours

Frank J. Hall

FJH/EH

MRS. E. P. HAWORTH, SUPERINTENDENT
MRS. NELLE T. McEWEN, SECRETARY
IN CHARGE OF ADOPTION

ADDRESS ALL COMMUNICATIONS TO
THE WILLOWS
OR
MRS. E. P. HAWORTH, SUPERINTENDENT

THE NURSERY
OF
The Willows Maternity Sanitarium
2929 MAIN STREET
KANSAS CITY, MISSOURI

February, 1933

Mrs. L. H. Brakhage
426 N. Broadway
Sterling, Kansas

Dear Mrs. Brakhage:

The approval of your home for a Willows' baby was received from the Court a short time ago. We are, therefore, giving you first opportunity to take a baby boy who was released for adoption by his mother this morning.

I should like to have written you earlier in regard to this baby, but his mother had planned even before he was born to keep him herself. A letter she received this morning disrupted her plans and made it necessary for her to give up the baby.

Baby Robert is an attractive little ones having a well shaped head and good features. He has very little brown hair and at present his eyes are blue.

The mother of this baby entered our institution early in December and during her stay here has been an exceptionally nice patient. She is quite pretty and neat and refined in appearance. She had been living at home up to the time she entered a nurses' training school where she intends to return to complete her training. Her father who was a mechanic and owner of a garage, died a few years ago the result of (Cerebral) a hemorrhage. Her mother is living and she has one brother who is a bookkeeper. This family owns a home and has lived in the present community for 22 years. All are members of a Protestant church.

The father of baby Robert is a bank clerk and is an only child. Both of his parents are living, his father owning a general store. The parents of baby Robert have known each other all of their lives. The health record of both sides shows no hereditary diseases nor is there Tuberculosis. The Wassermann test on the baby's mother is negative. Baby Robert has been examined by a baby specialist and pronounced to be a normal healthy baby.

Now, Mrs. Brakhage we feel that baby Robert is a desirable and that his parentage is well above the average. We do not have a nicer patient in the institution among the expectant mothers nor one whom we could recommend above Robert's mother. We, therefore, believe he

Page 2 Mrs. L. H. B.

would be an ideal baby for your home. Baby Robert is now about nineteen days old and started on the bottle.

If you and Mr. Brakhage are interested in his description and parentage, we shall be glad to have you come to see him Saturday morning, February 4th. As Kansas City courts close at NOON on Saturdays, it will be necessary for you to reach here reasonably early Saturday morning so that we may have time to complete the adoption procedure before noon. You may bring with you a quart thermos bottle and two or three nursing bottles or obtain them here at the institution.

Now if you are not interested in this baby, please notify us at once so that we may make other arrangements for him.

Awaiting your visit or early reply, I am

Very truly yours,

Lyra M. Haworth Supt.

MRS:EPH:HM

Mrs. E. P. Haworth
THE WILLOWS

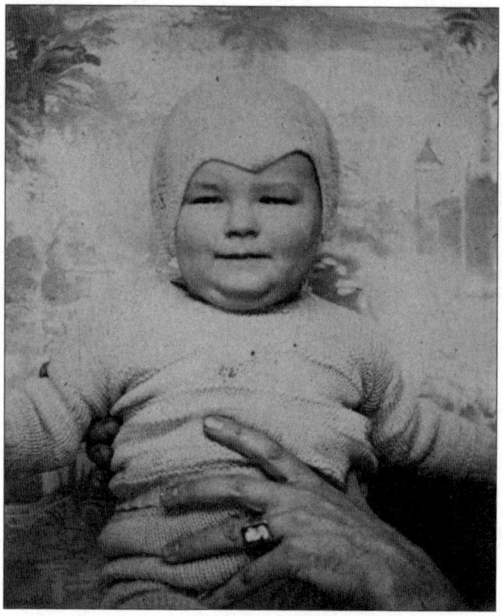

then Perkins would throw it all away, "The ice cream would have melted," he'd say.

Then in 1958 on a commercial job I was sent to Switzerland and Eugene Smith was there, the great still photographe r and after the day's work we'd sit in the kitchen together and drink. I don't usually drink very much but that job was far from what I was wanting to do. It's a good thing Eugene Smith was there and all that whiskey or I'd have made a scene. Anyway after about a week of good conversation and good whiskey, late one night after quite a bit to drink, he said to me, "I've been wracking my brains to remember who you remind me of and now I've got it." Right then I knew who it was going to be. "It's not that you look a whole lot like him," he said, "but you move like him and most particularly, you drink like him." By this time I was pretty sober. "My old drinking buddy, Thomas Wolfe," he said and then I told him all about it, about The Willows, and what Henry Keebles and that CU professor said. I didn't know Mirabell's name then but I knew my name was supposed to be Robert Sanders or at least so I'd heard. Turns out that Wolfe was an incredible rake, but he was also a wonderful lecturer so people would bring him to town for a lecture and then all the mothers in the know would keep their daughters home during his visit. I imagine Mirabell's mother, my grandmother, wasn't in the know or more likely Mirabell was on her own. But we found in a book on Thomas Wolfe much later that Wolfe had been in Kansas City in the spring of 1932.

When I went to Kansas City and found the teddy bear oilcloth, it was April. That'd be the month I was conceived. It was still winter in Colorado but in Kansas City the forsythias were in bloom and the tulips and crocuses and the sweet mad smell of spring wafted around in the streets.

Clara and Lou came and got me when I was three weeks old. Since a very few years after that, I always felt they had hired me to make their marriage work, but that I had failed.

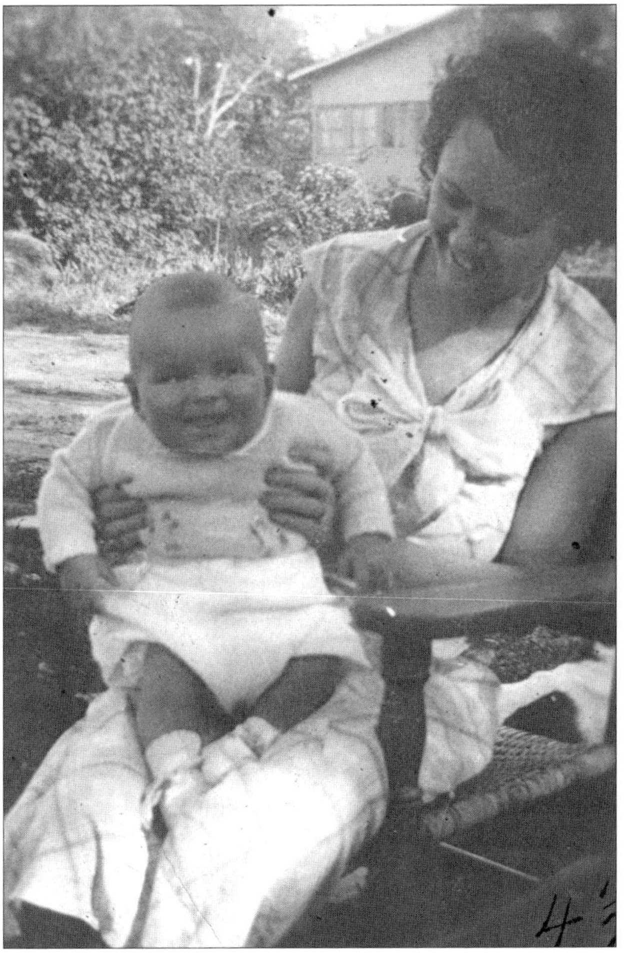

2

Grandmaw and Clara

IN THE YEAR 1901, in Winfield, Kansas, the Lutheran minister's wife went to her bed to bear her third child, another girl. As it happened she sickened in childbed fever, lay for three weeks there and then died. She must have been around forty at the time but she had a head of hair that was the pride of Winfield and that hair was still beautiful at the funeral. I imagine the whole town went to that funeral because, for one thing, who could be a more eminent citizen than Mr. Dubberstein, the Lutheran minister in a small town in Kansas? And for another, it was the last chance to get a glimpse of that crowning glory, the pride of Winfield, the golden-auburn hair of the preacher's wife.

The baby, however, survived, so although Mr. Dubberstein was well into middle age, he quickly found a young woman who would marry him, take care of the baby and perform all the duties of a preacher's wife in Kansas. Her name was Alma, but everyone who didn't call her Mrs. Dubberstein called her Grandmaw. The baby's name was Clara.

Clara's two sisters were considerably older than she, into their teens when she was born, but soon the young stepmother provided her with two brothers, Waldo and Herbert. Clara always felt that her stepmother cared more for the boys than for her. One time Clara heard her calling for her and she ran and hid under her father's desk in his study. Then she heard a chair creak and she looked up and there was her father sitting reading. Grandmaw called again and Clara looked at her father. Her father winked and turned back to his book. Clara felt warm all over. She had found a friend. Shortly after that, her father died.

Waldo and Herbert loved to tease their half-sister. One time not long after their father died, they found a dead rat and threw it at her. She started screaming and couldn't stop. They had to send for the doctor and he gave her a shot and eventually she calmed down a bit but for weeks afterward she was shivery and jittery. She never really got over it. If she ever saw a rat or a mouse she'd jump on the table and scream and scream.

After the preacher died, Grandmaw became a pillar of the church. She had to sell the farm and move into town where she bought a house with several garret rooms upstairs and began to take in boarders. Most of these boarders were students at the Lutheran College in Winfield.

Clara grew up quickly. By the time she was eighteen, she was teaching in a one-room schoolhouse twenty miles from Winfield, coming

home on weekends. It was a couple years after she started teaching that she met Ludwig Brakhage, or as his friends called him, Lou. Lou was teaching at the Lutheran College and Clara was sick of being stuck off in a one-room schoolhouse so she quit her job and married him and they settled down in a house in Winfield a few blocks away from Grandmaw's boarding house. By 1931 they realized they were probably not going to have any children of their own so they set out to adopt a child. Finally, late in January of 1933, they heard of a newborn baby boy at The Willows in Kansas City, Missouri, and in the first week of February Clara took the train to Kansas City to pick him up.

3

Winfield

I DON'T REMEMBER A WHOLE LOT about the years we spent in Winfield but I know this: Grandmaw, wherever she was, was the center of town. No one could say "No" to her, nothing she ever did was wrong, her morality was the moral morality. Kansas was a dry state, no drinking, no dancing. No card playing. No blaring radios, no neon lights. That was in the 1930's. Maybe it's changed now. The winters were horribly cold and the summers horribly hot. The streets were quiet and orderly. People sat on their porches. They never locked their doors.

Grandmaw's porch went across the front of her house and all the way down one side. There were chairs on it and, of course, a swing. The swing made a noise like cree-dung, cree-dung, cree-dung. In the back of the house was a screened-in porch where Grandmaw did things like make sauerkraut, shell peas, pot geraniums. In the backyard were the chickens clucking and chattering and sometimes singing out in the ecstatic hallelujah that comes to them when an egg is laid or sometimes in chorus for no reason at all. Behind them, the ground sloped rockily up to a ridge and on top of the ridge was a small hammer-type oil well slowly pumping day and night, summer and winter. It took

several seconds for each pump, creaking up and thumping down,

eeeeeee ... dump ... eeeee ... dump ...

And all summer long, the crickets chirped.

Grandmaw had worked hard on the front yard. The walk went up the middle. On one side was the lawn with the apple tree in it. On the other was a rock garden — lilies of the valley, violets, a weeping willow; a deep goldfish pond in which the fish could winter over; yard sculpture around the pond — a spotted fawn, a goose and a little black boy with a red cap and a fishing pole endlessly fishing in the pond.

As I said, the summers were horribly hot, often staying over a hundred degrees even at night. People slept, or tried to sleep, with no covers over their nightclothes, sweating. Some set up beds on the screened-in porch. They liked to sing the old song:

"I wear my pink pajamas in the summer when it's hot,
I wear my flannel nighties in the winter when it's not.
And sometimes in the springtime and sometimes in the fall,
I slip between the sheets with nothing on at all."

The winters were, as I said, terribly cold and the wind raged across the fields and into the town, piling drifts of snow here and there. In the spring the tornados came and once in a while we'd all run into our cellars and sit there for hours. It would be kind of fun at first, being snatched up, going through the slanting cellar door and down the steps with several people and there were shelves and shelves filled with canned goods, onions hanging in braids from the ceiling, barrels of tomatoes and apples and everybody sitting around on the floor. The ladies had to keep their cellars clean for these occasions. After awhile I'd want to get out and they wouldn't let me, they'd tell me scary sto-

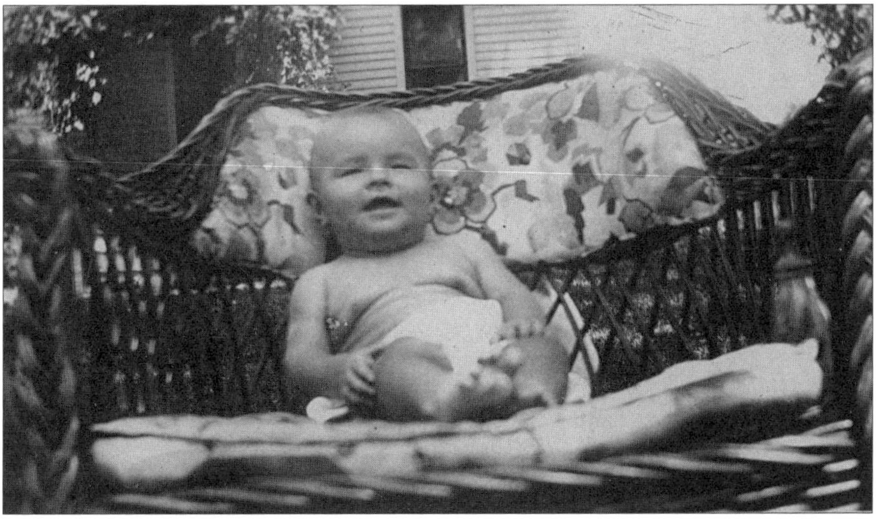

ries about monsters and werewolves so that when it was finally time to climb back up the stairs I'd be afraid to. But at the same time I loved the stories and listened to them avidly. Even at that age, I always sympathized with the monster. Somewhere inside me I thought I'd grow up to be in the pitiable position of a monster.

One time I was being babysat at some woman's house and, I guess to get me to do what she wanted me to do, she got a whole big scene going with a bogeyman in the basement, intimating that she could control him as long as she could control me, until in an anguish of fear I somehow managed to call up my grandmother. I don't remember my conversation with the telephone operator, though she must have been an extremely knowledgeable and sympathetic person, since I was two or three years old at the time. My grandmother somehow gave me the strength to face this babysitter, said I'd have to put up with her. I was rather a celebrity for having made a phone call so young.

Grandmaw had five rooms to let, the three upstairs, each with the slope of the roof narrowing it and a small, low window. The best room was the front bedroom downstairs where there were two windows so that in the summer there was cross-ventilation or at least the hope of it in that one room. Of course, everyone could and sometimes did sit on the porch. The boarders were all students at Saint John's Lutheran College and a very serious studious bunch of young clergymen-to-be. Whenever we went to see Grandmaw, there were these boarders always about, all well-behaved but there to bump into on the porch, in the living room, and at dinner, almost always carrying a book. I can't remember any of them very well, but the fact is that since I was very young I always have to carry a book wherever I go. It's soothing. And it comes in very handy sometimes, like in airplanes and waiting rooms.

My first trauma that I can remember had to do with the chickens, which I liked very much. I liked their chatter and their enthusiasm over laying eggs. But one day I was with Grandmaw on the porch and she got up and said, "Well, I'm going to go get dinner," and told me to play by myself. I wandered around to the backyard and saw her out there feeding the chickens. Then, as though she were picking flowers, she reached down, picked up two of the chickens and wrung their necks, then carried their corpses into the kitchen. I never liked chicken after that unless it was cooked to taste like something else.

The summers were made of watermelons and dust. The dust made everyone keep their windows closed, kept people indoors. But even then there would be the dust in our eyes, in the gutters, sweeping across the lawns and sidewalks, and in our food. There was no way to keep it out of the food. And if I'd laugh into the wind, there it would be crunching between my teeth. Maybe that's part of why dust bowl people are so grim-looking.

But the watermelons were the opposite. I never was clear whether people were brought together into parties because someone had some watermelons or whether people got watermelons because they were having a party, but the fact was that if there was a party, there was watermelon. And if there was watermelon, people had to go outside to eat it and there were seed-spitting contests and laughter and rinds were thrown to squirrels or fed to the barnyard animals or we'd all just throw them as far away as we could and figure some critter or other would be grateful to have it.

The heart of Winfield was the church. The church was a clapboard building so the heat tended to get in there and stay. The pews were hardwood and exceedingly uncomfortable. On the back of each one was a rack and in each rack was a Bible, a prayer book, a hymnal and in the summer, there was a fan. The fans were decorated on one side with pastel illustrations from Bible stories and on the other by advertisements from local merchants. The place was always full of people and we always sat close to the front. Since I was a little child I could turn around and see the congregation, the grim and somber faces, the women in their colorful but filmy chintz dresses with perhaps a pattern of holes to keep cool, the cloth so thin anyway that I could see their lace-trimmed petticoats underneath, the whole place quivering with the pastel flutter of these fans, an ocean of color with faces sticking up in rows. That many fans made a whisperiness that accompanied or was accompanied by the voice of the preacher below the altar. All these mysterious effects plus the sure knowledge that my grandmother was in some ways a powerful and central person in the church gave me an early and very intense feeling of devotion to the church, to God, to Jesus and to the Heavenly Hosts. It was here, in the Lutheran Church of Winfield, in the bellowing of the preacher, the muggy air and the, to me, vast room full of the shimmering multicolored fans that I felt the power of religion and began my trek along the wrackingly painful path to the love affair with the muse called art.

Oh, I suppose it could have happened earlier that I began to go in that direction. It could have been that it began at the age of one year when I got a smallpox vaccination and put Clara and Lou in a dither with my first asthma attack.

Much of Grandmaw's position of power in the church was because of her Christmas decorations. She started working on them in January, collecting everything, every rag and sparkle, every bit of cardboard or string. Her string ball was a family joke. Every piece of string that came to her hand went into that string ball, even if the piece was only two or three inches long and nothing there but two knots side by side. The Christmas decorations started at the tree, expanded throughout the house and out into the yard. In the house there would be cardboard angels and lighted tassels and mistletoe and sparkles everywhere but it was in the yard that she came into her glory.

Here, great figures of papier-mâché depicted scenes from the Bible all across the front of the house and around the fish pond, back into the apple tree and even to the alley, all cleverly lit with strings of lights and glowing with glitter. Every year she received the prize for the best Christmas decorations in the town of Winfield, every year the whole town and many people from the towns around would come to see what she did this year, for each year her decorations were new and different. Oh, she'd salvage things from the previous year but the scene would always be something new.

Once I was taken to some people's house where they had a miniature nativity scene laid out on top of a bureau and I asked my mother if I could have a doll like the one they had for Jesus, tiny lovely thing made of porcelain, or something hard like that, complete with eyelids and fingernails even though it was only the size of my thumb, and with a face on it that fascinated me, pure and clear and knowing-looking. She said to hush, she'd buy me one and some time later we went to Wichita and she bought me a doll which was made of rubber and bigger than the Jesus doll and had a stupid petulant look on its face and I hated it and threw it in the gutter.

The preacher was a fierce man with big bushy eyebrows and a great bellowing voice and being Lutheran and in Kansas and having the lungs and the eyebrows for it, he did a good deal of shouting from the pulpit. One time he was going on about hell-fire and followed it up with a brief boring sketch of angels strumming harps and afterwards I went up to him and in my piping but also loud voice said to him, "Hell seems a lot more interesting than Heaven. Do you suppose I could go there when I die just as a visitor?" Nobody remembers what he said back to me, but I was the talk of the town for weeks afterward. Grandmaw defended me because of the child Jesus arguing with the Pharisees.

Although we saw an awful lot of Grandmaw and most of my memories of Winfield are centered around her, the fact is that we lived in a house of our own down by the tracks. I guess we were renting the downstairs and two old ladies lived upstairs. When I got old enough I sometimes went to visit them or took messages to them. They were always perfectly kind to me but I didn't get to know them very well because they had a way of graciously and amiably sending me right away as soon as I arrived.

I wish I could remember exactly what happened with the little girl in the red wagon. It may have been that I did something precocious in the sexual line, or maybe it was something else. She was dark with an olive Mediterranean skin and must have come from the poor immigrants' section across the tracks. I pulled her in the red wagon and there were her bare feet and the sound they made on the rusty bottom of the wagon. Then I remember being seriously lectured by Clara and her looking very stern in the living room as she lectured me. I don't know why the sound of bare feet scraping on cement has made me quite ill all my life long, but perhaps it began on this occasion.

My very first memory is in that house. I was on the floor in the dining room building something out of blocks. There was a cupboard under the window, and something in the window so that the light came through in three beams, and I remember the beams of light shining, and glittering dust motes moving around in them.

Lou was teaching at Saint John's Lutheran College and I sometimes visited him in his classroom. It was in the basement, there were dugout basement windows, and I got into one of those and watched him teaching from above that way.

Sometimes I sat in the back of the class too. I was always delighted to visit him when he was teaching because he was jovial then and moved about talking cheerfully and winningly, and all the young men who were his students listened to him, and sometimes he made them laugh and sometimes they'd raise their hands and answer.

I was proud of him then, proud to be his son. If the students or the neighbor boys played baseball, he might be the umpire, and that was exciting too. At home he wasn't near so interesting. He'd talk desultorily to Clara and read the newspaper and after he ate he'd always rum-

mage his tongue around in his mouth and suck his teeth. And when he did this, Clara would tell him to stop, that it was a disgusting thing to do.

One time I had a dream. I was a student in Lou's class. It was his class because of the dugout basement windows, only the teacher was the devil. It was very hot in the classroom and I was uncomfortable and wanted to get out of there. I raised my hand and said I'd like to go out to get a drink of water and the devil said no, I couldn't go for a drink of water, so I raised my hand again and said I had to pee. The devil said I could leave the room to pee and this way I got out. I felt at the time, and still do feel, that in this dream I discovered a wonderful and very useful way to get out of things and I've always used this and I'm grateful for having been given this dream.

In the thirties there were people who did all kinds of strange things to support themselves. Many of them wandered from town to town with some service or other. There was a man who came to Winfield with a quiet pony, a few children's cowboy clothes and a camera, and he took pictures of the children on his pony and sold them to the parents. I still have mine.

There was an older boy who lived a couple doors down the street and he and I used to play together. One time he came over to show me that he'd gotten golf clubs for his birthday and how they worked. He took me out in the backyard and carefully stuck a little colored tee in the ground, then placed the ball on it, took his club in his hand and stepped back and forth on each foot a couple times like a cat, pulled back the club and swung it around, walloping me violently on the temple. I cried and cried and wouldn't stop and all through my childhood I had a dent there and it showed whenever I laughed or cried.

As my grandmother represented religion in Winfield, the Waxman sisters represented culture. There were two of them. One, big and fat and jolly, was the one in charge of music. The other was thin and had big teeth and she was in charge of posture, dance and Shakespeare. They lived together some blocks away and I took piano lessons from the fat one when I was three years old. This was during the era when all the parents wanted their child to be Wolfgang Amadeus Mozart or Shirley Temple, and, along with our toilet training, we were all seriously encouraged to flower. It was a hard time for money and everyone knew that Shirley Temple was making more than probably the whole town of Winfield put together. So I got piano lessons at three and Clara and Lou were told that I "had an ear" and was a good little student. Miss Waxman came to our house to teach me. I thought it was the regular thing but I suppose it was really because her willowy sister was teaching posture, dance and/or Shakespeare at their house.

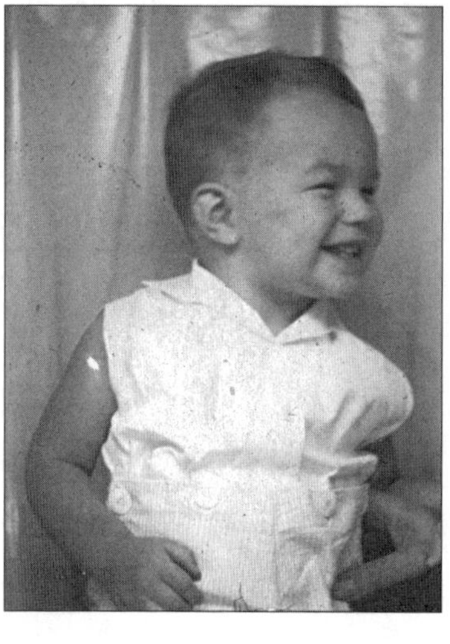

My best friend in Winfield was my cousin Ronnie. He was the son of my uncle Herbert and he was less than a year younger than I was. Uncle Herbert was good at sleight-of-hand tricks and would often greet me when he came to visit by saying, "What is that you have behind your ear?" and reach back there and there'd be a penny. But Uncle Herbert and Aunt Maryann broke up

PROGRAM

*Swinging To and Fro - - - - - - - Steele
BOBBY KUHLMANN MILLICENT MORRIS
STANLEY BRAKHAGE

Mothers Know - - - - - - - - - Gillman
MARY LOU BIRD

Left Right - - - - - - - - - - Williams
Up The Hill - - - - - - - - - - Diel
RUTH KUHLMANN

I Can Play - - - - - - - - - - Diel
Dolly Dear - - - - - - - - - - Pendleton
MARY LOU BIRD

*First Duet - - - - - - - - - - Kohler
The Squirrel - - - - - - - - - - Diel
Gold Fish - - - - - - - - - - Pendleton
MILLICENT MORRIS

Wishing - - - - - - - - - - Oldman
MARY ESTHER EDENS

The Star - - - - - - - - - - Williams
Indian Dance - - - - - - - - - - Diel
STANLEY BRAKHAGE

The Big Clock - - - - - - - - - - Blake
Sing Tra La - - - - - - - - - - Blake
JENNESS PHILLIPS

A March - - - - - - - - - - Blake
The Country Band - - - - - - - - Blake
BOBBY KUHLMANN

Ginger Cat - - - - - - - - - - Clark
NANCY WALDRON

Climbing - - - - - - - - - - Williams
MARTHA MADOLE

Swimming - - - - - - - - - - Graves
PATRICIA BIRD

I Fell Down in the Mud - - - - - - Goodman
MARTHA MADOLE

The Surprise - - - - - - - - Haydn-Schmidt
The 'Cello - - - - - - - - - - Blake
PATRICIA BIRD

Hot Biscuits and Honey - - - - - - Sweeney
RUTH MOBERLY

Tarantella - - - - - - - - - - Goodrich
MARJORIE ANN KUHLMANN

Dolly's Funeral - - - - - - - Tschaikowsky
BETTY LOU HARRISON

Bobby Goes to the Movie - - - - - - Berry
JOSEPHINE MCALLISTER

The Wood Nymph's Harp - - - - - - - Rea
RUTH ANN BERGEVIN

Initiation - - - - - - - - - - Tarkington
PATRICIA GRAHAM

Evening Star - - - - - - - - Wagner-Liszt
PATSY JEAN MARTIN

The Anniversary - - - - - - - - - Berkley
GENEVIEVE DAVES

Quartette—Chivalry March - - - - - - - Webb
MARTHA JUNE HUDSON CHARLOTTE GUY
HELEN DEAN ARNETTE PATTY HUGHES

Between Two Loves - - - - - - - - Daly
Mia Carlotta - - - - - - - - - - Daly
PATSY JEAN MARTIN

Rustle of Spring - - - - - - - - - Sinding
GENEVIEVE DAVES

*With MISS FERN DIELMANN

and there was a day when Ronnie was very upset. We were running on a shiny floor and Ronnie slipped on it and fell and cut his lip and then started to vomit and I, in sympathy and shared nerves, vomited with him.

When Uncle Herbert left Aunt Maryann, he gave Ronnie a Boston Bull puppy. Boston Bulls were all the rage in the Thirties. People had figures of them as doorstops and lawn decorations. I was given one of glass. I still have it, though one ear is broken off. But Ronnie got a real one when his parents broke up and he went to live with my Grandmaw. The dog's name was Mugsy. Mugsy was a terrifically smart dog for learning tricks and Grandmaw loved to teach dogs to do tricks so she taught him a lot of them. She taught him to shake hands and roll over and play dead and sit up. Then she taught him to jump through a hoop and to dance. Pretty soon she could get him to roll over and over all across the room, jump through a hoop that was covered with tissue paper, get into a chair and sit up. She started making costumes for him then, a little red coat, a hat and glasses and when he'd sit up in

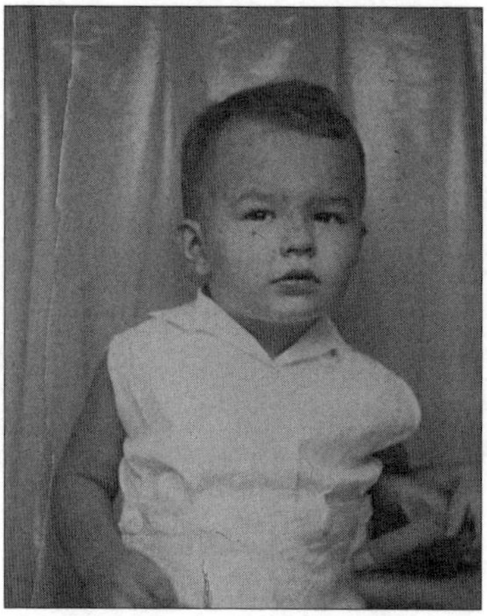

the chair he'd take a pipe in his teeth and sit there quietly for long minutes holding the pipe and balancing the hat and the glasses, and wearing his coat that fit him exactly, a red coat with mustard yellow lapels and big gold buttons. Then she'd tell him to take his hat off and he'd shake his head and the hat would come off but not the pipe or the glasses. But when he wasn't doing these tricks for Grandmaw he was a regular dog with Ronnie and they'd play together.

It made me want a dog real bad. I don't remember whether I hounded my parents for a dog then or whether they wanted one too but anyway we got one, a shorthaired terrier mongrel named Ritzy, my dearest companion for several years. He had had his tail bobbed, so when he wagged it, it wasn't enough, so he wagged his whole back end, and was very charming about it. Grandmaw didn't have a chance to get at him to teach him tricks, but she did notice his insatiable passion for burying things he was given, so she started giving him ice cubes and he'd take them out and bury them with everyone peering out windows and through doorjambs to watch and giggle as he did it.

Uncle Waldo was an adventurer. Actually he was an anthropologist and went to digs in odd forgotten and distant places. It was partly because of his travels that I began my postcard collection. By the time I was three, I was given all postcards that anyone in the family got and I pored over them with delight though I couldn't yet read. Uncle Waldo knew this, of course, and when he passed through Paris on the way to Persia, he found a postcard of a naked lady and sent it to Grandmaw. No doubt he laughed over it for days, imagining the embarrassment of the people in the post office, and knowing this would be a serious thing for Grandmaw because they went to her church and knew her, though the fact was that they knew Waldo, too, and his jokes. But by the time Grandmaw even got the postcard it was no secret so she treated it the same as she treated all the postcards, she showed it to everyone in the family and a few friends and then, at the end, she gave it to me.

This was now my most precious possession. Oh, I had many wonderful possessions, I had toys and dolls, I had a red wagon and a sailor suit. Until I got Ritzy, my prize possession was my teddy bear and I still loved my teddy bear because Clara and Lou wouldn't let me sleep with Ritzy and I always slept with my arms around my teddy bear. But now I had a woman, a real woman and in the privacy of my own room I looked and looked at her, gently touched the picture with my fingers and said to myself that someday I'd marry such a woman.

I gave up most of my postcard collection after that, only kept a few of the others as a protection for her. I felt that the collection had served

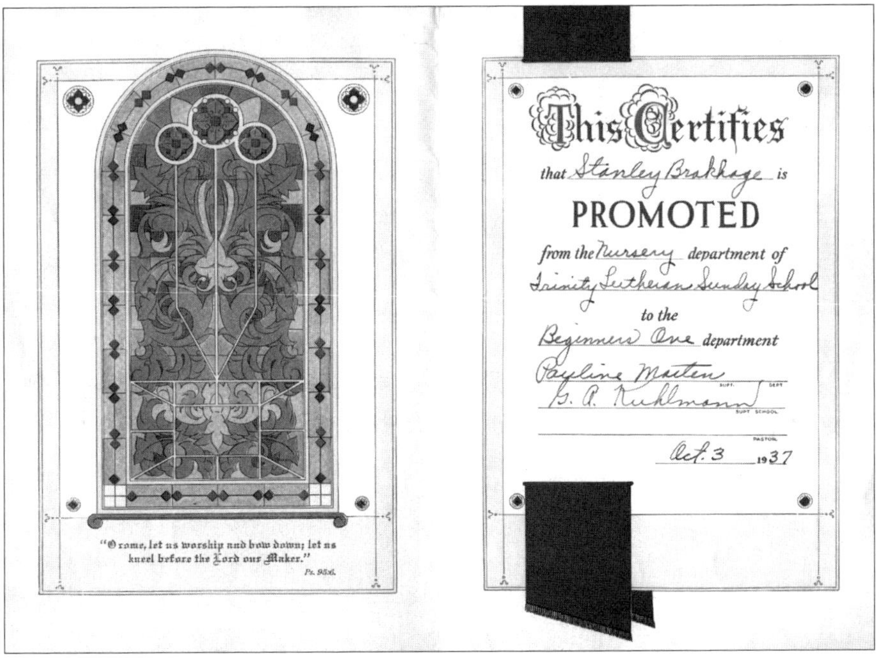

"O come, let us worship and bow down; let us kneel before the Lord our Maker." Ps. 95:6.

This Certifies that Stanley Brakhage is PROMOTED from the Nursery department of Trinity Lutheran Sunday School to the Beginners One department

Pauline Marten — SUPT. DEPT.
G. A. Kuhlmann — SUPT. SCHOOL
PASTOR

Oct. 3 1937

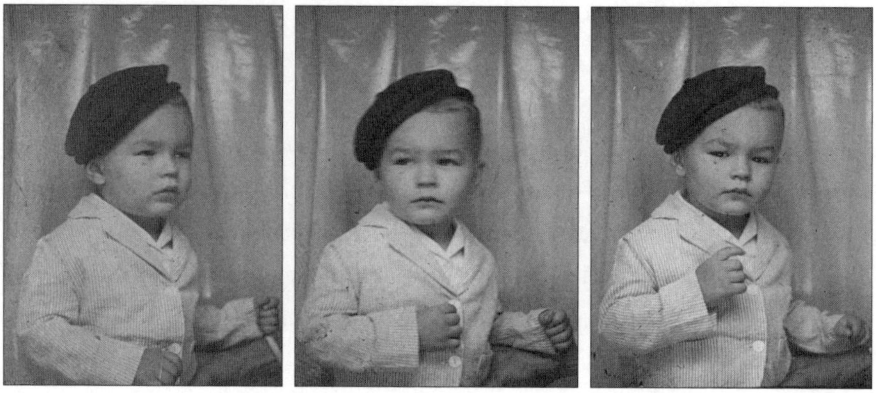

its purpose, that nothing finer could come from it and there was no reason to extend it beyond its usefulness. I still have that postcard.

When Uncle Waldo came back from that trip he brought everyone presents and to me he handed a walnut. I had been overwhelmingly excited at his return and the prospect of a present, and the sight of this walnut depressed and betrayed me. But everyone said, "Aren't you going to eat the walnut?" and I couldn't say, "I don't like walnuts," though it would have been true. And someone handed me a nutcracker and I finally opened it and instead of nutmeat inside there was a dollar which was an immense amount of money then, especially for a little kid. He was like that. I can imagine him carefully opening numbers of walnuts until one opened right at the seam then carefully picking out the insides, putting in the dollar and gluing it back together again. With Uncle Herbert it was, as I described before, sleight-of-hand.

It was Uncle Herbert who played Santa Claus. I don't know whether I discovered this when we were living there or whether it was later on a visit, as we tended to celebrate Christmas back in Winfield for many years. I saw him putting on a Santa Claus suit in the chicken yard, the same place where I saw Grandmaw killing chickens for dinner, and the feeling was so much the same as when I saw Grandmaw and the chickens that I have the two mixed up together in my mind.

The big thing to do in Winfield was to go to Wichita and Clara and I did that fairly often. She liked to buy a lot of clothes, especially shoes, and there were doctors' appointments, and it was in Wichita in 1937 that I saw my first movie, which was "Snow White and the Seven Dwarfs" and I cried hard and loud when the witch was climbing the mountain and the thunder and the lightning were crashing around her and when finally she fell as a piece of precipice that she climbed on broke off. Well, I made so much noise that Lou had to take me into the lobby and even then I went on crying and when he tried to take me back into the movie to see how the Prince comes, and everything is all right with Snow White, I'd scream again and it wasn't till later that I saw the whole thing and learned how it comes out.

Always there was Ritzy and he was a wonderful solace and delight to me, wagging his whole back end to greet me and trying to lick my face, though Clara said it was dirty and I shouldn't let him, and then he followed me wherever I went. He had one weakness though, and that was when bitches went into heat he'd leave us. Then we'd have to listen for the howling and follow it. He never seemed to get into fights or get hurt at these times, but when he'd see us he'd wag at us sadly because he knew we didn't like it and we'd punish him by putting a chain on him in the house and he'd have to drag it around and he hated it horribly. He'd lie still for awhile and seem to forget that he had it on and then he'd move and it would clank and his head and rear end would sag and he'd arch his back in misery and then he'd lie down again and get eventually to where he'd seem to forget again and then he'd move again and the sound and the weight of the chain would remind him of his disgrace and he'd go again into his expression of despondency. But the rest of the time he'd sit by me and encourage me in what I did and let me pet him or lean on him or sit with my arm across his shoulders and think about things.

4

Bisbee

THEN LOU GOT A JOB TEACHING in a business college in Bisbee, Arizona. I suppose he didn't too much like living in a town dominated by his mother-in-law. Bisbee was a famous town because of its history, having been a common hangout for Wyatt Earp and Doc Holliday and Billie the Kid and many more of those gunslingers of the old West. So even though it was a town about the size of Winfield, it had a very different character than Winfield. I loved Bisbee very much and I loved living there. In spite of the fact of my very tender age at the time and even though we were there only nine months, I feel I know Bisbee better than any other town I've lived in in my whole life. The structure of it is clear in my mind and seems to me right. I could tell you even now how to get to anything in the town, or so I feel. It sits in a canyon that's very steep and only a few blocks of the business district are on the flat at the bottom of the canyon. The rest of the town goes up the sides and the roads are very steep and winding, hard-packed dirt. The houses are dug into the mountainside and each one has a little terrace for a yard. When snow came to Bisbee, which was rarely, I could look down to watch it fall on the rooftops below. There were a few trees that people had planted among the houses and the people tried to have some grass and plants around, but directly outside of town, and even many places in the town, there was desert with sand and cactus.

I really liked the cacti a lot. They fascinated me and I liked to go and look at them with their spines protecting them. Everyone treated them with respect and left them alone. "Don't step on the cactus!" People not only respected them because of their spines but they loved them for their flowers, which were in many cases more beautiful even than roses. When I grew up, I thought to myself, I wanted to be like that.

The house we lived in was high up on the side of the canyon and I could see across the canyon to the school where Lou taught. It was, as a matter of fact, the biggest thing in view, more openly and closely visible than any of our neighbors, though to get there Lou had to drive down the steep and winding road to the bottom of the canyon and then up the steep and winding road on the other side. One could shout across to the school, hear its bells ring and even, perhaps, although I never tried it, sail a paper airplane across with a message.

Another thing Bisbee was known for was The Great Hole, the biggest man-made hole in the world. It was a copper mine and I stood on the edge of it looking down at tiny toy trucks creeping up the spiral road around and around, loaded with copper ore, slowly getting bigger, and when they came to the top they had tires bigger than a man.

I had been drawing sunsets in Winfield with my crayons and had thought them beautiful there. But now in Bisbee I went wild with my crayons. The sunsets were incredible. They were brilliant, luminous, and had colors in them that I hadn't imagined using for a sunset. They even had green.

I believe it was here in Bisbee they told me I was adopted. I've always been very grateful that they told me that when I was little. I think it's important that people tell their adopted kids the situation when the kids are very young because it's so important to know the truth, and when one is very young one can absorb it, whereas if the parents wait till later the child feels he/she's been living a lie and it would be hard to get connected then. Anyway it was a relief to me because even then I was discontented with them and, although they were my parents and I yearned and strove constantly for their love, they also seemed to me stupid and insensitive, and their telling me I was adopted opened possibilities in me of fantasies and dreams of who my real parents were. It gave me hope.

In Winfield and again in Bisbee I had a picture over my bed, a reproduction of a painting by George Frederic Watts called *Hope*. In those days ordinary people would have things like that in their homes, reproductions of famous paintings on their walls, and they'd learn to play music by Mozart and Chopin on the piano and be able to recite poems by Robert Browning. So the picture called *Hope* over my bed was not at that time peculiar. It was a picture of a woman dressed in fluttering gray silk sitting on the world ... I think it was the world. Her eyes were bandaged and she looked quite miserable. She was barefoot. She was huddled over with her ear pressed to a lute and looked to be totally concentrated on the sound coming from the lute, as if it were the only thread she had to keep her from becoming part of chaos. I dreamed that she was my mother. She watched over me while I knelt and said my prayers by the bed at night and she watched over me while I slept.

First Clara and Lou told me the story that the people at The Willows had told them to tell me, which was that my real father had died in an automobile accident on Thanksgiving Day, less than three months before I was born, and my mother died of a broken heart after I was born. But then they told me they didn't know, only that my name was supposed to be Robert Sanders.

There was another picture on the wall of my room which I also liked very much, a picture of a log cabin in the twilight with windows glowing yellow and on a hilltop above the cabin was a wolf howling at the moon.

When we lived in Bisbee we did a lot of going for drives. Ritzy was very good in the car and enjoyed going with us, so he and I would sit in the back seat together. The grownups were always very irritable and argued and snapped at each other all the time but Ritzy and I enjoyed the traveling very much. Often they had flat tires and would have to stop and fix them and then they were extremely irritable but Ritzy and I always enjoyed the flat tires more than anything else because then we could get out and stretch our legs and play in the field or look at the cactus.

I was different from the grownups. Perhaps it was because I had hope.

Several times we went across the border to Old Mexico and Clara would buy serapes and things. One time we were coming back through customs and I was as usual in the back seat with Ritzy and a lot of bags, and the customs officials looked at me with my black hair and my dark skin tanned by the Arizona sun and my dark eyes and looked at Clara and Lou with their pink skin, blue eyes and light brown hair, and the officials thought I must be a Mexican child and that my parents must have kidnapped me. I don't remember it at all but evidently they kept us there for a long time until they made some phone calls or something and decided to let us through.

And as we had gone to Wichita from Winfield so now we went sometimes to Phoenix. I was having very bad headaches from sinus trouble and my tonsils were always inflamed because of the sinus trouble. There was a specialist in Phoenix they brought me to and he said he should take out my tonsils, which was a very popular thing to do in those days even if there was nothing wrong with them. And at the same time he'd drill holes in my skull or enlarge the holes that were there so that my sinuses could drain better. We had to take several trips to do this, first for consultations with the specialist, then for the operation, and then for checkups to see that the sinuses were doing all right.

One time early on during the consultation phase Clara and I were in a department store and I was following her in a dreamy sort of way, I was following her dress, which was a blue flowered dress, as she went about buying things, and then I looked up at the face above the dress and it was a black woman looking down at me. I started screaming. I screamed and screamed. This was about the time of the kidnapping of the Lindbergh baby and everyone was very conscious of the dangers of kidnapping. I was dressed up real nice with short pants and a matching jacket and I suppose I looked like I might be a rich kid. Clara had already noticed that I was no longer with her and she had gone out to fetch a policeman because the first thing she thought of was kidnapping, so when I screamed and when the department store announced my problem over the public address system, she wasn't there to hear. And so I went on screaming. Finally Clara came back in with the policeman and we got together again but it was a big trauma to me.

After that, I had a dream which came back to me several times, and each time I woke up screaming. It was in our house in Winfield and I smelled a horrible smell which was the smell of burning milk. Other people don't seem to hate it but I think it's awful. I went into the kitchen and there was my mother bent over a pan with steam rising from it, and when she raised her head, her face was black.

It may have been during this trip to Phoenix that I got my Raggedy Ann doll and heard my mother read the story of Raggedy Ann. This added two important items to my collection of important possessions, a doll and a book. Raggedy Ann was found in an attic. She was the leader of all the dolls even though she was homemade. Since she was quite independent, I felt she must be lonely but in fact she was always in cheerful company. One picture in the book frightened me, the picture of Raggedy Ann when she fell into the chicken yard and a huge hen was standing on her looking as though she might peck out Raggedy Ann's eyes. There was a lot of reference to her eyes, which were made of shoe buttons, and sometimes one would get lost and have to be replaced. Sometimes she got in trouble because she always wore a happy smile.

It was also about this time that I saw *The Ugly Duckling* cartoon, in which a very gawky and different duckling is severely and endlessly teased until he grows up to be something far grander than any ordinary duck. This affected me profoundly. It is so important for children to have heroes they can gain hope from. The Ugly Duckling was my great hope for my future. My favorite fairy tale was Hans Christian Andersen's *The Snow Queen*, but that was later.

There was another intense interest that was building up in me during this year and that I should tell you about here. Singing. I loved to sing. I must have discovered singing in Winfield because somewhere there was a picture of me with other children in Winfield dressed in surplices at the church. But in Bisbee I never stopped singing. I sang all the time while I played with my Raggedy Ann doll or outside in the sand. I sang even as I crayoned the glorious Arizona sunsets. Evidently I sang very beautifully because my singing didn't go unnoticed.

I don't know which came first, the nuns or the movie. The nuns lived at the bottom of our street and somehow they must have heard me sing, which was an easy enough thing to do if they ever walked up the steep roadway past our house, because, as I say, I was doing it all the time. Unless the movie came first and they went to it, which seems less likely than the other thing. In any case, what happened was that they asked my mother if they couldn't have the joy of giving me singing lessons for free, and Clara, always glad to accept anything free, especially babysitting, said they could, and for several months I studied singing with the nuns every weekday morning, but I don't remember any of it at all and I've always wondered exactly what those nuns did to me.

I've heard that the Catholic Church says, "Give us a child before the age of six and we've got that child for a lifetime," or something to that effect, and I am a very religious person with singing mixed up in my mind with religion.

Although I don't concern myself much with saints and the Virgin Mary, I do feel very strongly about angels. It seems to me that anyone who doesn't believe in angels is being insensitive, is blocking out large hunks of the obvious truth. I've seen angels, I'm all the time communicating with them. Angels are reality. Without angels, life is a hollow misery. If those nuns gave me angels, I'm eternally grateful. I couldn't live without angels.

The other thing, the movie, was a strange affair. We went to a lot of movies in Bisbee. There was one movie house in town and it changed movies once a week. I was older now and learned to enjoy going to movies. The movie house was run by a man who is now a well-known Arizona painter. He was very conscientious about his movie house and what was shown, and in addition to the movie and the cartoon and the Preview of Coming Attractions and *The March of Time*, he'd often photograph news events in the town and show them as *The March of Time of Bisbee*. Then one day he knocked on our door and handed my mother three complimentary tickets to the movie and asked her to be sure to bring her son to the movie that evening, so we all three went, Clara and Lou and I, and on came the cartoon and the preview and the news and then came *The March of Time of Bisbee*, and there was a little boy playing in the sand and it was me and I was singing and my voice came over the loudspeakers. I sat stunned in my seat watching myself digging up sand and putting it in my bucket and then dumping it out into a heap. I was sitting in a dark movie house and I was singing and playing in the sand in the bright sun, both at once. It was a most amazing thing to me to see myself in a movie, larger than life.

There was some preparation made for the cameraman's visit, my mother asking me what song I'd like to sing, and I had heard somewhere like on the radio a song I liked, "Mickey Mouse's Birthday Party," and insisted that that be the song. We had to go to Phoenix for the sheet music and I learned it with Clara accompanying me on the piano and then actually made a record for the man to play. But no matter what the preparations were, I had no idea I would see myself so big on the screen.

Of course I got praised and teased for this, no end. They called me the Spanky McFarland of Bisbee. Spanky McFarland was a little boy in a series of shorts that were often shown in the Bisbee movie house called *Our Gang*, in which a bunch of little kids get in and out of trouble. The reason I was tagged with that name was that Spanky McFarland was the fat kid and already I was quite fat.

I was fat and asthmatic, had serious sinus trouble and inflamed tonsils. My eyes were bad and my ears were always infected from the sinus trouble. I had chronic severe headaches. But I was a precocious child. I was smart. I emulated men of position. Clara dressed me well. I could sing. I could join in conversations and say brilliant things. I knew I was more interesting than other people, children and grownups alike. I knew I deserved attention. In Bisbee I started becoming bossy and usually people obeyed. Some people think I was spoiled. I think I was fighting for my soul.

One day Clara and I were walking along downtown and we saw a man who was very fat. I was acting naughty at the moment and she pointed at the fat man and said, "If you don't behave, I'll have Fatty babysit for you." This must have been shortly after Fatty Arbuckle, the famous silent movie comedian, became the image of the monstrous to everyone by inadvertently killing a young woman in a peculiar sex act. I stopped being naughty immediately, looked at the fat man and saw that, in being fat, he had a certain impressive power.

One time we went to visit a family for supper. They had a little boy. He and I were playing together in his bedroom and I wanted to see his feet and convinced him that we could both take off our shoes although I knew this was forbidden. At least that's the way I remember it. I don't know if we got caught or not.

Clara had one of those washing machines of the time with a wringer and, because they tended to spill, people usually ran them out in the yard in nice weather. One time I was sitting on the basement wall watching the clothes come through the wringer.

They would come oozing out and the top part of the wringer would go all crooked. I was sitting watching this with the usual fascination and Clara called me to her and I went over and she glanced over to where I'd been sitting and there was a huge tarantula. It was really big with hair all over. She screamed and ran and got the toilet plunger and killed it by hitting it again and again with the plunger. She told me that once a tarantula had fallen into the bathtub with some woman and bit her and she'd been very sick for days. She said, "You see how important it is that you come immediately when I call you."

The year we were there was the year of the great fire when the big two-storey department store downtown burned to the ground. We saw the glow of it from our house and we stood outside and watched it. The next day we all went to see it. It was astonishing to me. The department store, which we'd been in any number of times, the entrance, windows and aisles, the escalator and the pneumatic billing machine, the bright-colored scarves and the salesladies had all gone away and in their place were black rubble and twisted beams with smoke rising here and there in thin clouds.

There was a little girl next door. She actually lived in the house directly above us and I didn't like her very much even though it was good to have someone my age nearby. The problem with her was she was mean, and a few days after the department store fire she was standing above me on her terrace wall saying things like, "Fatty Fatty Fatty Fatty Fatty," and other endearments till I couldn't resist attacking her and beating on her till she ran home crying. I was spoken to severely about it. Not long after that she set fire to the curtains in her house and the fire truck came and it was night time and very exciting. After that, she'd scream every night because she thought she was on fire. It was strange.

The operation on my tonsils and sinuses happened right around Easter and my parents promised me a big Easter bunny if I were good. The nurses put the white cup-like thing over my nose and mouth and then I woke up and threw up all over my covers and my throat hurt real bad. But I could have all the chocolate malts I wanted and they brought me the Easter Bunny and the Bunny was totally satisfactory. It was actually better than I expected. It was two feet tall and stuffed and stiff. It had big pink ears and white fur and was wearing a blue coat and red corduroy trousers and a green bow tie. I was very fond of that bunny.

I also discovered while recuperating from the operation that a very nice airplane can be made by simply putting a pencil under the forefinger and the little finger and over the two middle fingers.

The doctor wanted to check my sinuses every day for some days so my parents took a motel room and we lived there. Even though my throat hurt worse than my nose, he was more concerned with my nose. I'd go back to the hospital every day and they'd stuff cotton swabs up my nose with stuff in them that was supposed to heal where they'd drilled holes in my skull, and they'd make me say "coffee cake" over and over. They said this would help it drain.

On the way home, Lou taught me about airlift, where you can make the wind from the moving car pick up your hand or put it down by the angle of your fingers.

I had to go back once a month for checkups. It was a large room full of apparatus. One whole side of it was all windows covered with

Venetian blinds. In the middle of the room was a chair like a dentist's chair and I'd sit in it while they'd probe my nose and I'd say "coffee cake" again and again.

Whether it was during these visits that we bought sheet music I can't remember. It seems hard to believe that we would have made a special trip to get "Mickey Mouse's Birthday Party" (the image of whose cover I still have clearly in my mind), as it was a considerable drive to Phoenix. There was other sheet music we got and also I learned to sing "Water Boy" and "You Are My Sunshine."

There was another recurring dream I had, a jungle scene with alligators. The main alligator is looking at me and has his mouth open and it's very red. This dream frightened me badly and I invented a way to wake up from my dreams because of this one. What you do is you squeeze your eyelids together very tight then open them with a snap. If it doesn't work the first time, try it again and you'll find yourself in your own bedroom with your own toys around you.

One day there was a school carnival and there was a game for little children where I could fish with a fishing pole over cloth that was water-colored and I'd put my hook down and then I'd pull it up and there'd be a gift on the hook. I liked that a lot. I did it again and again.

My father was a sad and lonely person, a ghostly figure mincing through the house, I suppose so that Clara and I wouldn't notice him and ask for something. I'm sure he was not happy in Bisbee. Lou was from a large farming family in Oklahoma and he liked farmers but there weren't any in Bisbee. Clara would occasionally try to find a place in society by inviting over some of the other faculty members and their wives for dinner or something, but Lou would sit there sucking his teeth and talking about farming or they'd be liberals and he'd be a Republican. Or he'd put on his Oklahoma drawl and talk about his family, because it was even more embarrassing than being a business teacher to be the son of an Oklahoma farmer. He had been born the youngest of a family of thirteen and he was the one his parents had chosen to send to college to get out of the mud and become a teacher. But he would, I think, have preferred to get back in the mud if he could have.

I'm afraid I was a terrible disappointment to Lou. He wanted more than anything to be a regular guy of the sort that was in the rural community he was brought up in. And since that seemed to be impossible for him, he would have been happy if I had shown signs of becoming a regular guy, but on the contrary I was already clearly even less regular than he was. That was what he wanted from me the most. What Clara wanted from me was that I be a child star, and she used every opportunity to keep him away from me. He felt awkward with me, mostly did stay away from me.

One time he was the umpire for a baseball game, he did a lot of that, being umpire, and I got hit by a baseball. He was ineffectual, not having enough of a relationship with me to be able to soothe me. The event simply discouraged him, pulled him even farther from me, and I felt a failure about it too.

The strongest memory I have of Bisbee, and strangely in some ways the sweetest, was going walking with Lou one night after a snow, ending up at City Hall in the middle of town where a lunatic was being held in the jail, which was the top floor of City Hall. Some other people had gathered also and the lunatic was screaming and shouting through the bars of his window, "I'm going to come and get you at midnight! I'll be there at midnight!" I was terrified. I felt that he spoke with conviction and I was afraid he meant me. I was sure the lunatic looked right at me and that he knew, or could find out, where I lived. I clutched Lou's hand and noticed that Lou was unperturbed. "He can't get you," he said, and we stood there awhile holding hands and listening to the lunatic rave. Then, still holding hands, we walked home.

5

Macomb

WE SPENT THE SUMMER IN DENVER. Lou had a summer job selling shoes at Sears. This was the pleasantest job he ever had. Maybe he got a thrill out of fondling feet. Or it might simply have been that in the shoe department at Sears he encountered the salt-of-the-earth people that he knew how to talk with and who accepted, even shared, his values. Whatever it was, he was extremely successful and popular there and he was happy with that job as with no other.

We lived in a fine old house on an old street with tall trees and full blooming bushes half a block from Colfax Avenue. At that time Colfax was cheery, busy and handy. The house was made of red stone with beautiful dark hardwood trim inside, lighted and colored with stained glass windows. There was a glass-covered bookcase in one of the rooms with a set of encyclopedias in it, which Clara let me look at. It had beautiful covers with gold filigree, fine paper and many wonderful pictures, and I spent a lot of time reverently and avidly looking at the pictures in the encyclopedia.

Clara supplemented our income by taking in boarders. She had a deal with several motels. If the motel was full, they'd send the tourists to Clara, then Clara would give the motel a commission. It worked well, the house was always full, and Clara was kept very busy washing sheets and cooking. This left me freer than I had ever been.

One of my duties was to water the lawn. It was also one of my great pleasures.

There is something extremely satisfying to a man in holding a hose in his hands and the water keeps coming out and out all over the ground. I liked to take the nozzle off and hold the hose in one place till there was a big puddle. I had a great stirring fantasy that if I watered the lawn long enough I could drown the world like Noah's flood and then we'd have to go around in boats. This, I think, was a very important fantasy for me that by making love to the world I might change it.

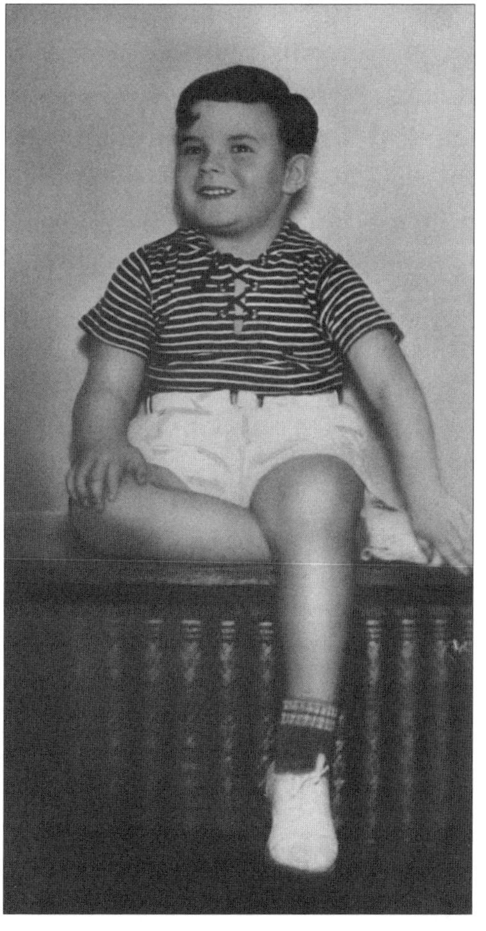

In spite of the sinus operation I contiued to have serious ear trouble. It was very painful and people were always pouring medicine in my ears.

The only other memory I have from that time was from a box of chocolate-covered cherries someone had brought. They were the kind that come in a pretty box and each piece is a swirled shell of chocolate which contains one red cherry in sweet white creamy stuff. They were wonderful. I ate most of the box one afternoon and then broke out into hives all over my body. Red and swollen with welts and wildly, insanely itchy. Clara covered me all over with white paste, which dried to a white powder and dribbled around aggravating the itch. I was told very severely that I must not scratch. It was an agony.

Then in the fall we went to Macomb, Illinois. Lou got a job there replacing a teacher who was on sabbatical for a year and we lived in that teacher's house. It was a big house, bigger even than the one in Denver, two storeys plus an attic and very modern for its day. There was no porch in front, only a stoop at the top of several cement steps through a large green lawn. The door was white with a great brass door knocker. Inside the door was a hallway leading back to the kitchen. On the right was the stairway to the bedrooms upstairs. The bathrooms were new and bright. Before the stairway on the right were the doors to the dining room, which were of glass, and in the dining room were a big table with chairs and a cabinet full of nice dishes and a sideboard. Behind the dining room was another bedroom where I think Clara and Lou slept. Across the hall from the dining room was the living room with newish comfortable furniture and big windows and a fireplace. The kitchen was shiny with chrome and tiles. The whole house inside and out was brightly colored and cheerful beyond anything I'd ever encountered. Here, I got my training to be very careful of everything.

The driveway curved around the house to the garage in back and beyond the garage was more lawn with the clothesline and many trees. There was no alley.

On the other side of the driveway beyond a stretch of grass was the rock garden. The rock garden was a sort of pit with a tall thick hedge around it, a tangle of flowers, shrubs and trees with paths through them all leading down to the bottom where goldfish swam in a pond. This rock garden was my Eden with Ryda Rue.

It didn't take me long to get to know Ryda Rue. She lived next door. But she wasn't anything like the girl next door in Bisbee. She was dark and small with round cheeks and long eyelashes and almost exactly my age. She always wore pants and a baseball cap and had her hair in bangs. She wasn't cruel at all. She was very nice indeed. She was never mean to me and I was never mean to her and we never argued. We spent hours most days together in the garden playing and talking. Sometimes we'd hold hands for a while. At first the grownups thought it was cute and then when it went on and on they thought it was strange.

I made other friends there too, quite an assortment of friends. In that neighborhood it seemed easy to make friends. Everyone was nice and everyone was friendly. It was the strangest thing. It had never happened to me before and has never happened to me since, that everyone was nice and everyone was friendly. I've brooded about this a lot. If we had stayed in Macomb I might well have had a happy childhood and if I'd had a happy childhood would I still be a genius? I was already very precocious, very inventive, smart, had perfect pitch and sang like an angel. I put on shows for guests, used big words, and discussed politics. But where would I have got the push, the flame, the raging need to become an artist without trauma and misery to whip me on?

The school where Lou worked was a teacher's college and there, in 1937, they were very excitedly studying the possibilities of having a pre-school. It was something that hadn't been tried before and they were trying it out. Unique and quite experimental. Clara, eager as always to get me out of her hair for a while every day, used Lou's position and my precocity to get me enrolled in it.

To get to the pre-school I went half a block to a busy street, went a block along that and crossed at a crosswalk. This was dangerous. After I got across that street there was a very nice park with multicolored trees in the fall and flowers and shrubs and grassy knolls and water running through. Across that park was the pre-school and the whole college behind it. The school was bright and modern with several teachers, all women. There were little tables and chairs spread around for us and we each had a mat for exercises and naps. We were read to and we did projects with crayons and scissors and paste. We worked on music too, it may even have been Carl Orff, and I played the triangle though I liked the tambourine better. Sometimes we put on concerts in our room and invited the parents to come and there were cookies and lemonade. Sometimes a teacher would come with her college students and they'd all give us tests with blocks.

By this time I was troubled because, even though I could do many things, I could neither wink nor whistle, and I confessed my handicap to a young teacher. She was blond and thin-faced and she took me out on the back steps of the school and we worked and worked on these problems. Finally I did manage to wink one eye but not the other and, after a long and arduous labor, I somehow pushed out a whistle, but I've never been very good at these things and still feel shamed and embarrassed about it.

I don't know where I learned to read. It could have been that the nuns in Bisbee taught me. Or perhaps I naturally picked it up singing. I had to learn to read the notes. And then there were the words I was to sing down below. How could I help but learn to read? Or maybe Grandmaw taught me to read like she taught Mugsy his tricks.

However it happened, I could read when I went to pre-school and the teachers let me take home books. I was very excited and proud about this. And as I carried these books home from pre-school, my classmates bullied and harassed me. They threatened to beat me up. They tore the books from my hands and threw them in the mud. They ganged up and pinched me and hit me. It was a nightmare every afternoon after school.

In this situation I think is the key to my social problems all through my life. Where it actually began I couldn't say, but here, in pre-school, when I was four years old, it showed itself in full flower, and it's been like this every since. Therefore we should probably rummage around here to see what we can find.

Here I am, age four. I can read, I can converse and strut around like any grownup. I know how to cross a street. I can pace with my hands clasped behind my back like any professor and shout impressive things. On top of all this I can, as we know, sing, and, as we are soon to see, put on circus acts and amazing shows. I am an amazing phenomenon. I deserve attention. I merit attention. If you pay attention to me, you will not only be momentarily satisfying me but you might well be delighted or even, and here is my most wonderful reward, you might even become inspired. This is my great hope, this the purpose of my life, the driving desire behind all my actions, that I might fulfill my destiny by transforming the mind of man by whatever means, if not with the garden hose then with conversation or, if I may express my understandable impatience, a monologue would be better, and, with the monologue, and I have always been generous in this area, a show, with bright colors and splendid dreams and magnificent rhythm that puts popular music to shame.

You know, the more I think of the shows I put on and the way I acted at such a young age, the more I am reminded of Mugsy, the very smart little Boston Bull that Grandmaw trained. Maybe I saw the honors he got for his act and I wanted such honors, too. Maybe it was as simple as that. Maybe I wanted to be smiled upon by my grandmother as she smiled upon him. But although I have always vociferously defended Sigmund Freud as a discoverer of truth which his followers have been trying to obscure, nonetheless, I am as fiercely defensive as anyone, as Freud himself was, of my neuroses and my illusions and my delusions. Ezra Pound was called insane with the epithet "delusions of grandeur" but he was grand! He was accused because, or so say the rumors, he called himself the greatest poet alive — and he was that! And I too am great, I am very great, it's not a delusion, it's the simple truth. I'm great and I have a destiny and anyone who gets in my way must be working for the evil one!

So perhaps, dear reader, you can understand how in pre-school as with the rest of my life I didn't look around, as the other children did, to see how to act and where to fit in. I scorned that. I made an entrance. I showed them what I was and what I needed. The teachers, very excited to have the opportunity to work with such a very bright child, gave me encouragement and help. Brazenly I moved in to make use of what materials were available, but the other students rebelled, called me "bossy" and "teachers' pet," and when the teachers let only me take home books because I could read and they could not, they flew around me like hornets and gave me no peace.

The thought never occurred to me to change what the bullies were asking me to change, that is my behavior in the classroom, my equality with the teachers, and my obvious superiority to the other students. "Don't rub it in!" they said but I never heard them, still don't, and if anyone suggests something of the sort I say that would be hypocrisy. If they don't want to recognize what I am, they're the walking dead, they're evil. They ask me for false modesty and though there is much that I can give, I cannot give that. False modesty erodes integrity and integrity is what my destiny is made of and without my destiny, I die. I would rather die fighting than false. This I proved in pre-school and have been proving ever since.

And so although I loved pre-school, the walk home was torture. I tried leaving later than the others but then it would be getting dark and the path through the park would become eerie. The tree branches would sway and if the bullies found me then, there would be no one to appeal to for help. I don't know how this was resolved. Perhaps as spring came on they took up baseball or something. As for me, I had learned to fear, and had I been able to see ahead of me all the bullies waiting for me on all those walks home from school and on into adult life, I might have quailed and quit right there.

On Saturday, Ryda Rue and I were taken to the Saturday afternoon matinee and we'd sit side by side and watch the news and the cartoons and the serial and then the feature. *Scarface* was wonderful. Paul Muni in the life of Al Capone. And the one about the man who was sentenced to Alcatraz and, although he knew there was no way to swim to shore, he tried it anyway and died. That one was all grand and moody with foghorns and searchlights. When we got back to the garden we would try to reenact the movie. We worked very hard and seriously on this and went over things and made improvements. We had to make do with what we had, and so for San Francisco Bay we made do with our goldfish pond, and for the rocky shore of Alcatraz we had the biggest rock in the rock garden.

It was the serials, though, that made us go week after week with an eager solemnity. At the end of each chapter, the hero was left in some terrible situation, and then at the beginning of the next chapter it was resolved and he'd get himself into another. There was one where a helicopter took off from a roof. It was full of bad guys and Dick Tracy was hanging on the strut. Then a bad guy climbed out and was stamping on Dick Tracy's hands and in the last shot we saw his body falling through the air. For a whole week Ryda Rue and I worried and fussed together trying to imagine how he could possibly survive this one. Perhaps he could land on something soft? But any number of mattresses after such a fall would not be enough. So with frantic solicitude we went the next week and saw that Dick Tracy had grabbed the ankle of the gangster and knocked him off balance so that the body we saw falling was that of the gangster and all was well.

Then there was the time Dick Tracy was fighting with the bad guys on the dock and a barrel rolled off into the water beside a big ship and was crushed to splinters by the rolling of the ship. Then Dick Tracy was pushed off just where the barrel had gone. And the next Saturday I was sick in bed and Clara wouldn't let me go to see how it came out. I said I would stay in bed if Ryda Rue could go and then come to my room and tell me how it came out. So she went by herself to the movie and I waited and she came and told me the solution, but I honestly have forgotten what it was.

I do remember her showing me another thing that I thought was very interesting. Dick Tracy needed a telephone number very badly and someone wrote it down on a pad of paper then tore off the page with the number and threw it in the fire. Ryda Rue got a pad of paper and wrote on the top sheet, tore it off and threw it away. Then she got my pencil sharpener and sprinkled the fine carbon dust onto the pad, blew gently on it, and there, lightly etched on the second sheet, was what she had written on the first. I was very impressed.

Clara tried again in Macomb to be a socialite and we often had people over for parties. The discussion was often about Hitler, who was casting gloom on the world already. Most of the people were frightened and outraged. Everyone listened intently to their radios and pored over their newspapers. They all said those damn Germans were starting up again, a great ugly beast growing in Europe. I had some idea of what they were talking about because I saw it in the newsreels at the movies. I even knew what Hitler looked like and had seen pictures of his troops and some of the devastation he was making. Clara was defensive about the Germans, being German herself and raised in a German community. She said they'd been mistreated after World War I, they'd been set apart and were fighting because of that.

It was at that time that Oswald Spengler's book, *The Decline of the West*, came out and everyone read it, or at least glanced through it, and it was as much news as Hitler was. There were great arguments about that, too, about whether this was a decadent society, whether

America was really the last dregs of the greatness that was Europe, whether America wasn't perhaps a new beginning culture. Lou was unimpressed. He scoffed at the whole idea. He made a fool of himself not only by his constant vulgarity but also by his perennial optimism. And he did go on sucking his teeth.

Then there was William Saroyan's book, *The Daring Young Man on the Flying Trapeze,* and everyone talked a lot about that too. I don't believe I had been taken to a circus but I must have seen something of one, probably at the movies. I got much of my education at the movies. And then perhaps in pre-school we walked around as various animals as part of our exercises. In any case, I always put on a show at these parties and I was encouraged to do so by Clara, and my shows at this time were mainly circuses where I impersonated the elephants and the lion tamers and the tightrope walkers. I used any props I could get together, a jump rope with one handle broken off for the lion tamer's whip, a piece of string stretched across the floor as my tightrope, a top hat for the barker. I couldn't do anything athletic, of course, but I had a lot of energy. It was as the barker that I shone the

brightest. The barker was my own part.

I got so excited about my circus act that I enlarged it into the neighborhood. All the kids around got into it and we did it in the yards and on the sidewalks. It got quite big. Some kids wanted to pull their wagons as horses and others were clowns and did somersaults and danced around. I tried to get Ritzy to jump through a hoop like Mugsy had, but he'd only step through it amiably if I got on the other side and called him. I always tried to have Ryda Rue be the star of all the shows we did. She was always agreeable and encouraging. But the garden with just Ryda Rue and me was the best thing. Winter and summer we played together there. There was one hole in the thick tall hedge around the garden and that hole was her entryway. We talked a lot about the movies and about our lives. We made hollyhocks into dancers and floated them on the pond. When the newsreels carried stories of war, we played with toy soldiers. We had dolls and toys and blocks. We built houses and castles, made up stories and acted them out. Ritzy was always lying around not far away. Sometimes other children would come into the garden and then we'd make a bigger production, maybe play blind man's buff on the lawn or act out a play.

There was a caretaker who came by once or twice a week to mow the lawn and mind the flowers. He was fat and red-faced and white-haired and he was nice to me, too, and sometimes we would converse for a while.

That spring it became very hot very early and on weekends Ryda Rue and I started a lemonade stand in front of my house. Lemonade and Kool-Aid. The Kool-Aid was a nickel and the lemonade was a dime. Clara made it for us and we were very successful.

Pretty soon she ran out of sugar and makings and we paid her to buy some more. We had other children we paid to wash the glasses and pitchers as they were used. We were so successful we moved our enterprise around the corner to the big street by the park and employed the other children as runners to carry the dirty dishes away and bring more lemonade and more glasses. Ritzy lay under the table all the time.

Ryda Rue and I took care of the customers and the money. Our customers were lined up and coming very fast It was a tremendous success and we were making a lot of money. However, the parents of some of the runners started to worry about the dangerous street and we had to stop. But by this time I had filled a good-sized piggy bank with money and I was rich. Clara said we should save the piggy bank to help me go to college.

It was a wonderful world. There was so much to do and everyone was kind and everything was interesting. I had a great fondness and joy with all my neighborhood. Life was grand. If Lou had gotten on with the staff at the school there and if Clara hadn't done what she did that summer, we could have stayed in Macomb, and if we had done so, what would I have become? Life was so very very good there.

6

The End of Eden

WHEN THE SCHOOL YEAR WAS OVER in Macomb, Lou was invited to come back the next year, since the teacher whose place we took didn't plan to return. We went to Denver again for the summer and Lou went back to his job as shoe salesman for Sears.

The house we got in Denver was a tremendous disappointment to me. It wasn't big. It didn't have books in it. There was one front porch (with no swing) which we had to share with the people in the other half. The yard was a tiny spot of bare hard dirt with nothing in it but gum wrappers and dog poop. Of course, there were no boarders. The neighbor children were stupid and sticky. Why Clara and Lou chose that place to live after the tall trees and oak-paneled house of the previous summer, I can't imagine.

I don't know what I did that summer. With no children who interested me to play with, no books to read, not even a lawn to water, there was nothing for me to do except to be with my mother wherever she went.

The other half of the duplex was inhabited by the landlady and her grown-up son who drove a taxi for a living. She was very fat with glasses and she was jolly and fun-loving and liked to sit around the kitchen table and talk. Her son was about Clara's age and had been married and was now divorced. His name was Adam. Clara spent more and more time visiting them in their kitchen while Lou was away selling shoes at Sears. I think they were the only people we knew that summer and the only thing for either Clara or me to do was to visit with them.

One time we went to City Park with Clara and Lou and Adam and his mother. It was nighttime and the fountains in the middle of the lake were lit with colored lights and the band played marches and popular tunes as the colors changed on the fountains; the shapes of the fountains changed from a peacock tail to a mound of water to a circle of fountains to a tall pillar with side sprays, all with red, green and blue lights changing in synchrony with the music of the band. It was the most beautiful display I ever saw in my life. I wanted it to never stop, and in my mind and my eyes after that I could always see red and green and blue balls and falling water and shooting stars whenever I wanted to.

In the daytime when Lou was at work, we sometimes went out with Adam in his taxi, always in his taxi.

In August, Clara and I took a trip to Wyoming with a young woman friend of Clara's. I don't know where she found her. She looked like something out of a fashion ad in a magazine. She had red hair and bangs and was very stylish indeed. We saw the Tetons and the Glory Hole, blue and steaming. We thought it looked like a big morning glory. We saw bears and we gathered with everyone else at Old Faithful and everyone was looking at their watches and it went off right on time. We stayed in a room at a log cabin lodge where there was a little shop out front. Clara's birthday was coming up and I had decided to buy her a birthday present, the first one I ever gave. I had been saving up my allowance for it and that was hard for me as I was very fond of candy and there were certain small toys I might have bought also. But I saved

it up and then on her birthday I went to the little shop and bought her a ceramic wall hanging with a profile of an Indian woman on it, black hair, bangs, an orange headband which hung down in back, gold earrings and red red cheeks. It was oval and a few inches across. I thought she'd like it because it looked like what her friend wore.

I bought it and I carried it upstairs and gave it to her but she simply didn't seem interested. She was, as it happened, distraught and excited about something else. I was very disappointed but she swept me out of the room and down the stairs again and there was Adam standing outside waiting for her. Clara told me not to tell Lou that Adam was even here at all, and we stayed another couple weeks there with Adam and then went back to Macomb.

Oh, I was glad to get back to Macomb and Ryda Rue, back to the garden and the nice people, the open and friendly neighborhood. I was so glad. Ryda Rue and I returned immediately to our old intimacy, playing together in total peace and harmony in the garden, dappled by golden sunlight. We went everywhere together, to Saturday movies and to play with other children.

But in the house with Clara and Lou, something was terribly wrong. Clara and Lou shouted at each other all the time and it echoed through the house. After I went to bed, they'd shout even louder and I had to cover my head with a pillow. Or there would be the silences. Long tense silences. In the kitchen, the sweet golden sunlight of Macomb turned gray with their silences.

When they shouted, they very often shouted about me, Clara going on about how sickly I was and how I needed clean air for my asthma, and Lou saying she liked me being sick all the time, that he'd like to have a healthy boy who could play baseball.

It was about this time I developed my hernia and had to wear a truss. I was constantly examined by doctors. The truss was made of springs covered with leather around my hips. There was a big spring with a big ball on the end of it that pressed into my crotch between my right thigh and my testicles. I was told that if I didn't wear this truss all the time, my innards would come down through the hernia and press into my left testicle and I'd strangle and die. And if this ever happened, that someone should push against my left testicle until my innards went back in and then I could breathe again. Whether this ever happened or not I can't be sure. I have such a creepy horrible feeling about it, but that may have come from what the doctors said and the ghastly image they created in my mind.

It may have been then, or it may have been earlier, that my teachers discovered that I had very bad eyes, and from then on I wore thick glasses.

The ear trouble, of course, kept coming back, and the hives, and the asthma. The holes in my head seemed to have cured my sinus trouble more or less. And if I was fat in Bisbee, now I was becoming really fat.

At this time I developed a delight in certain foods, like salmon patties or mashed potatoes with creamed corn and cheese, and though I was terribly sickly, I always had a good appetite. Clara always enjoyed giving me second and third helpings and Lou always hated to see it and sat there at the dinner table sucking his teeth and glowering out the window. The more Clara succeeded with me, the more Lou resented me. He'd hardly speak to me and never took me anywhere or played with me.

Clara decided to take in a boarder. When she showed him around downstairs, I went into Clara and Lou's room and got two powder puffs from Clara's dresser. When she brought him upstairs to show him his room, I ran down the hall and whapped the two powder puffs together in his face laughing wildly. He decided he didn't want to live with us and Clara gave up the idea of taking in a boarder.

Constantly, constantly, Clara and Lou screamed at each other and I got the habit of sleeping with a pillow over my head. The tension was continuous and the talk about me was often and Clara screamed about my needs and Lou shouted what I should be and they yelled other things too, about money and social status and sex, but I didn't understand those things so much.

There was a poor kid that Ryda Rue and I knew. He lived in a house very like the duplex we had lived in all summer, and he had a birthday party. It was a small house with grates for heat in the floor. It was hot and dowdy and there was very little to do. Ryda Rue and I were quite uncomfortable, but we had been dropped off and weren't going to be picked up for a long time so I looked around the house to see if there was something. There were chairs and a table and a couch and curtains and a fan. It was the fan that gave me the idea. I asked the boy's mother if we couldn't use the fan to make an airplane and she said yes, so we turned over the chairs in the shape of an airplane and had the fan in front like a propeller. We turned it on and off and crawled about under the chairs. We really had a good time with that, and I was proud as could be that I had invented the airplane.

I have no memory of church in Macomb at all though I do remember singing to visitors, and I believe it was at this time that I made a record at a studio of "Water Boy" and "You Are My Sunshine." "You

Are my Sunshine" was Adam and Clara's song together. They had me sing it to them again and again in Wyoming and as I sang it they'd smile at each other or hold hands. Maybe I hoped Clara and Lou would smile and hold hands if I sang it, but they didn't. And when we proudly played the record for Lou in the evening, he fidgeted and looked bleakly out the window and finally read his newspaper.

There was no way I seemed able to get through to Lou. If I could transform myself into Babe Ruth, his eyes might light up and he'd say, "That's my Boy!" But as it was, there seemed no hope for that from him, ever. On the other hand, Adam had brought me presents, taken me places, and listened smiling as I sang, his head bobbing with the rhythm. No doubt it was purely as a seduction of Clara, but I didn't know that and I had enjoyed it. Now, however, there was the endless screaming in the house, contrasted with the sweet peace of the garden with Ryda Rue.

But one Friday afternoon Ryda Rue and her family went to spend the weekend with relatives in Ohio and I was left to my own devices.

On Saturday afternoon I went to the matinee by myself. I don't remember what it was but it must have been very good. Somewhere along toward the end, I had to use the toilet real bad, but at the same time the movie was at such an exciting point that the thought of getting up and going to the bathroom seemed quite mad so I stayed where I was and let it go into my pants. When the movie was over and the lights came on, I stayed in my seat until everyone else had got up to go and I managed to be the last one in the aisle, but in the lobby things got stirred around and I felt that someone or other had seen or smelled the unmistakable. I stood outside the movie theatre in misery, back against the wall, waiting for my mother to pick me up. Finally she arrived and I had to walk to the car even though some older kids were there and might see. Then in the car I rolled down the window, though that seemed a needless precaution since Clara was concentrating on her own problems. We got home and I sat in misery on the grass of the yard for a while until finally I couldn't stand it any more and I went in and told Clara, who changed and bathed me with no pity or sympathy at all.

On Sunday, Clara and Lou were screaming again as had become usual, and I decided to go out in the garden and play there by myself. There was a certain rock wall I had always admired, and I had recently noticed a sack of red cement in the garage. I got out my wagon, gathered together some loose stones, and got to work. But somehow the cement didn't hold the stones where I put them. The wall kept falling over, and there was red gunk everywhere. I finally decided that I had failed at building a wall. Not only that, I had made a really disgusting mess and didn't know where to hide it all. Unless I put it in the goldfish pond. I loaded up my wagon again with the stones, icky now with red cement, hauled them to the pond, dumped them in, and went back for another load. When I brought the second load, I saw that the water of the pond had turned red and the fish were floating belly up and dead in the red water. Some of the fish were orange and some were spotted and a few of them were very old and very big and I had watched them swimming around and had fed them crumbs. The pond and the fish had been a connection to my grandmother in my mind, as she had had a similar pond with similar fish in it. I was so horrified by what I'd done, and so discouraged, that I just sat and pulled off the tops of the grass with my hands until the red-faced, white-haired gardener came, as he always did on Sundays, and I saw him then talking to Lou and then he went away again. Lou spanked me hard and it wasn't much more than a week or so later that Clara and I drove to Denver.

7

The Great Trek

WHEN WE ARRIVED IN DENVER, we stayed first at a sleazy motel on East Colfax. We didn't stay there long. We moved to a downtown hotel which was dowdy and dusty with faded flowered wallpaper and worn green rugs. Some of the wallpaper was faded brown. The toilet was down the hall. There was overstuffed furniture in the lobby with the stuffing coming out in places. Everything was old and dull. Even the people that ran it were. Adam was there most of the time.

I discovered two pleasures during the month or so we were there. One was toast and tomato juice. When I had toast, I'd dunk it in the tomato juice like Adam dunked donuts in coffee. There was a little coffee shop next door to the hotel and every morning I went there to have toast and tomato juice. The people were nice. They smiled and said hello when I came in. It was a pleasant place. I still love to eat my toast and tomato juice. I had it every morning there without fail.

The other pleasure was climbing on statues. Our hotel was right near the capitol building and the little Natural History Museum, and every day Clara took me there and I climbed on the statues. There was a bear I particularly liked. I think it was a grizzly bear. He was black-bronze and smooth and soft as fur. I liked to pet his feet. When I sat under him, he protected me, like Ritzy, who had always slept under my bed before we came to Denver, had protected me. There were statues on the lawn of the capitol building too, terraces up to the building, and on some of the terraces were sculptures, all of them realistic, of course, men and horses and lions and such. One of them was an Indian who was huge and powerful and imposing, and I'd climb up the pedestal and then reach 'way up and touch his thigh. There was one time in Wyoming when we saw a cigar store Indian and the adults were getting a big kick out of it, but he was made of wood and man-size and I didn't care for him and was embarrassed because they did. But this one was smooth hard metal and bigger than anyone and beautiful and I hugged his leg and stroked his thigh and felt safe with him. Someday, I thought, I'd be big, too.

When the sun shone on them, they'd shine reddish-orange through dark brown. Some of them were smooth and black, others were pitted like skin is. In a sort of traffic circle nearby was a fountain with statues in the middle of a pool. It wasn't working because it was winter, but I could get into the dry fountain and clamber up into the middle. The ones in the fountain were rough with green streaks and I didn't like them so much, though it was fun to clamber around at the bottom of them while Clara and Adam sat on a bench and held hands. I never cared for going to museums because there were things in glass cases and I couldn't touch them. And I have never understood looking at scenic views. I'd rather have them on a postcard where I can touch them. Except in Wyoming when the bears came up to the car.

A few years later when I was mowing lawns, I mowed the lawn one summer for the lady who had made some of the stone animal sculptures. Her name was Mrs. Fisher. She and her husband lived in a little house by the alley and I worked for them the whole summer in exchange for an old typewriter. She was quite well-known all over the

OAKHURST CABINS
"Just a Nice Place to Stop on Hi-Way 40"
11325 E. Colfax Ave. Ph. Aurora, Colo., 285

state but they had little money. They were very kind to me.

But the thing about toast and tomato juice was it was always there. It was something I had control over. When I get started on a certain kind of food, I want it all the time. I want to know I can have it. I know that's neurotic, that one should like a variety of foods, but I want always the same food. If I don't get the food I want, what's the point of living? I'd get my toast and tomato juice and then in the rest of the day any kind of chaos could fall on me, but I'd had my toast and tomato juice and I could make it. Knowing I'd have it again the next morning gave solidity to my life. Lately I've suspected I might be allergic to tomatoes and wheat so I've been eating rice crackers with chutney on them, and just in the last few months I've switched from chutney to caviar. I vary this with grapefruit and English muffins, and now I've learned how to make beef stew in the crockpot with Tamari in it and wine. I can't drink wine but I like it in stew. I have to always have the same brand of whatever food I like because then I know I will get precisely the same taste at the same time of day .. so it was always Libby's tomato juice and now it has to be Bay's English muffins and Romanoff's whitefish caviar, and

Major Gray's chutney. I have had food neuroses from the time we met Adam in Wyoming and I felt my world quivering. Though it may have started before that because, you remember, I was already fat in Bisbee.

The bedstead was brass with knobs and the bright gold was peeling to reveal the dark metal underneath. And, of course, it sagged in the middle. But I didn't sleep there. Clara slept there. And Adam didn't live with us yet. So they had the problem of what to do with me so that they could be alone together. Again and again I sat in the musty hotel lobby, a spiffy sailor suit on my fat body, reading magazines through my thick glasses under the dour glare of an aged clerk, one of the many Dickensian scenes in my childhood.

Everything was so strange. The whole world had turned into weird things. Clara was always these days having hysterics. With her strict

Lutheran upbringing, she was trying not to face the facts of what she was doing, so she laid it on me, saying she was on the way back to Phoenix to check my sinuses. She cried all the time, which disturbed me, and when she wasn't doing that, she was making up to Adam and acting totally silly, so I had no security in her at all. Adam was what would be called a member of the low-life, and so the people we met were unlike any I had ever encountered before. They were grotesque in some sense, separated from me. Adam was sandy-haired, thin and angular with sharp features, a seamed, pitted reddish face. He wore a taxi-driver's cap, a World War I leather jacket, and cheap plaid shirts. He dangled his cigarette out the side of his mouth, drank whiskey out of the bottle, and liked to crumple his beer can and toss it into the corner of the room. He used a lot of dirty language, knew the whores and gamblers, enjoyed their repartee. He loved travel, gambling and drink. When he drank, which was often, he was at first thrillingly warm and friendly, plying Clara and me with gifts, and I was ecstatic with the warmth of it, with getting things I wanted. But always later that night he was extremely cruel and nasty, shouting, insulting me, hitting and kicking, destroying the gifts he'd given a few hours before. When he was sober he talked of what he wanted, and he alternately thrilled and embarrassed both Clara and me with his dreams of power, glory and revelry. When he was half drunk, he was an angel of happiness, which led inexorably to meanness when he got drunker, and especially when he was hung over.

Clara, who had taken a lot of money out of the bank in Macomb, after weeks of hysterical dallying, finally backed up again and we drove away with Adam in her car. It was the beginning of our great trek. The first stop was Phoenix, and we went to the sinus doctor's. I found it extremely comforting to be in a familiar place. There were the same doctors and the same room with the same wall of Venetian blinds and the same dentist chair. And they probed my nose while I said, "coffee cake" again and again. I sat in the chair and hungrily absorbed the familiarity, the middle-class style of the doctors, and the stripes of light coming through the Venetian blinds.

Then we hit the road again. Riding in the car was no pleasure. The views, as I say, were not interesting to me. The roads were bumpy and dust was always in the air. It was either hot and muggy and I'd bounce gasping in the back seat with my clothes sticking to me, or it was cold and drafty and I'd sit in a silent agony as numbness crept inexorably up my legs. The seats, made of heavy upholstery with buttons here and there to hold the stuffing in place, smelled of vomit and exhaust fumes. I don't know which was worse, the endless feeling of trapped boredom or the increasingly desperate urgency when I had to pee. At least when I had to pee, they took me seriously and began searching for a gas station. The only joy was that of stopping, either to eat or because of car trouble. Eating was great. We'd go into a cafe and it might be like the one near the hotel in Denver and the people would be friendly and notice how grownup I was in ordering the food I wanted. It may have been at this time that I discovered the cheeseburger. And apple or lemon pie. Lemonade was good and, of course, tomato juice. I didn't like milk. I've never liked milk.

The car broke down pretty often. It seemed like tires weren't very trustworthy in those days and cars were always boiling over too, so there was always the hope that there would be the regular thump thump of the flat tire or the cloud of steam when the water escaped the radiator or some other mechanical problem and Adam would pull over to the side of the road and they'd have to fix the tire or find water or flag down someone while I played in the field at the side of the road. And although Ritzy wasn't with me now, I did enjoy that.

I had toys I could play with in the car. I had my postcard collection for one thing, and during this time, it grew when we stayed anywhere long enough to receive mail. And sometimes Adam would just buy a postcard to add to it. Or if we were in a town for any length of time and happened to see a dime store, they might buy me a lead soldier. I had all different kinds of lead soldiers. They were shellacked and they were in all different positions so I could arrange them on the seat of the car and down on the floor so they'd be in a battle. One thing about travel was we could find every kind of lead soldier made, so I had a fine collection. I didn't like any but the lead ones. I liked to hold them in my hands and feel their weight and the ridges and bumps of their bodies and their weapons.

There was a song I used to sing, but I've forgotten it now, of a little boy who plays with his tin soldier, then puts it back on the shelf and goes to sleep. The boy never wakes up and the tin soldier waits and waits for him, very lonely. The prayer I was taught to say was the old standby where it says, "and if I die before I wake …." It seems strange now how much children were taught to think about dying in their sleep in those days.

The next stop was Las Vegas. Riding in the back seat alone, listening to the ghastliness of Adam when he was drunk and the hysterics of Clara, the endless sameness with fields going by, then the confusion of various motels, but perhaps mainly because of how horrible Clara and Adam were, I had no security in them except that of being fed, plus the fact that Clara was the only person in the world who knew the complexities of my medical needs. And so I was tied to them and followed them, but I was alone with nothing for myself but my postcards and my lead soldiers to hold onto. I think I must not have laughed or smiled that year.

There were essentially three kinds of motels at that time. The best was the stucco kind like the one we had in Phoenix, with carports between the units, pile rugs on the floor, maybe an overstuffed chair, a bush or two in front and a few flowers, gold threads in the bedspread and lamp shade, and the soap was wrapped. The log cabin type economized with rustic charm. They smelled of wood and surrounded one with splinters. They'd have a hook rug on the floor, a rough wood closet, an outdoor toilet, a rocking chair, drawers that stuck, a washbowl with a bent dipper, and leftover soap.

The third kind, the real money saver, was made of clapboard and had screen doors with holes in them. They smelled of people and garbage. There was a naked bulb on the ceiling, the folding chairs and beds were wobbly, the linoleum ragged, the toilet seat cracked, and there was no soap at all.

There was always the problem of where I would sleep and we attacked this problem with a great deal of ingeniousness. Since Clara and Adam liked to stay up late and have some privacy, they preferred that I sleep in a different room than they had. There was a character in the Andy Gump comic strip, a child who always slept in a dresser drawer, and I felt very akin to that child. Sometimes they could turn an overstuffed chair around and I would sleep in that. Or there would be a big closet, and pillows and coats could be made into a bed for me. Many times I slept in the bathtub. The first time I did that and Adam came into the bathroom to piss. I was shocked at his vulgarity in doing so and impressed with his penis.

Adam was in his element in Las Vegas and Clara was jolly. "Ain't we got fun?" she said. I have an image of lots of glass everywhere and rows upon rows of one-armed bandits. But we didn't stay there long. In Los Angeles there were weird plants and the city was huge and exotic. There were lots of peculiar strangers and lots of driving around to see things which I hated. Sometimes they'd put me in a movie and other times they'd have people watch me like the hotel clerk did in Denver.

I do remember the big fair in San Francisco. It must have been the Golden Gate International Exposition, with extraordinary lighted shapes and weird modernistic buildings. Any picture of any world's fair haunts me in a strange way. There was a carnival atmosphere, there were real barkers, but the main thing was the freak show. It was in and around a canvas tent held down by ropes. One freak outside affected me vividly. He had a distorted tortured face with tusks and he had holes in his cheek that he could blow smoke through. I looked at him, thinking of my sinus operation, and I thought, "I have holes in my head too." I knew about faking already from doing my own shows in the living room in Macomb but this man had no fakery about him. He had true tusks and true holes in his face and he was truly and simply miserable and nasty and it seemed to me that he hated to be looked at but I looked at him and I saw the power of his authenticity.

But inside the tent one could see the mysteries of life. We all wanted to go in and do so, but since it was one of those adult things they went in and left me outside. I was angry and wanted to go in, maybe crawl under the tent flap. I wanted to see the mysteries, I was being denied the mysteries of life. But people were all around and I couldn't sneak into the tent, and then I became frightened. I was alone yet I was being watched and couldn't do what I wanted to do. Adam always said, "He'll be all right."

But they weren't in there for long and we went on into the carnival grounds. Adam won numbers of toys and gewgaws at the rifle range and throwing the ball to hit the bottles and gave his winnings to me.

In San Francisco, I noticed a good deal of fear and nervousness in Clara. Adam, of course, was not controllable and while we were there he was drunk a lot, which made him really nasty, and Clara was afraid of him. She took every opportunity to go into hysterics. I think the problem was that the money was running out. I have a dismal image from this time of the Golden Gate Bridge with a cold white mist drifting across it.

The next stop I can recall is Reno, with the mountains in the distance, the glittering lights, and the even then old-fashioned and dowdy look of it. We stayed in the crummiest dismalest motel in my memory, with the naked overhead bulb, the curling linoleum, the ingrained filth and the stench. Here, in this motel, Adam and Clara quarreled violently. The quarrel ended in Adam taking the rest of the money and driving away in Clara's car. I don't know how long we waited, Clara frantic and me miserable, but he did come back and he had lost all the money gambling. He was very drunk and very nasty. It was awful. I started to cry and he hit me and hit me again and again. I lay in pain and misery, unable to sleep, beside the sink. He came in and I thought he would kill me but instead he pissed in the sink and I was shocked again.

It must have been that Clara sent to Lou for money. We all went to Phoenix after that and actually rented a house. It was small and brown outside with white plaster inside and whorl designs on it. The yard was bare with a few dry cacti. Of all the places I've been in, Phoenix seems the least real, the most like a dream. Rows and rows of indistinguishable little houses with little dry yards on a flat flat ground with very little that was green, very little to see or touch. A few trees that looked like the trees in Los Angeles.

Adam started driving a taxi and I was put into school. It was, I believe, kindergarten. In any case I was some months late and was the new kid in the class. By this time my loneliness and fear and misery of the last few months separated me from the others and I was as alone as I had been when I was left in front of the freak tent. The only way I could get the kids to play with me at all was on the teeter-totter because I was so fat by then that two or three kids could get on the other end of it. Then they'd have me move forward or back to balance. I was so grateful to have any attention from kids my age that I put up with the indignity of it, put up with being called "Fatty" again, and managed even to smile sometimes. But there were no friends.

Every Saturday I went alone to the movies. This time the serial was *Deadwood Dick* and as it happened I started on chapter one. What a joy it was to know him from the beginning. He had a trick which rendered him invincible. He had holes in the bottom of his holsters and could shoot, without drawing, from the hip. This made him faster than the fastest draw in the West. Later, when I met the photographer Eugene Smith, I was fascinated with him because he could do that too. He went about the streets with several cameras dangling about him and when he'd see something he'd grab one and snap it. I asked him about it, asked wouldn't it be better if he'd aim, and he said that he had each camera set with a certain lens and knew almost exactly what was in the frame. There was no need to hold it to his face and look through the view finder so why trouble himself to do so. Anyway speed was important to him, too.

I watched *Deadwood Dick* in joy and fascination in Phoenix for several weeks. I never liked popcorn but at a movie I really enjoyed hot dogs with lots of mustard. Some time later, when I got a pair of holsters for Christmas, I was very disappointed and upset because they didn't have holes. At that time, no holsters had holes but as the years went by the style changed and most holsters did have holes except for those of the police and I thought, "Why don't they wise up?"

I believe it was in Phoenix that Adam took me to *The Wizard of Oz*. My God, what a delight that was! Of course I felt terribly close to Dorothy, who had been ripped and whirled away from her home, found herself wandering in a place where nothing and nobody were familiar, where terrible things happened that were disconnected with anything she knew before. And all the time she wanted to go home. I was thrilled when at the end she actually managed to get home again. It made me think that maybe somehow, somewhere, there was still hope.

We were in Phoenix a couple of months I guess, time enough to get deeply involved with *Deadwood Dick*, time enough to be sorry when we left, even though I found the place ugly. I don't know where we went after that. From the time we left Phoenix until the following September is in my mind a confusion of motels and misery, of being enrolled in schools and taken out again. Always the new kid in school, the fat kid with glasses who can't do anything. The hernia, the asthma, the ear trouble, and by this time a solidly entrenched hostile loneliness, defensive, sour, and coldly, bitterly, hopelessly arrogant. I knew what I knew, which was not what the others knew, or what they thought was so. I had known love and warmth, the power of my grandmother's position in Winfield, I had known the spotlight, had sung publicly, been in a movie, organized a circus and run a successful business. I had had a dog who slept under my bed and guarded me wherever I went, I had known and loved Ryda Rue. And what I knew now was that it was all gone, that all securities and joys and recognitions could be taken away, and when they were, what one had was filth, quarreling, drunkenness, danger, despair.

The feeling of danger came essentially from Adam. When he was drunk or hung over he was not only cruel, he was violent. He hit me hard and Clara too. He pummeled, kicked, slapped my face, he shouted vile and insulting things, hopeless frustrated things. I can't remember what things he said when he was drunk, but sometimes I think I've been saying those same things myself all my life. Knowing him, I swore never to be a drunkard and never to be physically violent, but I guess it seemed to me that what he said he proved was true, that society was disgusting, life a garbage heap, and success impossible.

Adam knew all the cities we went to like a taxi-driver. The only glory I had left was that of knowing a man with that cap and being able to get into his taxi. He had no trouble finding work in the city, even in the '30's. And if he didn't make enough money, Clara would get more out of Lou by lying about me. Adam knew where the whorehouses were and everything else that was shady and seedy. He had a great sense of the romance of the streets and delighted in showing Clara "what life was all about." Money flowed through him like through a sewer pipe. I have no memory of him showing me his gun but I do remember fearing that he'd use it. He seemed the embodiment of all that was exciting. Many many movies were being made, still are, about how romantic his world was and is. And, I later found out, many novels too.

And he could be so nice, so kind and effusive, and had such a sentimental affection for children. His main idea about child-rearing was "He'll be all right," thus persuading Clara to be less frantically protective, leaving me out and on my own in the street or wherever. His insouciance forced on me a sense of independence, of self-assurance. I don't believe he cared if he or anyone else lived or died. The thought of "purpose" or "destiny" to life surely never entered his head. Life was something to spend.

Although there was no security in movies because they always ended, I found in them something like a continuity. In this whole blanked-out several months of moving and new schools, I can find only one happy memory. We arrived in a town and I went to the movie and there was Deadwood Dick in the very next chapter after the one I saw in Phoenix before we left. I was so excited, but after two or three weeks we left that town too and I never found that serial again.

At another town I saw a couple chapters of *Flash Gordon* and found it quite thrilling. The cliff-hanger before we left that town was the image of a spaceship hanging in space, another spaceship bumps into it and it "falls." I saw it again about forty years later and it was sequins and toy spaceships, chintzy and stupid. I was embarrassed, amazed that it could have impressed me as a child.

For succor I still had my lead soldiers and postcard collection. I had lost *Hope*, the painting I said was of my real mother, but I still had the French postcard of the naked lady. And I had my teddy bear to sleep with.

I have forgotten the quarrel Clara had with Adam that caused her to make another stab at Lou. But she said we were going to Macomb to say goodbye to Ryda Rue and pack up the rest of our stuff. I don't remember saying goodbye to Ryda Rue either. Where we went was somewhere in Indiana where Lou was starting to teach at a college. I hadn't seen my father for almost a year.

Clara started to rent a duplex in the town but Lou already had prepared a nice house for us, a small-town house like the one in Winfield, two or three storeys, white frame with a big lawn and big trees. And Ritzy, Ritzy was there, wagging his whole back end and I was so glad.

Clara was a bit huffy because she had been knocked down at the start about the duplex. Lou was unaffectionate and aloof as before, if not more so. Quite a shock after Adam's effusiveness when he was sober. But oh, such a relief that he never got drunk and never never hit me.

I started first grade right at the beginning of the year in a nice red brick schoolhouse with a big playground. The teachers were nice and the kids accepted me.

I have a great warm memory of raking leaves with Lou. It was a beautiful afternoon, crisp and cold, with hardly any wind. Ritzy was there and we raked multicolored leaves into a big pile. Lou gave me a farmer match and let me set it on fire. Then we stood to watch it, a father and son and their dog burning leaves in the fall like other people. It was grand beyond description, so rare to be doing something with Lou in the best of times. The smell from the fire was wonderful, some of the leaves were really big and I watched them burn with fascination. It was a very lovely feeling.

I began to seriously believe that the movie *The Wizard of Oz* was right, that what Adam called "the real world" had been only a dream and it was all over. I was so grateful that I began to sing again and smile and laugh and I was open and friendly with the kids at school.

On Saturday afternoons I again went to the matinees. I don't remember what the serial was.

Then one Saturday Clara said to me, "I have a surprise for you," very sly and secretive. "You're not going to the regular movie," she said. "There's a special treat." She took me downtown and there was Adam. I was horrified. I was very frightened. I knew then that the dream was back, the nightmare had been reality and there was no escape. But Adam was effusive, generous. Clara left me with him and he took me to see *Gone With the Wind*, which in spite of — or perhaps because of — the frightful revelation of Adam's reappearance, I was extremely impressed with. He took me to movies every Saturday after that for several weeks and I was back in the routine of keeping the secret of his presence from Lou, not being able to be open about what I did on Saturdays. "See no evil, hear no evil, speak no evil." But Adam continued on his best behavior, buying me ice cream, taking me to the zoo, being very kind indeed. One of the movies he took me to was *The Arkansas Traveler* with Joe E. Brown, and I thought Adam was like that when he was at his best, though he was not so funny. Another time we went to a small circus, which I enjoyed tremendously. I began to think that if Adam went on behaving himself, it was real nice having two fathers.

But then late one night Clara came in to my bedroom, which I dearly loved, a cozy tiny room with a slanted ceiling and a little funny-shaped window. She was very upset and hugged me desperately. "You'll have to be my little man," she said, and I knew it was over. I tried to work up a feeling in myself of strength and responsibility but it didn't work too well.

An attempt must be made here to understand Clara. The problem is that, strangely, although children spend a great deal of their time with their mothers, their relationship is such that no thought is given to an understanding on either side, and if any is, it would be the parent understanding the child. But in our case there was emphatically none of that either. Although she was constantly my closest associate until I was well into high school, nothing like understanding ever entered into our relationship.

I can say with every assurance that she was a manipulator. Even as a doddering senile old woman, that remained her most basic and obvious trait. She mainly manipulated through guilt and through hysterical helplessness, but she saw also that the Waxman sisters were highly respected in the town for knowing something about cultural things. Clara did play the piano, though not very well, and I would often hear her plunk away at Chopin or Schumann or Debussy. It's a hard thing and boringly time-consuming to learn to do anything well and Clara's yen for a position of power was not the right incentive to get her to learn these pieces or to develop much skill on the piano. In Bisbee and in Macomb she tried to build herself up as a sort of salon, but here in Indiana Lou's hickish love of earthy things thwarted her, although by this time I was becoming useful by singing and putting on shows.

Her sneering scorn of Lou was constant in my memory of the few years of their relationship. She said that she married him to be a professor's wife, that she left him because he lacked ambition and would rather sell shoes at Sears than teach. And because he sucked his teeth. She said also that he never cared much for sex. She never set her cap for another professor, perhaps because she didn't find there the power she yearned for.

But there must have been another feeling mixed in or she would have found someone more high-class to run away with than Adam. Perhaps it was something to do with class. When Uncle Herbert divorced Aunt Maryann, he had to leave town and become a low person. In the '30's, divorce, although not unheard of, was a thing that only wild people did. How Grandmaw, with all her respectability, could have raised two such offspring in such a time is hard to fathom except perhaps that her very power stifled them and both Herbert and Clara had to kick off to another class to feel their own existences, to develop their own power.

Uncle Herbert went back after some years, married a Cherokee woman named Marie, lived thirty miles from Winfield and raised children more or less respectably. At least more so than Clara did. When Grandmaw died, he died too. It was his heart. But that all happened decades later. Clara never went back to Winfield. She didn't ever want to go back even for Christmas, even for funerals. She said she felt stifled there, couldn't take the heat or the wind.

So the two realities that I felt tearing apart in me were a function of Clara's release from the smothering folds of Grandmaw's power. I always yearned to go back to Grandmaw's world but by the time Clara was through with me, I never could. Because, although she never achieved anything like culture herself, her ambition for it burned high for me to achieve it and achieve it I did, much to her joy. Yet doing so has left me, as an adult, with a great sense of loss. Always, daily, every moment of my life I yearn for what I call "a place in the world." A position like Grandmaw had with her Christmas decorations in Winfield, Kansas. Bach had it, playing the organ in the Lutheran Church, the same as Grandmaw. I yearn for a whole community that believes in me, that is open to my work and comes to see it as a matter of course, as they'd go to church and hear Bach on the organ, something new every Sunday. And I yearn for people from other towns around to hear of how good my films are as they heard about Grandmaw's decorations and as musicians all over Europe heard about Bach, and they'd come, they'd come to my church to see my films and be inspired, naturally. Something like the position of the shaman in a tribe. Hard work for me but, in the German tradition of my grandmother and of Bach, I have never balked at hard work. Matter of fact, I can't stop working hard. My sweetest dream of happiness would be if the Lutheran church of Winfield, Kansas would invite me to live there and work and show my films every Sunday and the congregation would come and see them and love them and their eyes would open and the light of the films would shine across the land like the Star of Bethlehem. For this dream I still have hope because I feel it's the center of my destiny. But at the same time it's seeming lack of fulfillment burns in my gut like gall and I am bitter bitter bitter because it appears that it will never happen and my destiny will be swept away by the blind frivolity of the times. My feeling is that humanity is washing away, doomed, that I have the answer that could keep it from doom but, try to sell it to them as I might, they won't buy it.

The next day in school I was told to get my things together, that I was leaving. I collected what I could of my workbooks and pencils and crayons. I went out and there was Clara all dressed up. "Hurry," she said, "we're late." The steps of the school were of stone and as she dragged me down them, I dropped my crayons and they spilled all over those stone steps. "It's not important," she said, and pulled me along in a frantic hurry. I saw Adam on the curb and the yellow taxi and she stuffed me into it. I looked back at my crayons, they looked horrible all over the steps of the school. I was upset that she wouldn't let me pick them up. Then as we drove out of town another thought occurred to me. Ritzy. Couldn't we please go back to the house and say goodbye to him. I had missed him so much. "We'll send for him," she said, and I knew that this now was reality and that the other had been the dream.

8

Chelsea Court

ADAM DROVE US IN THE TAXI to Denver where we moved into a four-storey apartment house called Chelsea Court at Thirteenth and Pennsylvania. The building was a dark, square box of sooty brick with tall, narrow windows in rows surrounded on all sides by a few feet of caked dirt. Our apartment was furnished with ratty furniture and threadbare rugs. It was quite small, the living room, Clara's bedroom, a tiny kitchen and a bathroom. The kitchen had a dumbwaiter to put trash in and send it down to the basement where the landlord would take care of it. I slept on a sagging cot in a sort of cranny by the broom closet. The place had a temporary feeling to it and was quite dirty with the filth of much time and many different people.

I enrolled in Emerson School some blocks away. It was also sooty, and old, and dowdy, and decrepit, with sagging splintering floors.

On the first day in school I sat by the radiator, hunched and glowering. Clara had given me a new box of crayons to replace the ones we left lying sprawled on the school steps in Indiana. It was a cold day and the radiator was very hot. I opened the box and one by one I took these new crayons and pressed them each one on the radiator. I watched as they dripped in bright colors down the bumpy radiator, the streams stopping and swelling at a bump then slithering quickly down steep places. Some of the streams ran across other streams and their colors blended and changed when they went on. Then I noticed the smell, hot burning wax, and with a start I realized I was doing something wrong. I was shocked. I looked guiltily up at the teacher but she was blithely reading to the class. I looked again and saw that smoke was rising dimly from the melted crayons and wavering the view of the buildings across the street. The heat blasted mercilessly from the radiator and the smell increased. The streams of color were drying now and cracking. Some of the wax had made it to the floor and these drops were hardening again.

Miserable and very much afraid now of being punished, I sat and squirmed in my seat. What would they do to me if they caught me?

When the bell rang at the end of the day I still hadn't been caught and I never was caught. The next day some of the mess I had made was cleaned up but most of it remained and I sat all the rest of the year in that desk with the peeling colored streams always beside me.

The fondest memory I have of that school is the wavy glass in the windows and the way it made the things ripple if I moved my head as I looked out. The playground was surrounded by a high chain-link fence and I could make it waver with the bumps in the glass as though it were a curtain waving in a light breeze. In Winfield I had had a curtain on my bedroom window, clean and white and heavy, woven in knots of thick strings, scalloped on the sides and fringed on the bottom, that had waved like that on summer evenings. So that seeing the chain-link fence rippling with the ripples of the glass sent me into memory and soothed me.

I was distant from the other kids at Emerson school, distant and depressed. There was a dismal, dreamy quality that seemed to be all over the school. The children played quietly, learned little and without enthusiasm, and mostly didn't know or care about each other. I was not bullied there. Perhaps it was the subdued aura that pervaded the school but probably it was because in my misery, I didn't try to shine out as I had in Macomb, so they hardly noticed me. The playground was small and cramped, the schoolrooms were stuffy and hot, the desks carved and bumpy, the paint chipped and peeling, and the teachers dreary with wispy hair.

Our neighborhood was dismal all around with tumbledown, divided-up old houses and dingy apartment buildings like Chelsea Court. Filthy, dimly lit hallways, busted tricycles in arid yards, alleys littered with bed springs, cracked gray boards full of nails, rusted car parts, and bedraggled people who loitered and stared and shuffled along cracked sidewalks. Colfax Avenue was again not far away, two blocks, with a semblance of bustle.

Happily, Clara got a job right away in a Rexall drug store, but she had to work until seven or eight in the evening so she arranged for an old woman to mind me after school. I was to walk from the school to her house and stay there until Clara came to get me.

My route took me through a vacant lot. This was a great new discovery for me, the vacant lot. It was fairly good-sized, big enough for three or four houses. It was hilly, too, and the different hills had different characters. One was thick with tall dry weeds, a wilderness of mid-winter vegetation, while another was totally barren and hard-packed, embedded with broken bricks and hunks of cement. I dawdled through this vacant lot after school. It was a real pleasure and a fascination. There were different kinds of weeds, some tall and stiff and hollow like bones, some low and knobby like coral, and other grasses gone delicately to seed. And here and there all through the lot were abandoned things, old shoes, a tattered shirt, pieces of metal from cars or other things I couldn't fathom, cans and bottles, a magazine, a broken chair. It was fascinating and I spent as much time there as I could, marveling and searching. There was a pink naked doll without arms or head, a broken toy truck. There were worlds here for my imagination to create. It was all here.

But I couldn't stay long. I was supposed to arrive at the old lady's house right away and if I didn't, she would get upset, she'd tell Clara, and Clara would get hysterical. Whenever she got hysterical, I lost something. The last fit of hysteria she had had, I lost Lou and Ritzy, the nice house and raking the lawn in Indiana, the nice people in school. And a box of crayons.

The old lady and I had nothing to say to each other and there was nothing to do at her house. She was tall and straight, white hair arranged nicely in an upsweep. She was nervous and arch and looked like an aristocrat. She lived in an old gray stone house full of knick-knacks. She'd ghost about silently fixing supper or whatever and I would stand around looking at her knick-knacks. There were pictures in little stand-up frames that I could pick up. There were doilies that I could run my fingers over and follow the threads. I could do homework. At supper we sat and ate in silence. Our forks clanked on our plates. The clock ticked. These were the only sounds I heard from the old lady and her gray stone house and they haunt me.

My favorite of her knick-knacks was an ashtray. It was made of brass which was mostly darkened and had on one end of it a little statue, a knight in a full suit of armor. His helmet could tip back to reveal a cigarette lighter, which was grand enough, but also he held a sword in his hand that could be pulled out and had a moderately sharp edge. Perhaps to cut the ends of cigars. He was like the Indian by the capitol building, he was made of metal, but he was small like my collection of lead soldiers. Also he could be removed from the ashtray and one day I took him out of the ashtray and carried him home in my pocket.

Right away, the old lady missed him and she told Clara. I had never done anything like that before. Since my birth I had constantly been sickly and demanding, but until the incident of the crayons on the radiator I hadn't done anything really naughty. And for that act I hadn't been caught. When Clara accosted me with the theft of the brass knight I denied any knowledge of it. But there was no other explanation to cover its vanishing and finally I had to admit to stealing it and then I had to give it back.

Whether it was because of this incident or because Clara couldn't afford to pay her, I don't really know, but I stopped going to the old lady after that. Clara was working odd hours, sometimes getting home around eight and sometimes not until midnight. I saw Adam only rarely and then they were usually quarreling. She complained about her feet a lot, standing behind the counter all day, and she would get hysterical about that and about Adam, too.

After mooning through a day at school I would go home to the apartment and sit around alone, play with my toys, open a can of Campbell's soup, cook it, and have it with a piece of cheese or two in it and some saltine crackers, my latest food pleasure, one which I still enjoy. If Clara was going to work late, she'd come and get me on her dinner break and take me to a double feature movie. Usually she worked on Saturdays also and then would take me to a double-feature movie in a theatre that was not far from another movie house with another double feature, and what with the newsreels, the cartoons, short subjects and coming attractions, as well as the two features in each theatre, and time for a hot dog between them, this arrangement filled an eight-hour day very nicely and kept me occupied the entire time she was at work.

She gave no thought to being on time for the beginning of a movie, but the place where I'd be waiting for her to come pick me up was firmly settled every time.

Nonetheless, there were mixups when I'd be waiting in front of a different theatre than the one she came to pick me up. The car seemed to often break down. Then she would arrive an hour late on foot and we would wait together for a bus. She would be, of course, hysterical. Waiting in front of the theatre became a big thing in my life. Again, my activity was very limited. Until the theatre was closed, I could wait in the lobby — maybe, if I had the money for it, I could eat another hot dog. I could look at the pictures on the wall. Then when they closed up I'd have to stand outside. I'd look again at the pictures and again and again in the pool of light in front of the theatre. It got bad when they'd turn off the lights and the ticket woman would leave. Then I'd stand frightened, cold, miserable, in the dark, wondering if Clara would come to get me at all. Being in the movie was a time of peace and security, rich with a multiplicity of visions and vitality. The rest of life was dreary, insecure, and seemed dangerous. I'd stand in front of the theatre every time unsure that she would come at all. Snow would be falling perhaps or there would be a cold wind and I'd shiver alone there. Many times I would be crying when her horn would beep and there she'd be, tired and upset.

She was a terrible driver in the best of conditions, but ice on the roads and snow falling through darkness was hell and madness to her and hell and madness also to me. Driving has always been a problem to me, and driving at night with snow coming at me pulls me into an agony of terror and I go into fits of hysterics like hers, screaming of hopelessness and of giving up everything.

It was strange to me that she would turn me loose like this. She had always been so protective, hovering over me and fussing about my various illnesses. But Adam always said things like, "I know kids that age that're making a living shining shoes." Perhaps it was his influence that caused her to loosen her grip. My feeling was that I was a drag on her love life and she'd just as soon I'd die. Times were different then, the streets safer than they are now, but she told me never to take candy from strangers, never to get in a car with them or to speak to them. There were certain lines I could say to them like "No, thank you," or

"My mother's coming to pick me up." I don't remember any incidents with strangers in spite of all my being alone. Though I never was at all sure that she would pick me up. But some days I was allowed to go to the movies on the bus and come home on the bus.

The Mummy's Hand was as important to me as *Scarface* had been, and happily I saw it from the beginning. It was another really well-made movie too, with Karl Freund the photographer and Lon Chaney, Jr. as the mummy.

The story goes that in ancient Egypt a commoner loved a princess, and since she loved him too he was given this doom, that he would be mummified but never die. It shows them wrapping him up to his socket-like eyes in long strips of cloth and burying him in the tomb. Then in the present, there's an anthropological expedition with the girl and an evil guy who knows the secret of how to open the tomb (he burns tamris leaves in a bowl on a tripod and says certain things), at which the mummy rises up and breaks out of the tomb, killing everything in his way, his left arm and leg dragging, his wrappings in gray tatters, his right hand reaching out for his beloved princess who, as it happens, is reincarnated as the girl of the expedition.

I was completely captivated and overwhelmed by this movie, went home on the bus and found Adam there with Clara. I told them the story with great excitement, acted it out, my left arm pressed against my side, left leg dragging, all around the cramped and dingy living room. That night I had terrible nightmares and for some time I wasn't allowed to go to horror movies.

But at that time movies seemed to me inexhaustible. There were the big central theaters, the Denver, the Paramount, Orpheum, Tabor, Denim, there were neighborhood theaters around, too, and all of them changing their movies every two or three days, except for the really big shows, those would stay longer. I liked the Coming Attractions very much, they were so lively and mysterious.

And the newsreels were amazing. I knew they were the news, that they were telling something of what was happening somewhere. They were showing war in Europe, buildings burning, Hitler and Mussolini talking to cheering multitudes and signing treaties that they later broke. I have, strangely, little sense of the serials at this time but the newsreels took their place and Hitler and Mussolini, particularly Hitler, took the place of the heroes. In a strange way he took Lou's place, too, as by far the strongest and most constant adult male influence in my entire childhood. He was there, always there, in newsreels until I was in my teens. I saw more of him than of any other man. I saw how he acted in different situations and how there were big results from what he did. He changed the world and changed it again until the world couldn't go back the way it was before, didn't even remember how it had been. All he had to do was speak and it was done. "Take Czechoslovakia," he said. "Take Yugoslavia," and I saw shots of the invasions of these countries and he took them. He had the most power of anyone, ever. He had power in his voice, in his generalship, and in the wealth and passionate loyalty of his country.

There was a movie house across the street from the Orpheum called The Newsreel Theatre, which only showed the short subjects, no feature-length movies at all. There was a plethora of shorts at the time, fascinating things. There was a boa constrictor killing a lion, the lion thrashing, scratching, panting, dying. There was Frank Buck in puttees and safari hat with his dramatic voice and the picture moving through the jungle. I saw tightrope walkers and jugglers, seals juggling and dancing about, which Joseph Cornell was also fascinated with, I saw magic shows, volcanoes emptying. I watched with fascination as an octopus ate something, saw again the Golden Gate Bridge, looked down into the Royal Gorge, saw a bridge buckling in the wind, an image that shocked the world and which Bruce Conner used in a film. There were racing car accidents and circuses, *Our Gang* comedies, and old silent films with sound put on. I never liked the travelogues but I liked just about everything else. Some people came in for half an hour or so on their lunch breaks but I always stayed for the full two-hour show.

The movies were now my life. I wished they'd go on forever. Everything else was variously uncomfortable. There was school, in which my only pleasure was the wavery glass. There was Clara having hysterics and sore feet and being late. There were my old standbys, asthma, sinus and ear trouble, being fat, the thick glasses, and most of all the hernia truss, which was a constant source of self-disgust and an irritation besides.

I have two memories in the bathtub from this time. One was, I was being babysat by a young woman. I was in the tub bathing and as I rubbed my leg I saw my skin coming off in little rolls. I rubbed my other leg, then my arms and saw that it was the same everywhere. I became very frightened and called for the babysitter, asked her what it was all about. She told me it was all right, that it happens to everyone all the time. I was reassured but I couldn't understand why it would be.

The other bathroom adventure became a haunting which dogged me. It was this. I was alone in the apartment. I had just stepped out of the bathtub and was looking in the mirror. The light from over the sink was throwing my shadow down darkly behind me. I felt suddenly that if I fell back directly into my shadow, I'd fall into black space, I'd fall forever through space surrounded by stars. I could turn my head around and see that there was the floor and the wall, but then what was behind me was still behind my head and I could never turn my head around fast enough to be able to see what was there. Looking in the mirror, I blocked the view behind me with my own image. A few days later we went to a clothing store where there were three mirrors and I looked long into them. They showed me an infinity of myself, endless duplicates of me, but still the image of me was blocking my view of the shadow at my back. I looked and looked at the picture of the girl on the

Morton's salt box carrying a Morton's salt box and on it a picture of the little girl carrying a Morton's salt box and on it a picture of the little girl carrying a Morton's salt box and on and on for infinity. The picture of her didn't have a back really, the box was round so that didn't help. It never occurred to me to look behind other people. It was the shadow man again, though I didn't think of it that way.

Often I was alone in the apartment for hours at a time, but no matter how often I was alone, no matter how much I had to do, I was always afraid. Fear became my companion, my familiar, my guide. In the movies I was full of apprehension too as the movie built up tension, but there in the theatre behind me (for I always sat down in front so I could see) were the other people of the audience, and I could hear them eating popcorn and rustling, feel them looking at the same thing I was looking at, and know I was not alone. Practically every movie was filled with, and based on, suspense, and as I squirmed in my seat I reached out for security to sense those around me, and they were there. So, it developed in my heart that whenever I was afraid, I was not alone. If I had ever thought it through I would have seen the fallacy of this feeling, because when I was alone in the apartment and I was afraid, I was still alone. But even there I found comfort in fear, although the apartment was not a nice place, the streets were worse, I wasn't at a movie, and I never knew when Clara would come home.

One afternoon after three or four months of this, I was as usual alone in the apartment. The dumbwaiter had trash in it. Perhaps I was thinking about my last lovely memory of Lou, when he gave me a farmer match and let me light the autumn leaves. I took a match from the box, lit it, and set fire to the trash in the dumbwaiter. Then I took the rope and ran the burning trash to the bottom of the shaft until it landed with a bump in the basement.

Fortunately, as it happened, the manager was there in the basement and I heard his yell echoing up the dumbwaiter shaft. He put the fire out frantically then stormed up the stairs and knocked repeatedly on the door of the apartment. I simply didn't answer the door. When Clara came home hours later, he told Clara about it and how it had to have been me that did it. When she spoke to me about it, I denied it. But he was clear that it couldn't have been anyone else and at last I confessed. Clara beat me then and the manager told us we had to leave.

9

Duplex on Pennsylvania

SO WE MOVED TO A DUPLEX not very far away. It was a long narrow space, a very thin lot, the front porch almost smack up against the sidewalk. The incredibly long living room narrowed even more in the middle by the bathroom and Clara's bedroom on one side; a dust-filled couch at the front beside the door, overstuffed chair next, a window, with a view of the neighbor's window and with a string-laced curtain, much like the white one in my bedroom in Winfield only filthy and greasy and shredded, the chest with the radio on top, and, at the end of the long room, a dining room table. Beyond that were the kitchen, directly behind Clara's bedroom, and my bedroom beside it. Through the kitchen you could go out the back onto a screened-in porch, with two sides for the two apartments divided by a partition. It was full of stored stuff in boxes. Then, down rickety steps to a tiny yard, not even a weed to grace it, and the alley. I always went through the back door.

The other half of the duplex was inhabited by the landlady, a stumpy little German who was grossly fat and always wore a shift that went straight down below her voluminous breasts. She wore spectacles and waddled when she walked. With her were her daughter, who was always away at work, and her grandchildren, a girl several years older than I was and a boy only a year older than I with blond curly hair, pug nose, and freckles. Athletic and domineering, he bullied me into playing with him, decided what we would play, always took the winning position. Still, he was someone to play with, something I hadn't had for over a year. I can't remember his name.

The area we had to play in was extremely constricting. There was the crowded house, the little bare yard, and the alley. There was no fence between our yard and the alley, and we could go up and down the alley but we couldn't cross the street, and there was no vacant lot on our block so the alley didn't lead to any place to play except itself.

I encountered him again when I was almost thirty and went in desperation to work for Educational Television. I didn't recognize him. He was something up the ladder and climbing fast. I heard not from him but from someone else that he recognized me. He was one of my bosses there, he was autocratic and cross with me, even cruel, so I quit the job. He reminded me of the SS officers in the newsreels and later in the war movies, harsh, powerful, heartless. He wasn't even condescending.

I was still going to Emerson School and when I got home the boy's grandmother babysat.

Clara told her all about my hernia and my truss and what to do if the hernia popped and I have a memory very v ague that it did pop once. Not that I remember the trauma itself, but I think I remember Clara telling me that the fat old German lady told her that I hadn't worn my truss one day and had consequently fallen down in the yard unable to breathe, and that she had rushed out and done the prescribed cure, i.e., shoved my gut muscle back in by my left testicle and thereby saved my life. I do remember that she had the very irritating habit of feeling me up all the time to see that I was wearing the truss, and I disliked her perhaps more than I disliked her grandson.

But there was one blissful moment with that family which I should record here. One day shortly after we arrived, they invited me over to their half of the duplex and they were all there in the kitchen smiling, the heavenly smell of German sugar cookies baking in the oven. A strange man was there and a movie projector, and as the grandmother took the cookies out of the oven and put them in bowls for us to eat her daughter hung up a pillowcase and covered the windows with towels. Then the man ran the projector and the movies were there, tiny on the pillowcase, Charlie Chaplin, I don't remember which ones. It was an hour or two of delight and enchantment. There were other neighbor kids there too, and all the cookies we could eat, there was warmth and laughter. I felt myself back in Winfield with my own German grandmother and her cookies which smelled and tasted just the same as these. I have never found anything in the world to compare in warmth to a German kitchen.

Another wonderful thing I discovered at this time, probably from the boy, was comic books. Comic books were wonderful. Of course I was very fond of *Dick Tracy*, but the *Green Hornet* was my favorite. I never cared for *Superman*. With Superman there was no danger, no excitement, nothing. His power was too great. But Dick Tracy and the Green Hornet were always in danger and very brave.

The Green Hornet had a chauffeur named Cato who was his dearest companion and the only person who bridged the gap of his two lives. During the day, the Green Hornet was a gentleman whom nobody would ever think of as a hero. But at night, he and Cato would go out in their elegant car with its hornet insignia painted on it and they'd catch criminals. He wore a snap-brim hat and a trench coat and a very stylish mask which covered the lower part of his face and part way up his nose, leaving his eyes free. His gun didn't kill people, it was a gas gun and released a puff of gas which knocked the criminals out long enough for him to turn them in to the police. Some time earlier I had seen two movie serials of *Green Hornet* and it may have been that the time I whapped two powder puffs together to get rid of a boarder in Macomb was as a result of having seen that puff of gas. It was appealing to me to have the possibility of handling bullies without being like them, and the Green Hornet's gas gun was to me a suggestion in that direction. In Phoenix I discovered the *Green Hornet* radio serial although it came on well past my bedtime. I was crazy to hear it, mainly I think because of the theme song, Rimsky-Korsakov's *Flight of the Bumblebee,* and the other piece they'd play parts of also, Stravinsky's *Fire Bird Suite.* Of course I didn't know their names then. I pleaded and begged to be allowed to hear that late serial and was often permitted. If I wasn't, I'd sneak in to the radio, turn it on very low, and press my ear to the speaker. The music thrilled me and I had a passion to hear it every week — and the car gunning with a tremendous noise away into the night.

As I had to hear the *Green Hornet* radio show every week, I now also had to read all his comic books and others besides. The problem was that although there was a drug store only two blocks away on Colfax, and with some care I could sneak away to buy them, I was very often without the dime that it took to get them, and so I began stealing money from Clara to buy comic books. Whether I actually told the neighbor boy next door about it, whether he weaseled it out of me, or perhaps he caught me at it, I don't recall. But I do remember that he told his grandmother, his grandmother told Clara, and Clara beat me.

One time the boy and I decided to play Green Hornet and Superman, me to be the Green Hornet and he to be Superman. His grandmother made capes for us out of towels or pillowcases and a mask for me. It was quite a production. But when it came to the actual playing we bogged down very quickly because we couldn't agree as to whether or not Superman would be affected by the Green Hornet's gas gun.

I played by myself for the most part.

Adam still came around occasionally, in and out of our life and although the weekday movies were no longer available because the boy's grandmother watched me after school, there were still the two double features on weekends.

I do have a sense of going to a movie with the boy and his older sister. It was about a man being blackmailed. He and his blackmailer go out in a rowboat together for the money exchange. Again there are the foghorns of San Francisco Bay. The man then decides to kill the blackmailer next time and he does, he hits him and throws him overboard. And then the man becomes like the blackmailer.

In that movie I recognized a familiar problem, the danger of becoming like the enemy. In fact, at this time, I was already becoming the enemy. I was at this time very much under the influence of the boy who was in all the effective ways my superior. He was superior in age, beauty, health, strength, and position with his grandmother who was minding us both. Endlessly, everywhere, in the newsreels, on the radio, and in conversation, people were presenting the Germans as bad and hateful. Knowing the boy and his grandmother as I did, I felt it was true, Germans were hateful. Yet every once in awhile I was reminded of my own German grandmother by the smell of cookies baking or by a sense of comfort in their kitchen unequalled by any other, even perhaps exceeding at moments that comfort I found in the movie house. My mother was German. And there was Hitler, always Hitler in all the newsreels, the one man I could depend on to see. I understood the Germans. I hated the Germans. And in hating the Germans I hated myself.

When the Hindenburg exploded, I was able to see it in a newsreel. It was an extremely striking and powerful newsreel, a huge, silent and dignified dirigible approaching the landing area, then bursting into an inferno with people falling visibly from it through the air. The camera jerked and shook, following the flaming action with a passion of its own. The incredible emotions of the cameraman shone through and I was deeply moved.

Soon after that, I took some of Clara's menstrual napkins from the bathroom closet out into the backyard, stuck them on sticks and lit them with my farmer matches. I think it must be that Lou had a fondness for these matches which everyone else calls kitchen matches. He called them farmer matches and always carried a few in his pocket. They were like a badge for him of his origin on the farm, and they were, and still are, some connection for me to him and his daring and rebelliousness in always letting people know who he was and where he came from.

So the boy and I stood in our little yard with Clara's menstrual napkins flaming high on sticks. In those days those napkins were round, bulky things with long tassels at each end like a fuse, and they burned very well, and created a great sensation in the neighborhood, other kids laughing and blushing and calling each other to look. I don't think I realized until then that it was not only wrong to light a fire but also wrong to have and show to the world my mother's menstrual napkins. For the moment, though, the response we were getting was terrific, and we held our flaming napkins high and slowly lowered them wobbling and breaking apart till we let them land in flames, took them off the sticks, and lit more. Finally the boy's grandmother realized what we were doing and rushed out to stop us and it was over. Except that Clara beat me for it when she got home.

Although my truss was presumably keeping me alive, it was a filthy thing. But it was expensive to replace. As I grew bigger and fatter, its leather, leather-bound metal, buckles, snaps, straps and the split egg-shaped ball which pressed always into my groin, became tighter and got ragged, and stank of old sweat and urine. It endlessly dug into me so that throughout my childhood, from its pressure, around my pelvis, I had marks which often became welts Then the greasy slimy horror of creams and ointments would be added to the already hideous monstrosity of the truss with its struts and buckles jabbing me whenever I moved. Then the holes in the truss would fill with dried blackened creams and the ball would change color and stick to my skin. The ends of the leather straps curled and broke off and the truss was always hard to put on. The only time I got to take it off, except when I was asleep, was when I took a bath, which I did with pleasure every day. But then I had to be very careful to be sure and put the ghastly thing back on again. Sometimes in my delight at not having it on, I'd forget to put it back on and there would be a big fuss. So then always I was being felt up to see that it was there. Then people were always wanting to see it and I didn't want to show them, show them my fat nakedness and my ragged stinking truss, my welts and my stomach hanging over. If I forgot to put my truss on, Clara would beat me.

My glasses were getting thicker already and troubled me very much as they pressed on my nose, making it hard to breathe, which was already hard enough. Then if I wanted to play I was to take them off because, as Clara endlessly told me, "If you fall down and break these glasses, you'll cut your eyes and then you'll be blind." So I'd put them down and lose them, or I'd carefully put them in their case and into my pocket and they'd fall out and be lost or broken. And whenever such a thing happened, Clara would beat me.

Then I got the measles. I had to lie in bed with the shade drawn over the window. I couldn't read or look at comic books and I couldn't get out of bed. I couldn't have any visitors and I couldn't play. It lasted two or three weeks. When I got sick it was winter, the trees were bare. When Clara finally pulled up the shade on the window, the trees were covered with new leaves. The light of my bedroom with the shade drawn was a dull orange. Clara was, of course, mostly gone to work and so the German woman next door brought me food. She'd come in and put the food on the dresser, keeping far away from me. I was contaminated and she'd leave right away. She kept all the doors locked in case I tried to get out. I was trapped, isolated, sick, and bored. There was only one thing I could do. Listen to the radio.

I had heard the daytime soaps before, probably during summers in Denver. I didn't like them near as much as the evening shows like *Green Hornet.* Mainly, the music wasn't as good. I've never liked the organ very much outside of church and most of the soaps used an organ theme song. Somehow, it was wheezy and wrong. Each one was mainly a theme. The music would come on, the theme, the soap ad, then the narrator would describe what the situation was. Nothing really changed much so that even months later I could listen and could pick it up with ease. There was *Ma Perkins.* I liked her a lot. She was a wise old woman and was always helping people out. There was a soap where they played "My Bonnie Lies Over the Ocean" but I can't remember what that was about. *Fibber McGee and Molly* was for grownups. I didn't like that one. I got a big kick out of *Our Gal Sunday,* which every day started out with the announcer saying, "*Our Gal Sunday,* the story that asks the question — can a girl from a little mining town in Colorado find happiness with England's richest and most handsome lord?" The English Lord was especially delightful with his British accent and his wit.

Somehow the Lone Ranger didn't please me too much. The Shadow seemed all wrong to me, sounding so bad and doing good. I liked Jack Armstrong, though, the All-American Boy. There were two news commentators, too, that I could listen to, Walter Winchell and Gabriel Heater. Walter Winchell always came on saying "Hello, Mr. and Mrs. America and all the ships at sea," and everyone around me seemed to like him much better. But I liked Gabriel Heater best. I always liked best what everyone else didn't like so much, except for Jack Armstrong, the All-American Boy. So the radio and particularly the soaps carried me through the vast desert of the measles to spring.

When I was sick, I thought a lot about Ritzy. If Ritzy had been there with me, I wouldn't have been alone. He could have lain on the bed with me. I could have petted him and he would have wagged his whole back end when I spoke to him. He would have been a tremendous solace. So when I got well I asked Clara when we were going to send for him. I was standing at the end of the dining room table with the whole long living room stretched out before me. Clara was standing to my left at the side of the table, and she said that Lou had killed Ritzy. At first I didn't believe her, I thought she was just being cruel to me again. I screamed at her, "He wouldn't do that!" But she said Lou got tired of taking care of Ritzy and had had him put to sleep. Then I cried and cried and wouldn't stop. I cried for days. I cried myself to sleep at night and I woke up crying. I didn't cry in class at school but I'd go to the bathroom often to cry there. And after school I sat in my bedroom or in the living room and cried. I blamed Lou of course but I also blamed Clara because Lou wouldn't have done that if we had been there. She wanted me to put all the blame on him but I didn't. From that moment my relationship with Clara was changed from a pretense of a normal mother/son relationship to something much more cold. The truth that we'd never never go back now was undeniable and unavoidable. I felt myself an orphan, totally alone, trapped with a woman who didn't love me in a world in which now there was no one at all who loved me. I felt that if my real mother had kept me, she would have loved me, that adoptive parents couldn't love the children they adopted. I was without defenses and without hope.

After a couple of weeks I stopped crying and became very quiet. One day after school I was sitting in the living room by the radio, which was on the chest beside the overstuffed chair. On the other side of the chair was the radiator under the window. The window was open a crack and the string-knit curtain billowed a little in the breeze, that curtain that was a grotesque twin of the one in my bedroom in Winfield. It was dowdy, cream colored, frayed. The strings were rather thick. There was one string in particular that stuck out into the room in a way that irritated me. I pulled a farmer match out of my pocket where I'd taken to keeping them and, with the final theme of "Our Gal Sunday" playing on the radio beside me, I lit that one frayed string.

My, what an impressive conflagration. Both curtains caught immediately and within seconds flames were snarling up to the ceiling. I screamed, "Fire!" and stood entranced as the strings blackened and curled and the flames went lashing all the way across the ceiling to the other side of the room. The German lady heard my scream, came in, grabbed the dishpan full of dishwater, swished it across the window, and put it out. I was still standing there staring dreamily at it.

"What happened?" she asked me.

"I don't know," I lied, "Maybe it was the heat from the radiator." I was still holding the match in my hand.

I didn't have a sense of its being too bad. Sort of a boyish prank that got away. The boy came in after his grandmother had left and told me that when she heard me scream, she had stuck her head out the window wondering where the fire was. I got to giggling over that and couldn't stop for a while.

When Clara came home she had a look on her face I hadn't seen before, black rage. She beat me with a strap until I crawled under the bed to get away. When she left, I got out and she came back in and beat me some more. Then she went away and I thought it was over and she came back in to talk and I told her I didn't think it was so bad and she beat me again until I thought I was going to die. She went away again and came back again and beat me, it seemed, all night long and by morning I was covered all over with swelling red and blue welts.

The German woman wouldn't speak to me any more and we had to pack up and leave right away.

10

930 Washington

930 WASHINGTON HAD A LOT OF STEPS. It was on a slight hill and the apartment was on the third floor. And, as far as I can remember, there was no one there to help carry our things, just Clara and me. And I was only seven years old and sickly. The apartment was really tiny, one small room with a kitchenette and a bathroom, a day bed for me and a fold-out sofa for Clara. The ceiling sloped under the roof. At one end of the living room was a nook with a window in it. The kitchenette and the bath also had a window each. The place was so small that we couldn't get nearly all our stuff in it, and the house had lockers in the basement, big wood-slat cages, one for each apartment. We could put the rest of our things in our locker. It was a weird basement with a dozen such cages containing boxes and heaps of everyone's things that had been set aside. We put a lot of my toys down there and games and comic books, there was so little space in the apartment. But at least I didn't have to carry it up the three flights of stairs. I was appalled at how small our place was. I had been accustomed to at least the length of that living room in the duplex.

So we got settled in by supper time. Clara had a date that night so she just fixed me something to eat, and left me there alone. My day bed was all made up, the radio was there. I was to eat supper, listen to the radio, and get to bed by nine. So I did. I ate supper, listened to the radio, and, at nine, I turned off the radio and the lights and got into bed.

It was then that the house began to express itself. It had been a mansion, a fine old residence, and had then been broken up into apartments. Stout and solid though it was, it creaked and snapped. There was a breeze that night, too, and the big old trees whipped and tapped the glass of the windows. The gables and crannies under the roof, where I lay alone, whistled like demons. The radio shows had been particularly creepy that night and I lay there in terror with these sounds like nothing I had ever heard. I couldn't imagine what these sounds were coming from, but I knew it was coming to get me, it was going to get me that very night for my sins.

I got out of bed, turned on all the lights and the radio, and sat looking at the clock. It was around ten by now. I wondered when Clara would come back and if I would survive until she did. I walked around and looked out the window at the flailing treetops. Even the traffic of the street sounded different than it should. I turned up the radio until I couldn't hear all those other things, the wild whistles and the tapping on the windows and the creaks and moans of the old house. I took the clock in my hands and looked at it and, as the radio blared, I watched the second hand go 'round and 'round, slowly moving the minute hand, which in turn very slowly dragged the hour hand further and further on the dial. I watched, clung to the time passing visibly in my hands, sat on my bed and watched those hands go around on the clock.

It was one o'clock when she finally returned and I was still sitting with the clock in my hand, trembling, sweating, exhausted and wild-eyed.

The next morning, we got to meet the neighbors across the hall. They had a little girl just my age named Patty. She was a nice girl

although she was plain and rather drab. She had some dolls and she mostly played with her dolls. But she was always kind to me. Her father was a rough, warm sort of fellow who reminded me somewhat of Adam, who seemed now to be gone from our life. It was Patty's mother who was a real jewel and a blessing to me.

Their name was Johnston. One time I tried to call them up and was totally defeated by the pages and pages of them in the phone book. They were classic Okies, poor, rough, simple, raucous, and warm with a drawly twang. They liked to listen to country music and some of the funny popular music that was coming out at this time. Mrs. Johnston was "tickled to death" with Spike Jones and all his chaotic hilarity. She could sing all the verses to the songs of *Hellzapoppin* and would sing them interspersed with her hard cackle.

They were poor people without much intelligence, calloused by life. Patty had very little to play with except her few ragged dolls. Clara and Mrs. Johnston liked to talk together and became fairly close. They'd talk about gossip and sales, how to save money, the new skating rink, each other's hair and how to fix it like a movie star in her latest movie. They discussed magazine articles and ads, radio shows, the soaps, exchanged tales of getting a run in their stockings on the way out the door. They gave each other advice on what lipstick to buy and what soap to use for what, kept themselves up on all the latest things. It was nice to hear them talking, nice and easygoing, pleasant chatter, and I was delighted to hear it, liked to listen to it, loved Mrs. Johnston's rough laugh.

Clara immediately got Mrs. J. to look after me until she came home, so I played with Patty after school. That was pretty boring because she wasn't filled with fantasies and thoughts like I was, and she only kindly indulged my invention. Still it was better to suffer her kindly indulgence than play with her dolls. I liked dolls if they had some class, but these didn't. And Mrs. J. fed me supper, which was very strange. It all seemed to be fried mush of one sort or another, Spam and grits and such. I never felt very related to the Johnstons, never felt with them that there was room for me to flower or show my worth. Yet they were dependably kind, roughly sweet, and good to me. They were good neighbors.

Right away, Patty showed me the house and I realized that, although noisy in its age, it wasn't the monster I had thought it on my first night there. Quite the contrary. It was a grand old house. No doubt it had been a fine residence at the beginning, and the third floor where we lived must have been the servants' quarters. It could only be reached by the back stair, and all the third floor apartments had sloping roofs. The Johnston's apartment and ours were tiny. The other two on the third floor were big and spacious. There was a small attic above one of these apartments. Mr. Frye let me look in it once through the trap door.

Mr. Frye was the landlord. He was a square, hefty man with a red face, a long jaw, and huge red hands. He always wore a black suit so his huge red hands were always there hanging out of black coat sleeves. He never smiled, but he was friendly and nice in a blunt sort of way. I soon learned to respect him, even though he sometimes spoke sharply, because he was reasonable always. He had a wife and two teenage kids, a boy and a girl, and lived in the back apartment on the first floor. He was a model of a landlord, always around doing things. When he was called upon to fix something, he'd be there immediately with his tools and he'd fix it right. I grew to like him very much and I think he liked me.

The second floor had a lot of stairs. There were two sets going down, a straight, narrow set that continued the back stair from the third floor, and a very narrow stair going to a little apartment that had a huge balcony over the drive. Then there was a grand staircase to the front door. It had a landing and an elegant banister with close-set carved spokes from behind which one could easily watch and listen to what went on below without being seen. There was a lot of space on the big stairway and it was a good place to play. The front door was huge and massive with ripply, leaded, mother-of-pearl-colored glass in it. The lead was so soft I could dent it with my fingernail. Under the stairs was a dark, mysterious space with soft chairs and couches where the older people would sit sometimes and talk.

Across the hall were the mailboxes and the apartment of an old man who always coughed and who later died. There were fourteen apartments in all, four on each floor and two between floors.

The basement was down a winding stair and was a very magical place. There were the lockers like cages making a set of hallways filled with rejected treasures. There was the huge great furnace, so big that you could burn a horse in it standing up if he'd keep still. And leading out from it were great round silver pipes going to the apartments. There was the coal bin, too, and Mr. Frye had to be down there often to keep putting more coal in the furnace. I loved to watch him do it. There were several washing machines and laundry baskets and clotheslines. Usually some of the machines were going and the soapy steam deepened the magic. Each apartment had a round electric meter and you could see their dials going around at different speeds. And from these meters, like the pipes from the furnace, silver coil conduits reached into the ceiling.

The house sprawled and the backyard was narrow, enclosed by a brick wall that I liked to get up on, but otherwise devoted entirely to clotheslines, trash cans, and a gigantic brick incinerator. Plus the garage. The garage had once been a stable and held a dozen cars. It was a magnificent place to play in, had massive beams and posts, and it echoed. On the side of the garage was a stair leading up to a concrete porch with a roof and railings from which I could look down at the glowing coals in the ash pit or out onto the roofs of the neighborhood. It was nice in the rain if there wasn't any wind, and it was nice to push snow off of it. The snow would fall two storeys and go splat. That porch was also a nice setting for telling ghost stories, partly because of the hayloft above the garage, the big hay door which was always locked, the vast dusty space of the loft, and the strong admonishment I got never to go in there.

The house was heavy and solid, red stone and brick with cream and light green trim, a steep dark green roof, and a solid front porch with arched pillars, green wire chairs and a wooden rocker. In front of that was a strip of green lawn and a three-foot brick wall topped with ironwork. On the south side was more lawn and one or two big old trees whose branches had frightened me so much on the first night. On the other side the cement driveway was partly covered with a big balcony supported by a brick wall which I could get up on. North of that, another big old tree had a seat under it.

Everything about the house was massive and mysterious and grand. It was the most magnificent playground I'd ever had access to or even imagined. I settled in.

I was still going to Emerson School to finish off the few weeks left of my year there even though it was some distance to walk. At last the school year was over and I got my report card.

Most of my grades were E's and I's. Because I was used to the top grade being A, I thought that I'd failed. This didn't surprise me because of the dismal dreamy feeling in the school and the amount of time I had spent looking out the window. But I was afraid I'd have to go back there and do it all again, that I'd spend eternity in that Purgatory, and I felt that it would be better if I died. I walked the long, long walk home crying and climbed the stairs with tears still streaming down my face. Of course Clara was at work and Mrs. J. was taking care of me. She heard my sobs as I dragged up the stairs and she came out into the hall. "What's the matter?" and I handed her the report card, my head down. "But what's the matter?" she asked. "These grades are wonderful!" For a moment I thought that by her low-class standards, failure was considered a good thing and my heart leaped at that possibility. She plopped down on the floor and pulled me to her and hugged me. "E for excellent," she said. "You got the top grade!" I lay in the warmth of her embrace as her raucous laughter rang through the halls and Patty stood giggling beside her. I wasn't sure but that she might be just saying that to make me feel good. But from that moment on, Mrs. J. was dear to me.

At the beginning of the summer we moved into one of the big apartments on the third floor. It was very large, after the tiny room we had been living in. The living room was huge, and there was a smallish kitchenette, a bathroom and a bedroom. It was wonderful to have space and oh, the light, it was light. It came into the living room from four windows, on the north side, which looked out on green waving treetops. The kitchen and the bedroom had windows that looked down onto the alley. We weren't prepared with furniture and couldn't afford to buy any. Mr. Frye let us have some chairs. We brought up much of the stuff we had stored in the cage-locker in the basement, but there was nothing to put it all into except trunks. So we had trunks as low tables or hassocks. Clara slept in the bedroom and I in a fold-out couch in the huge living room. It was very nice.

There was one peculiarity about this apartment. Outside the window in the bedroom was a fire escape, the only one on the third floor. Going through our apartment was the only way to it, so, to conform to fire code regulations, Mr. Frye had put a frosted-glass door on our apartment with a sign on it which said in big letters: "Fire Escape. In Case of Fire, Break Glass." And beside the door was a hammer hanging on a little rack. I was told to never ever touch the hammer and never, never play on the fire escape.

In the summer with Clara working all day I was in Mrs. Johnston's care, but she was very casual about it. I was to be there for lunch and that was about all there was to that. The rest of the time, I was on my own.

Patty introduced me to a lot of neighborhood kids. And there were really a lot of them. The neighborhood was a weird conglomeration of the fairly poor and the well-to-do. Next door to us was an attractive house, brown wood with thick beams. Miss King lived there, a white-haired lady who was always either puttering in her huge garden or teaching piano lessons. Her brother was, at the time, Premier of Canada. Directly across the street was a big rich white stucco house with a swimming pool. Next door to us on the south side was an even richer house owned by some relatives of a previous mayor of Denver. They were always having parties with people in evening dress and with expensive cars parked in front. Beyond that house with the pool was a wall and beyond that a vacant lot. There was a gate in the wall, and we kids could watch the rich people swimming.

On the other side of Miss King's house was a set of little stucco houses, arranged in an L shape, with a big lawn and lots of kids. Across the alley behind us were pleasant, one-family, old homes with kids in many of them.

The alleys were wonderful places with hollyhocks and weeds and tree branches sticking out. People naturally put their trash out there and there were always strange things lying about. It was a constant treasure hunt keeping tabs on the alleys and what new marvels they contained. Our house was a great place to sit and talk with one or two friends or maybe to play hide and seek, but we were always admonished to keep fairly quiet there. If we wanted to be active we'd go to the big vacant lot down the street. Here, there were hills and ditches and green or dry plants. Here we could hide in the weeds and jump out at one another, we could dig holes and make caves or castles and be cave men or kings and queens or cops and robbers or soldiers fighting.

It was a joy having kids to play with and none of them bullies like the boy in the duplex. "Let's play cowboys and Indians." "I'll be a cowboy," "I'll be an Indian," and we'd go into motion, running, crawling, hiding, leaping out, dropping dead. I didn't do well at the active games at all but I played and the kids didn't mind. I was better at hide and seek in the house or the yard because, thanks to Patty, I knew all the nooks and crannies. Often I was the one they would give up trying to find. It was a fairly quiet game except once in a while someone would have to call out, "ALIALIOXENFREE!" Sometimes we'd play hide and seek until it was almost dark. Then I'd hear the kids' mothers call them and they'd run home to their families. I'd climb the stairs to sit alone and wait for Clara to come.

Although the kids accepted me, I was different and I knew it. I had open wounds, open and inflamed, in my soul. The loss of Lou, and a decent home, the killing of Ritzy, the lack of roots, and the empty apartment gnawed my innards, no matter how hard I played. It may have been that being different hurt the worst. I was hungry all the time and I ate. I ate and listened to *Green Hornet* on the radio and I was still hungry. Hungry for something, I couldn't say what, hungry and bitter and afraid. Sometimes Clara would leave coins on the bureau in her bedroom and I'd take a few of them and buy candy with them.

There was a gas station catty-corner across Tenth Street and sometimes when all the other kids were at dinner, or otherwise unavailable, I'd go over there and watch the men work on cars.

One time late in the summer when I was there I met a boy who lived behind the gas station. He was square-bodied with freckles on his face and sticking-out ears. He was pretty nice and we began playing together sometimes, and then he took me to his house and showed me his collection. He had a collection of knights made of tin. They were incredible, they were brightly painted and beautiful. I told him I had a collection of lead soldiers and the next day I brought over my soldiers and we commenced to battle, his knights against my soldiers, and it was grand. His knights had shields and horses and helmets, and my soldiers, although much less colorful, had gas masks and cannons and tanks. But I coveted his knights. I had stolen and had to give back a knight only a few months before, a grand knight with wondrous things about it. I contemplated stealing one of his knights but I didn't do it because I couldn't have brought it to show off to him. Instead, I haunted the shops looking for knights but not one could I find. I didn't know where he got his collection. I did, however, see in the five-and-dime store one or two more soldiers that I didn't have, and I stole them. There were other stores too, tiny shops that sold yarn and potholders and candies and lead soldiers. I'd go in, palm a soldier, buy some candy with money from Clara's dresser, and escape with a new warrior to take to battle the next day, to show off to the boy who had a whole set of beautiful wonderful knights.

I wish I could remember this kid's name. He was a nice kid. He was a member of the choir in Saint John's Episcopal Cathedral and he asked me if I'd like to join. I hadn't sung for a long time now and I missed it, so one Wednesday afternoon I went with him. It was only a few blocks away on Fourteenth and Washington. Anyway, I knew that in singing I might shine out as exceptional. I didn't have knights, but I had a voice. And if I had to carry the burden of being different, I might as well go whole hog and be exceptional.

The Cathedral was very grand indeed. It was acknowledged to be one of the most magnificent churches of any denomination in Denver. Glorious peaked stained-glass windows with wondrous biblical pictures gleaming and coloring the air, pillars and arches inside, an amazingly high ceiling curved and peaked like the windows, dark mysterious depths on the side with square pillars and nooks and plaques. At the far end was a raised platform, a stage, a space full of marvels on display. The organ was on one side and on the other a pulpit surrounded by ironwork. Behind the pulpit was the choir stall, three pews where we were to sing during the church service. Across from the choir stall was the door that the preacher came through. Beside it, a throne, a chair with a back that must have been fifteen feet tall, all carved in flowers and angels curving gently into a spire on top. There were organ pipes everywhere on the walls. In the center of the back wall was *The Last Supper,* a bas-relief carved in wood with Jesus and the Apostles around a table.

I had never seen or imagined anything so overwhelmingly grand in my life. I was very impressed.

On my first glance at the choirmaster, I thought he was a double for Hitler — little toothbrush mustache and a strand of hair fallen down across his forehead — but when I came closer and my friend introduced me, I saw that he didn't really look like Hitler at all. A long smooth musical face, high forehead and a pointed chin, a fine nose and sensitive eyes, a delicate mouth. His hair was wavy. His name was David Pew. I liked him immediately.

Then in that vaulted Cathedral, I sang. My high clear voice rang out in perfect pitch. Most of the hymns I didn't know and I wavered and stumbled, but some of them I did know. I spun them out of my rotund and bespectacled body with my head high and one eye on David Pew. And he heard me and he got very excited. I was not surprised.

The deal was that the members of the boys choir got two dollars a month, and more if they stayed. They got a dollar extra if they brought a new member who stayed. I spoke to Clara about it afterwards, stressing the money angle, and she agreed that I could join the choir. Then every Wednesday afternoon from four to five, every Saturday evening from seven to nine, and every Sunday morning at ten, I went to Saint John's and sang. It was only the boys on Wednesday, but on Saturday evening and Sunday morning, the adults came, men and women, and the whole choir practiced together in the choir room.

On Sunday, we wore deep purple robes with clean white surplices over them and we'd walk out and around to the front door, then down the aisles singing. During bad weather, we'd go down long hallways and get to the front that way. Then, after walking down the aisles, we'd go into our choir stalls row by row, still singing. Mr. Pew had a fine sense of theatre.

But before I quite got the hang of the processional and the hymns, school began and along with it a tangle of troubles.

11

Transitions

DORA MOORE ELEMENTARY SCHOOL on Ninth and Corona was twice the size of Emerson School. It took up a whole city block. The playground was enormous and full of fun possibilities. It was, like Emerson, surrounded by a chain-link fence. The building was really two buildings connected by an overhead hallway. When I arrived, the noise was immense and I knew this was going to be different. This place was alive.

I wasn't in the playground two minutes till I heard the old refrain, "Hey, Fatty, move outta the way!"

"My name is Stanley," I said, pushing my horn-rimmed glasses back up my nose.

"Fatty Four-eyes, Fatty Four-eyes, Fatty Four-eyes!"

Gym class was bad. We had to change our clothes for gym and shower afterwards, so every day I had to be naked in front of them, struggle with my truss while they teased me about it, teased me about how fat I was, and what a small penis I had. Then we'd go out on the gym floor and they'd tease me because I couldn't do a somersault. Even the teacher got in on that. "Come on, Stanley, let's try a somersault today." And my heart would sink and I'd stand there. They'd insist. They'd all gather 'round as I got down on the mat with my head to the floor. "Now, push! Push with your legs! Bend your neck! Just do it!" Then they'd start laughing. "He's too fat to turn over!" they'd say, then they'd go to climb a rope. I couldn't do that, either. I can tell you just how to climb a rope. Put the rope between your legs, reach up, let go with your legs and pull your weight up, then grab the rope with your legs, reach up and on you go. I couldn't even get the rope between my legs, and if someone helped me with that, I couldn't pull my weight off the floor. If I tried very hard, which I often did, my truss would slip, I'd have to stop and adjust it, and the kids would tease me about the truss.

There was one boy in my gym class who was also in the boys choir at Saint John's. He was a bright boy with golden curls, thick lips and a prominent nose. He was a bit pudgy, but not nearly as fat as I was, and he did all right in gym. He kind of kept away from the others because his right hand lacked three fingers. There was just a thumb and a little finger and a web of flesh between. But he was strong and athletic, and besides that, he could affect a cuttingly indignant tone, almost a British accent, though he'd spent his life in Denver. I hadn't yet gotten to know him in choir, but in gym class he became my champion. He came up to the circle of bullies around me and said that some people could do some things and other people could do other things. He scattered my assailants with the force of his eloquence. His name was Jon Stark. I loved him immediately. He stayed with me in gym class and, from that moment on, although I never learned to do a somersault or to climb a rope, and was clumsy and troublesome at everything else, too, I had a friend there with me.

The worst time for the bullies was on my way home from school. If they saw me they'd come to me, tease me, call me "Fatty Four-eyes," snatch my books from my hands and throw them in the mud. Then they'd insist on a fight. There was an honor code even among the worst of the bullies never to hit someone who was wearing glasses, so they'd tell me to take them off, and of course I wouldn't. They'd call me chicken then, and make chicken noises, one would punch me on the arm, another would kick me in the shins and a third would get my glasses off. Then they'd light into me and I was helpless. The next afternoon they'd be back and do it all over again. Jon went home the opposite direction, across Cheesman Park, and had to be home by a certain time, so he couldn't help me in this. I tried to take other routes home, but they found me. It was a nightmare.

Then when I'd get home, sometimes there was nothing to eat, at least nothing I could fix. I knew how to open a can and light the stove. I could fix Campbell's soups with a piece of cheese and I discovered at this time canned spaghetti, but if these things weren't in the cupboard; I was lost. I'd open the refrigerator and it was disgusting. Maybe I could heat up some leftovers. I told Clara about this one time and she got predictably hysterical, told me we didn't have a lot of money and there was plenty of food. Mrs. Johnston had gotten a job now, too, and wasn't there to feed me. So I took money from Clara's bureau, from the table, even from her purse, to buy candy. The two dollars a month I got from the choir was not enough for the amount of candy I wanted. When Clara was there but out of the room where her purse was, I'd open it, and usually there were coins in the bottom. Maybe I'd take one coin so that she wouldn't miss it. Then, if we were out of soup, I could buy something to eat. I had, however, no sense of saving money. If I had it, I'd spend it. I got the taste for spending money this way, being hungry, finding nothing to eat, finding money, taking that and being comforted by it, going out and getting something with it, something to eat.

The question in my mind is why did the bullies pick on me so much. I suppose it was a combination of factors. In spite of the bullies, I was overwhelmingly grateful to be away from the hypnotic dismalness of Emerson School. At that place there were no bullies, true, but also I was not interested in anything. Here at Dora Moore, everything was exciting. In class — and here's one of the factors — other boys would be called on by the teacher, they wouldn't know the answer, and immediately they would be dealt a very painful public shame. Then, while they were still blushing, I would raise my hand, the teacher would smile upon me, and I would give the right answer.

Being an only child, raised by people who didn't think to try to understand me, losing all the basic securities that might have opened me to the needs of others, I was by now entrenched in a solitude in which the possibility of diplomacy didn't enter my mind. I knew what my needs were, they were enormous, and with all that I'd lost it took all my efforts, like Alice's Red Queen, to stay where I was, to keep what I had. In the classroom I could shine, I could therefore know I existed. I had a place where at least the teacher acknowledged my existence and my specialness by calling on me with a smile.

I did not smile back. I took her smile as meeting my needs, and I showed my being with my intelligent answer. The possibility that the other boys might have such needs also never occurred to me, and if anyone had suggested it I could only have said that I hadn't energy to spare for them, they hadn't given me anything but bruises and nasty words and I found it hard enough to defend myself from them. Actually they provided me with one thing — a comparison to shine against. They were wrong and I was right and why, then, didn't they change their ways.

This, I think, is the most important factor or the central one. I was a fighter. They were fighters too, that was obvious. They had strong bodies to fight with in the normal manner, but in their arena I was less endowed than the weakest girl in class. With my fat, my glasses, my ear trouble, sinus trouble, hernia and asthma, not to mention the shameful and endless degradation of the truss and the solid recognition in my mind of the fact that if I over-exerted myself my truss would slip or I'd have an asthma attack, I knew myself to be in a hopeless situation in a fight. One thing my parents had given me was that they had bragged about my intelligence and encouraged me to put on shows. On those occasions I was the only kid with an audience of adults or I was the organizer, the director, the barker in charge of the show. And I knew I deserved that honor. So in the classroom I shone. In the classroom it was clear who was tops. Through my energetic participation in class I fought, fought, as everyone fights, for my existence with what tools I had. My body was a shambles and couldn't be used, but I had a mind, I had imagination and energy. Through showmanship I beat them in class. It was too bad we couldn't stay there all the time. If we could stay in class, then my values, the values that seemed right, that I could prove were right, would prevail.

But then the bell rang, the show was over, and the other boys fought back. So it was that the more I won, the more I was beaten and the more empty was the empty apartment where there was nothing for me but another can of Campbell's soup and a few coins. But I couldn't give up shining in class. It was the only place where I could win against the other boys. I fought to win, I won to exist. At home, I studied hard to win again.

When the leaves turned, we moved to an apartment on the second floor, I suppose because it was cheaper. Certainly it was smaller than the big apartment on the third floor, less than half the size, but it was well arranged and had plenty of windows and the golden leaves out the window were gorgeous. Being lower down, we could see the grass and trees. Clara's bedroom had four windows and opened into the living room with French doors with little panes of glass in them. The kitchen was narrow with one pretty window, the living room was small but very pleasant.

Soon after that, Clara brought home a career soldier named Pete.

He was tall and straight with a deep voice, a khaki uniform, a hat with a bill, and medals. He looked like Gary Cooper in the Foreign Legion. And he was kind to me. He was my hero immediately.

On his first or second visit, he brought Clara a book. After he left, Clara opened it, was horrified, slapped it shut. She was terribly upset then and shouted and cried. I was really curious and wanted to look in the book too, but she wouldn't let me. The next day Pete came and they had a serious talk. The book was Kahlil Gibran's "The Prophet." Being full of pictures of naked bodies, Clara thought it was about sex.

Another time he took her into the mountains. I didn't go along but they told me about it afterwards. They went walking through the woods to a steep place where there was a lovely view, out onto a rock slab at the edge. Clara's foot slipped a little and she was unable to move, frozen in terror. The footing was such that Pete couldn't simply grab her and lift her away, couldn't even reach her, so he talked and she crouched, frozen. Finally he convinced her or softened her into enough movement that he could take her hand, pull her away, and get her off the edge.

We went again, as we had years before with Adam and Lou, to City Park to see the fountains in the colored lights and hear the band playing. We went to the zoo. Pete wanted me to lose weight and tried to get me to do exercises. But my hero-worship didn't extend so far as that and the project was soon abandoned.

Very often Pete spent the night at the apartment, but he had to get back to the base early, so I slept in the bedroom and they in the living room. It was nice in the bedroom, with all those windows and the autumn leaves still in full display. I'd wake in the morning inside a golden tree.

One morning Clara shook me awake. Her face was red and she shouted at me, "Have you been playing with the clock?" I don't know now if I had or not. I suppose I had. I had never been told not to play with the clock. But Pete was late to the base because the clock was an hour off and Clara beat me with a strap, her face red, screaming and shouting as she beat me.

Clara's feet were hurting her more and more. Her job at the Rexall Drug Store required her to stand up all the time. She had many pairs of shoes, but none of them now were at all comfortable. When pus began coming out from under her toenails, someone at work persuaded her to go to a doctor and recommended Dr. Best, so she went to him.

Dr. Best checked her over and told her she had to have a hysterectomy immediately, that uterine cysts had filled her body to the toenails with pus. She, of course, said she didn't have time or money for such a thing, and who would look after her little boy? Dr. Best said she'd be dead in a week if she didn't have the operation. So suddenly Clara was gone.

As to who would look after her little boy, I had become accustomed to looking after myself almost entirely, had been doing so for years. During the two or three weeks Clara was in the hospital I had more solicitous care than I'd ever had in my life. People were pestering me constantly. The Johnstons, of course, and Mr. Frye the landlord and his family were constantly keeping an eye on me and feeding me. Two ladies who lived across the hall up a little stair invited me over all the time and tried Chinese checkers and dominoes, which I didn't like very much, then they'd put me to bed, which was astonishing. I hadn't been put to bed for years. No one took me to the hospital to visit Clara, but they were all telling me there was nothing to worry about. So much so that I began to worry. Evidently she came very close to death. Pete visited her in the hospital whenever he could, then he'd come by to see me. He'd tell me Clara had told him to tell me this or that, then he'd take me to a movie. I was so busy being taken care of that I wasn't able to hear my radio shows. One time after the two ladies had put me to bed, I got up and turned on the lights and the radio after they left. Pretty soon they were knocking on the door again, asking what the matter was. After that I'd keep the radio turned down low and listen to it in the dark.

Clara's illness secured her relationship with Pete. He rose to the occasion like the radio hero Jack Armstrong, the All-American Boy. He visited her, brought her flowers, kept watch over me, and generally stuck with her through her ordeal.

When she got home she was very weak and tottery. I'd fix soup for her and bring her things. She'd hobble around but there was no way she could work yet.

When my birthday was coming up, Pete decided I should have a birthday party on the Saturday. I'd never had one before. I had gone to that one in Macomb, that was all. It was my eighth birthday. Pete went all out, with a cake, hats, party favors, crepe paper and other festive stuff around. He and I sat down and cut out formal invitations out of colored paper for six kids in the neighborhood. We didn't have room for more than that. I was thrilled when Pete said they'd all bring presents. Finally the Saturday came and the parents all brought the kids and sure enough the kids all brought presents. Clara was still feeling sick so she sat and Pete put on an apron and did the work. It was a fine show but the presents were a bust, and I had looked forward hungrily to them. Stupid, useless things, and then I had to thank the kids for them, I knew that much. I maintained my integrity by thanking them with a cold eye. Each gift made me sadder than the last.

There was one present, however, that I thought looked like it might be pretty neat. It was a model airplane. After the kids all left I opened the box, and inside were strips of wood and tissue paper and little jars of glue and paint. The picture on the outside was wonderful, but you had to build it yourself. I asked Pete but he was busy cleaning up and Clara said, "He's done enough for you, don't trouble him anymore." I tried to build it myself. It wasn't my kind of thing to do, but I felt that if I had such a thing as that model airplane it really would be great. And in my efforts to build it, I wrecked it. Well, I didn't know about that for sure, just yet. One time I had it laid out all in pieces on Clara's peach satin bedspread and the orange light of the late afternoon sun coming through the window and onto that shiny peach color so that the pieces of the model were colored orange from the sun and peach from the bedspread. I worked a long time at it as carefully as I could, but when I went to bed I thought it was hopeless. The next morning, Pete tried to save the airplane but he couldn't and I threw it away.

Finally Clara got well enough to get a job. I think it was the Fryes who found it for her, a bookkeeping job for a real estate company, Morrison and Morrison.

I got the idea then to clean the whole apartment, after school, her mess as well as mine. I did it every afternoon and when she came home she'd look around, her face would light up and she'd be pleased. She never failed to praise me and thank me for it. It was a great source of pleasure for me because it delighted her so much and then after complimenting me about it she'd tend to be kind to me.

I swear I cleaned the apartment to please Clara and to help her, she was still weak from being sick and I wanted to help as much as I could. The fact that I found coins that I wouldn't otherwise have found was secondary. Anyway, I deserved something for all that work, didn't I?

And besides, I was always hungry. Every morning for breakfast she made me toast and gave me tomato juice. I'd come home at noon and open a can of soup. After school if there was no can of spaghetti leftovers, I'd hope to find enough money to buy a hamburger. If I found less than that, I'd buy a candy bar. Although I knew well enough not to let anyone know I was taking money, I didn't entirely feel that it was quite stealing. I needed to eat after all, and she was supposed to be feeding me.

Jon Stark, my champion in gym class, was becoming more and more of a friend. We found we could talk with each other about all kinds of things, about school and the kids, the war in Europe. We could speculate and fantasize. So we got together whenever we could, at recesses and at lunch time. Often we'd leave the school yard and walk down the sidewalks. We found a drugstore across the street where we could get cherry cokes and talk about things in peace and quiet, and often we went there. But one time we went and discovered we had no money, so we ordered water and the drug store man kicked us out. Jon was indignant. We had bought plenty of cokes there in the past, we weren't strangers there, we just happened to be out of cash at the moment. Jon felt we shouldn't go back there again and for awhile we didn't. Jon almost always had pocket money and so, also, did I.

Then one day he invited me to come to his house on the following Friday after school and I said sure, that'd be swell. That evening his mother called my mother very formally and asked her too if I could come over on Friday. I didn't understand what all the fuss was about. Always if I went to a kid's house, I just went. Friday came and I walked home with Jon. It was great not to be expecting bullies at every corner. As we went along, the houses got bigger and bigger and nicer and nicer. They dwarfed the house of the ex-mayor's relative and the house of the people who had a swimming pool. When we came to Jon's house, I realized that he was rich. His house was huge and white. He even had servants. His mother was divorced and had moved back in with her parents. His mother was very, very gracious and pleasant. Jon introduced me properly to her and to his grandmother. The walls were covered with paintings and shelves of books, there were thick rugs on the floors and strange furniture. Jon took me to a gigantic cabinet with a huge curved horn on the top. It was a phonograph. He put on a record. He got impatient as it played. When it came to the end, he said, "Now, watch!" I watched as the phonograph needle arm rose up of its own accord and moved aside. Then a big round metal device rose up from the other side, glomped down on the record and picked it up.

A part came out from inside the device, turned the record over and glomped it back down onto the turntable. Then the needle arm moved back onto the record and started to play the other side.

Jon carefully took the needle off the record then turned, spread his arms, shrugged and said, "But it's useless!"

"What do you mean, it's useless?"

"When records first came out," he said, "the music continued on the other side. But now it continues on the next record, so we can't actually use this for playing long pieces."

I looked at the mechanism. It was thick shiny metal, scratched, with a mess of machinery below the turntable. The cabinet was beautifully carved wood and the horn on top was graceful and imposing.

"Besides," he said, "sometimes it breaks the records."

Jon showed me around the house. There was a lush conservatory full of plants, a library with books all over the walls, some of them in glass-covered cases. "Do you have a swimming pool?" I asked. "No, but we have a pool table." He took me downstairs to what seemed to me a gigantic table covered with green cloth and he taught me how to play pool. We had to be very careful not to scratch the cloth.

I was nervous at dinner with all the complicated equipment and the servants bringing things in. But everyone was very kind and friendly, and if I did anything clumsily they didn't seem to think it was wrong.

In the evening I was driven home by a chauffeur in a fancy car. Jon and his mother went along. When we came up Washington Street to my house, I looked at it in some trepidation. But the ironwork on the brick wall in front, the solid old house of red stone, the big tree, the care that Mr. Frye took to keep everything in good shape — it looked all right, it really did, it was really kind of nice.

Then he came to visit me and I showed him around my house, the great echoing garage, the balcony above it, the basement with the wood-slat cages of storage, the electric meters that went around at different speeds, and the great furnace like an octopus. And so we visited back and forth, always very formal in a way, with the invitations and parental consent. We had a lot in common. Broken home and only child, to begin with. Then we were freaks together, he with his deformed hand and I with all my complex of infirmities. What excited us with each other, though, was a developing similarity of minds.

We had both suffered a great deal from being "different," being unable to be part of the dynamic skills of physical play, being in fact inferior to the other kids. Both of us had enormous energy and vitality, however, and had found ways to redirect this energy into the various workings of our minds. Both of us brilliant, curious, wildly imaginative, and passionately, intensely dramatic. We each felt the urge to develop a set of values that was different from the norm, beyond the norm. And together at the age of eight we learned to converse, to express ourselves in ways that had meaning. We learned to inspire each other. And inspiring and being inspired became something we both valued very highly indeed.

Jon was a good boy. It wasn't his fault he was rich. It wasn't his fault that he was naturally given an allowance. It wasn't a whole lot, but it was enough for cokes and movies and candy. It wasn't his fault that he hadn't yet learned to worry about what it would cost every time he was thirsty and wanted a coke. If he wanted something, he'd get it. Not things, he didn't care for things. Already, he was disenchanted with that. The phonograph had shown him, if he hadn't learned it before, the irony of material goods. What he wanted, and could get without another thought, were satisfactions. The warmth of a chocolate bar on a park bench in a cold wind, the way a cherry coke in a corner booth of the drug store will stimulate conversation. Going to movies, taking the bus instead of walking in the snow.

It wasn't his fault. He was, after all, only eight years old. But to keep up with him and all his expenses, I had to steal more and more money from Clara's purse. If I didn't do that I'd be in the unmanly position of being poor, of being unable to go with him where he could go, unable to enjoy with him what he could enjoy without any worry, unable to keep up. Well, you'll say, why didn't I ask him to pay my way? But I knew that if I did that, we wouldn't be equal. I'd be a tag-along, a pet, a child, and then how could we talk together, like two little men?

12

Money and Malt Balls

ONE MORNING TOWARD THE END of the school year, one of my teachers was discussing the value and importance to the health of having a varied diet. This troubled me somewhat as, with my endless cans of Campbell's soups and spaghetti plus hamburgers and candy bars, I was having anything but a varied diet. I went home for lunch that day and instead of my usual can of soup, I decided to have my toast and tomato juice.

Every morning from the time we left Macomb, Clara had provided me with my toast and tomato juice for breakfast. This was inviolate and invariable and she was conscientious about always having these things in the house. I opened the tomato juice can myself or took it out of the icebox and shook it, my thumbs over the holes, to mix it back up. But she always made the toast for me.

It didn't seem like a difficult thing to do. We had one of the new kind of toasters that pops up when the toast is done. I plugged it in, put the bread in it and pushed down the lever. Then I went to the icebox for the butter and tomato juice. What with shaking the tomato juice and getting the butter out of its wrapper and onto a saucer it was a couple of minutes before I turned around, and when I did there was smoke coming out of the toaster.

Oh God, I didn't want to start another fire. I didn't want to lose this house. I loved this house. No, please, no fire, no! I tried pushing up the lever but I couldn't get the toast to pop up.

I tried to unplug the wire but I had butter on my fingers and I couldn't get a good enough grip to pull it out. The smoke was heavy now in the kitchen and pouring thickly out of the toaster. Yanking open the silverware drawer, I grabbed two knives to pry the plug out of the wall. I slid the two knives under the plug, saw a great flash of light as the electricity jolted through my body, and I toppled unconscious to the floor.

I have no way of knowing how long I lay there on the kitchen floor except that when I awoke the smoke was no longer visible although it still smelled strong. While I was waking up I was thinking how stupid it was what I had done. Really stupid. But the toaster was unplugged, the cord dangled down over the counter.

I sat on the floor shaking and crying. I felt weak and strange. I was scared. I got up and went sobbing and trembling upstairs to Mrs. Johnston. She went down and checked over the kitchen in our apartment, she looked me over, and she put me to bed for the rest of the day. When Clara came home, she was very upset. She thought I shouldn't be allowed to fix my lunch. I had to convince her I wouldn't do that again.

It was about this time that a new affliction was added to my long roster of ills, constipation. I think there was only the one incident in the movie theater when I actually shat in my pants, but the fact is I was deathly afraid of doing so.

I had, and have still, no sense that I can trust or control my system. My body has always been flimsy, pain-ridden and out of kilter. A poor tool, its only purpose to keep my eyes and mind alive. I was out of school often with colds which, with my asthmatic bronchial tubes, always struck me very hard. Stomach aches too would hit me unaccountably and I'd stay home pale and moaning. And now constipation with its sickly feeling and the terrible danger that it would solve itself uncontrollably before I could get to the toilet. I preferred to stay home, and stay home I did.

This got to be so common a complaint with me that Clara finally took me to Dr. Best. He said I had a sluggish system and prescribed a children's laxative. So every day I went to this big bottle on the counter and poured myself a teaspoon of thick white gunk. If I forgot, I got constipated. This would be an enormous trauma. Clara would yell at me then give me an enema. I'd have to kneel bare-bottomed on the bathroom rug so she could do it. Very soon I learned to take an enema by myself.

Summer came and school let out. What a relief that was. No more bullies for three whole months. No more gym class. No homework.

I went back again to playing with the neighbor kids, the hide-and-seek in our yard, cowboys and Indians in the vacant lot. The days were long and warm. The rich people swam in their pool. Treasures were to be found in the alleys. I played knights and soldiers with the gas station kid. Sometimes I'd go to the gas station and watch the men work on the cars.

This year, though, there were differences. There was Pete, who'd come when he could and take Clara and me out to a movie or to the band shell or a parade or a carnival. There was choir three times a week. There were exchange visits with Jon.

Across Tenth Street was a big apartment house with lots and lots of kids with long vast hallways. Many of these kids had no fathers or their fathers were away. It was a cheap place to rent and many of the people there were transient and I felt immediately related to many of them because I too had lost my father and was uprooted. But many of them were worse off than I was.

Sometimes I'd go home with one or another of them and there'd be very little to eat, maybe some cinnamon toast or a graham cracker, and mattresses on the floor. A sour smell pervaded the place. All the apartments were cramped, things were kept in boxes, and everyone was always ready to go on to the next place. Like me, their mothers were at work and they were on their own all day. I got along with quite a few of them pretty well but most of them didn't stay very long.

I must have asked Clara if she was going to marry Pete. She was very vague about it, said it would interfere with his career. I don't believe she was actually divorced yet. I think she was holding onto Lou as a security, something to go back to if times got really rough. And perhaps she got more money out of him if she stayed married to him. Even now in the '40's she was hanging onto the roaring '20's myth of the wild, romantic woman, untamable, unquenchable and impossible to understand. She was so full of lies, there was no knowing what was on her mind or what she felt she was accomplishing. It was as though her mind was sectioned off so that one part didn't know what the other part was doing or had just said a minute ago. She seemed to believe her lies and would defend them to the point of tears, then fight for another contradictory set, so I have no clear picture of what was going on with her except that I do know that she was getting money from Lou regularly and that she was very glad to have Pete. They were close for years.

There was a great new fashion that was sweeping the country now on the radio and in cereal boxes and candy. That was rings. It was very exciting to me, I got immediately swept up in it. The first one I knew about was the Superman ring at the Republic Drug Store. You had to buy a certain amount at the Republic and then you'd get the ring for free. The Republic was sponsoring a radio program and that's how I heard about it. It was easy enough for us to buy things at the Republic Drug Store — there was one by the Ogden Theatre — and

Clara indulged my new passion by buying all our medicines there until I could get the Superman ring. It was very pretty, with a blue lacquer background and a golden "S." It was adjustable too, and would fit any finger. It was a great day when I could go and get it, and I wore it and showed it around with excitement.

Some rings came in the boxes of cereal or crackerjacks and that was swell but those rings were pretty cheap. For others, I had to buy and eat a certain amount of Wheaties or Rice Crispies, save up the coupons and mail them in, then I would get the ring in the mail. The more coupons I was forced to save, the more of whatever cereal I had to eat, the more magnificent was the ring I eventually got. There was also always a tension and a fear about them because the ads would say, "as long as supplies last," and I'd stuff myself with whatever came in the boxes so that I wouldn't be too late.

There was a ring with a hidden compartment. It had a pretty top which you could slide off and then put secret messages inside. We were advised to use cigarette paper for the messages because it could be crumpled up real small. There was a ring which was a tiny whistle. You could blow into it and it would whistle and for a second or two after that you could hear the propeller or ball inside it still going 'round. There was one whistle ring that you could blow on and people couldn't hear it but all the dogs around would hear and they'd set up a big racket. Very mysterious.

They were all dream rings. Any kid that had one of these rings had a power that, practically speaking, could serve him only if he found himself in a comic book. But the desire for them was intense, it was a hunger, a greed, a yen for power. Clara understood this, she even got involved to some extent and, in spite of her pleas of poverty, would go out and cheerfully buy whatever was needed so that I could have the latest ring before any of my friends did. Then I could show them my new ring. "Be the first in your neighborhood," the ads said, "to have this wonderful ring!" and usually I was. Then I could show them what I had. And in the show was my power. They'd gather 'round me, they'd want to see it, touch it, wear it. But I wouldn't let them wear it. That would be to lose the power to the wearer of the ring. I'd show them the ring, show them the power I had, then I'd wear it myself.

There was one ring though that I knew had to be treated differently. It was the ring that glowed in the dark. In the light, it was actually rather ugly. Made of something like plastic, it was dull looking with a swelling black line down the middle. What you did, you held it under a light to charge it and then for some time if you had it in a really dark place it would glow green, looking like a cat's eye. The only way to get the power from that ring was in the pitch dark. In the summertime, it was very hard to find a place dark enough to show this ring. The only place was the bathroom with the light off.

There was a little boy who lived in the big apartment on the third floor, where we had lived for awhile. He was about four years old, dark and thin with bony knees and he always wore shorts. I had outgrown wearing shorts now and wouldn't be caught dead in them. I also held him in contempt because he wasn't allowed to cross the street. He was, I believe, a very nice boy. He adored me and followed me around. He bored me and I mostly ditched him, only playing with him if there was nothing else to do. But he couldn't play well either. He was too young, too stupid, too adoring. The only thing to do with him was to show him my toys and overawe him.

The rings especially would overawe him and there was some pleasure in that, but it had to be done with a great deal of solemnity and folderol. I'd take just one out of the box, hide the rest, and instead of showing it to him, I'd demonstrate. With the mirror ring, for instance, I took him out in the sun and said I could see behind me with my hands over my eyes. I placed myself so that the light was bright, held my mirror ring up to my eye, held the other hand there also and started calling off what I could see through the slits in the ring. "You're standing under a tree. Now you've moved to the sidewalk. You kicked a stone. There's a blue car coming down the street." People say if you have a secret you have power but I've never felt that was quite right. Where the power comes is in pulling the magic out of a thing without showing the thing.

When the cat's eye ring came I was disappointed because it was, as I say, dull and ugly. But I read the instructions, held it under the light for awhile and then went into the bathroom where it glowed very satisfactorily for some minutes, then started to fade. I tried it in other places but the bathroom was by far the best.

"I've got something to show you," I said to the little boy. "Come down to my place in a few minutes." I charged up the cat's eye ring under the table lamp. When he arrived, the lamp was off and the ring hidden. "I want you to see something," I said. I took him into the bathroom, sat him on the toilet, shut the door and turned off the light. Then I pulled out the ring. He started right off shrieking. I told him he'd better be quiet or the creature would get him. He stopped shrieking and all I heard were his suppressed whimperings, his trembling breaths. I brought the ring slowly closer and closer to him. It was a terrific sense of power. I heard his teeth chattering. It was delicious. I had never had such power in all my life. Closer and closer, deeper and deeper, the little boy sobbing and gasping and trembling.

Then I was afraid he'd tell on me. I said that if he mentioned this to anyone, the eye would come to him in the night. I hated to bring it to an end. But the ring was starting to fade so I put it in my pocket and turned on the light.

The boy was stark pale, his eyes wide and staring, unblinking. He had peed in his pants. I'll never forget how he looked. It frightened me to see him. At last I knew I was doing something wrong. I tried to soothe him, I told him that the eye was my friend and I'd protect him from it. He and I had a secret trust now. He wasn't to worry. But he'd better not tell anyone.

I knew I'd done a very bad thing. It was, perhaps, a technique related to and inspired by what that babysitter did to me back in Winfield, talking to the boogeyman in the basement. It was a form of bullying that really worked. There was, of course, the danger that he'd tell on me. Then I'd be punished and lose the ring. And I didn't want to lose that ring. I had suffered horribly all through the school year from bullies and now I had found my power. Oh, not the ring itself, the power of the show, of vision and drama and rhythm, the power of word and voice.

The little boy became distant after that. He'd do whatever I told him to do with alacrity but he avoided me now, didn't want to play with me anymore, and drifted out of my life.

Choir was a joy. I looked forward to it eagerly, went to it regularly, and sang in it with enthusiasm and a great deal of effort to sing well. David Pew was a jewel of a choirmaster, a very sensitive man, very delicate in his handling of us. He governed us by the look on his face. If we sang well, his face glowed with a pure angelic light that itself was sufficient to keep us in key and singing as well as we could. But inevitably there were times when we didn't sing well and then his face would darken, wrinkles of pain would shoot across his forehead, he'd stop us with a wave of his hand. His lips compressed, his nose red, his eyebrows bent down, he'd have us repeat the phrase or start from the beginning. "You must listen," he'd say. "Listen to each part and to the whole thing." Then he'd raise his hand again and his face would hold hope and fear mixed. Again we'd sing, trying to bring his face to that angelic listening glow that all good musicians have, that clear-browed look of purity. Sometimes, if we went on sounding bad, he would storm out of the choir room and leave us there in shame. Perhaps then he'd come back pale and grim, to raise his hand again. Other times his wife would come and tell us that we'd better all go home now and we'd file out in solemn humility and shame with the determination in every boy's heart that next practice, we'd show him how we could sing.

David Pew had a particular fondness for Bach Cantatas. Until I arrived though, there were many of them that he couldn't perform because there wasn't a boy's voice he could trust for the boy soloist. Now, however, with my sweet clear voice, my perfect pitch, he was freed to do certain Cantatas. I knew he was very excited about my voice. The whole choir knew. And they knew that he was right. Instead of being mean and jealous about it, the other boys honored me. As good athletes honor exceptional athletes. The excellence of my singing spurred them to do their best. How he achieved this, I don't know exactly except that the choir, like a football team, thrived on cohesion. Unlike my classroom teacher, he didn't give me special smiles. He gave me extra work.

He worked with me slowly until, by this summer, I was allowed to sing short solos in his beloved Bach Cantatas. Clara and Pete would come to church to hear the singing. There was a majesty about the choir at Saint John's Episcopal Cathedral while David Pew was there, and he was there for decades. If you wanted to hear great religious choral music done beautifully, that was the place to go. Like Bach before him, like Messiaen in his little church in Paris, David Pew had what I yearned for, a weekly audience, respectful and open to find the glory of God in what he presented.

David Pew played the organ as the choir wove its way in orderly fashion around or through the pillared hallways of the church, our deep purple robes flowing, clean white surplices gleaming. Then at precisely the cue note, we entered the church singing. David Pew was in the nave playing the organ and couldn't look as we proceeded slowly down the aisle and filed, row by row, into our places in front of the altar. We all watched him, however, intensely, as he conducted us by the bobbing of his head.

It was grand beyond anything. I sang hosannas with a religious fervor that was deep and heartfelt. I prayed with a faith that was of the essence of life. The great welling sound of the choir and the organ glowed up to Heaven as a worthy gift to a glorious Deity. I sang my solos to God and Jesus and I knew they heard me, knew they were delighting in the use I was making of the gift they had entrusted in me. I was proud and humbled at once, proud to be part of this choir, to be a vessel, a passage through which flowed beautiful music to the glory of God, humbled because the more I sang, the more powerfully I felt the greatness of God and Jesus and the Heavenly Hosts. The more magnificently we sang, the more I felt the omnipotence of God. With God and Jesus and Heaven was the glory, music radiating from us to Them was the power. Was the mercy.

The contrasts among the lives I was leading tore me to shreds. There was the fun of the neighborhood children playing together. There was the strain of the constant battle during school with myself winning in the classroom and losing to the bullies on the way home. There was the delight and the expanding horizons of my continued converse with Jon. There was the warm pretense of family life when Pete visited. There was my constant stealing. And now the shame of the cruel thing I did with the cat's-eye ring to the little boy.

I felt twisted into knots worrying about bad things I was doing. I yearned for help. I heard the Bible stories in church, I heard again and again about God's mercy, how he forgave sinners. If I joined the church, I could take Communion and the great tangle of my sins would be washed away. Besides, there was the triumph of my voice ringing angelically out among the smooth heavy pillars of the Episcopalian Church. Although I had been a Lutheran all my life, it seemed right that I should join this church and finally I did.

It wasn't hard to do. I had to study a few things, then one Sunday, along with a couple of other choirboys and a dozen or so other people, I joined. And I took Communion, and it was a tremendous relief. Not that I would quit sinning but that the weight of guilt wasn't on me and I felt better.

One day after church, Jon took me to visit his favorite relative, his aunt. He always pronounced it in the British fashion.

Jon's aunt lived downtown and we could go and have lunch with her, and the movie was right next door so we could go to that after lunch. In fact she lived at the Cosmopolitan Hotel. Surely, I said, she's just visiting? No, she lived there. A lobby with high ceilings, vast sparkling chandeliers, space, elegance, fine furniture, servants everywhere, silk curtains. We went to her room first and met her. She was all twinkling eyes with lace at her throat above a tailored suit. She delighted me with her humor and her charm. She took us to the main dining room of the hotel and ordered an elegant lunch. She was small and jolly, her hair was almost white, she wore pastels and was lovely, bright, and witty. She was like a modern fairy godmother or the image of the happy rich in the movies. She was a delight to talk with and full of fun. She asked me if I had ever tasted honeydew. I had never even heard of it. Honeydew. Just the sort of thing that such a lady would introduce one to in a dream. She asked me if I liked cantaloupe and when I said I did, she ordered honeydew. It was green! She insisted I squeeze a little lemon onto it. It was wonderful. I really liked it. I still do. And whenever I have it, I have it with lemon.

Then the summer was over and school started again. I was now in the third grade. Jon was in my class this year. On the first day of school the teacher conceived a game to introduce the kids to each other. We would each draw one of the other children on the blackboard and the rest of the class would guess who it was. And if the others could guess, the one who drew the recognizable picture would be praised and noticed.

From the previous year I naturally assumed a solitary fighting style in the classroom. By now I knew how to concentrate on learning, to be bright and special, to interrupt my classmates with their dull minds and dreary stumbling answers. I knew how to compete with other smart kids. But I didn't know how to have a friend in the class. A friend in class seemed a contradiction in terms. It was disturbing.

When my turn came, I tried to draw Jon. Curly hair .. but there were others there with curly hair. Round face, big features .. that didn't help. If only there was some way I could distinguish him, so that my picture would be recognized. I wanted to shine out. There was the hand, his right hand with only the thumb and little finger. Should I put it in the picture? I hesitated, wondering if I should or shouldn't. If I didn't the picture would not be recognizable as Jon and I would lose power in the classroom. This was important to me. There was the probability that Jon would be mad or hurt. But the hand was the truth wasn't it? The distinguishing feature? But wouldn't it be cruel? Wouldn't it be putting him in a painful position among the kids? What about his feelings? Weren't his feelings more important than a picture on the blackboard? Were they more important than my gaining notice from a new teacher in a new classroom?

It was one of those moments that come to all of us, when we choose our paths, and for the rest of our lives we find ourselves battered by our choice. Life had thus far been cruel and harsh to me and I had become cruel and harsh to meet it. That crippled hand was the truth, wasn't it? Perhaps a case could be made that Truth of Jon's deformity was more important than Jon's feelings. Because of all my deformities, I felt a need to point to the deformities I found around me, to present them as the Truth. I needed to feel that what I was doing was important.

With a few strokes, I put in the deformed hand and my picture was finished.

Everyone recognized him immediately. It was lovely. I shone. Then I looked at Jon. His face was red and pained. He was looking down at his desk. His hand, as usual, was hidden.

Jon was badly hurt. I had never seen his face so hurt and angry. At recess, out in the playground, I got the full brunt of his indignation. He told me I had been very, very cruel. I told him I hadn't meant to, that I didn't care about his hand. It didn't interest me. It was just the way to know who he was. But he wouldn't see my point of view. Nor did I care to see his either.

As I had denied stealing before, I now denied this act as cruelty. I said I was surprised that he was so hurt. I said I was innocent, didn't mean to do any wrong, was only doing the assignment. I interrupted him, couldn't bear to hear him call me cruel. I don't remember what he said except that he didn't care to be my friend anymore.

After that he stopped speaking to me. Our friendship was broken. I was alone in the playground, in the schoolroom, in the gym. In choir, though we sang side by side, he didn't speak to me. No exchange visits, no great discussions, no cokes at the drug store, no movies together, no sitting in animated volubility on park benches or on lawns or walking down sidewalks. No fine mind and kindred soul to delight and grow with.

I was very angry. Why must I always lose what I needed? Why was the center of my happiness always taken away from me? Why was I always left alone on the sidewalk? Life was sour. I didn't care about it.

At lunch hour, on the day I drew Jon's hand, I went to places where he and I had always gone. The steps by the old school, but kids came and chased me away. I wandered down the street to the drug store. I had gotten money out of Clara's purse to buy a cherry coke with Jon. I went in. I had no stomach for cherry coke. I bought two packages of malt balls and put them in my pocket, wandered out to eat them as I walked.

After school, the bullies came, three of them, and started teasing me about my fat, my truss, my glasses, my books. I didn't care. I reached in my pocket. "Want some malt balls?" I asked. "Sure." I passed around malt balls and they went away. They didn't hurt me at all. This happened several times. I realized I could bribe. Pretty soon we'd stand on the sidewalk eating malt balls and talking. I wasn't interested in their talk. But I very much liked not being hurt.

Some of the bullies, however, didn't care for malt balls. So the next time I encountered my malt-ball-bullies I spoke to them about it. There were two of them. "I'll give you 25 cents a week each," I said. "Each. To protect me." It was a deal. "Plus malt balls and extras."

After that I had, if not comfort and good times, at least some modicum of safety. My bodyguards didn't walk me home but if any bully teased me or threatened me, I'd tell my bullies. They were big strong boys and they'd tell the others to leave me alone. They'd threaten to beat them up. It was no friendship. It was a cold-blooded business deal. I never went anywhere without my malt balls. I ate them in class and at recess and I always had some left to give away. I had them in my pockets with my money. My pockets always bulged with money and malt balls. I'd put my hands in my pockets and feel the malt balls and the money and I'd know I was safe. I'd take a malt ball out of my pocket and put it in my mouth. It soothed me. My singing kept improving. I put my heart into that. Jon was right there, listening. On the way home from choir, I'd share some of my malt balls with the gas station kid and he and I would walk home together in a communion of malt balls.

One day after a couple of months of this, he and I were walking home from church and it seemed as though all the grownups had gone crazy. Usually after church it was pretty quiet except for other people going home from church and maybe a few little toddlers on tricycles but this day was different. There were people in huddles talking. Other people were standing just staring out into space. Ladies in aprons running out their doors and across the lawns to their neighbors. It was strange. I was getting low on malt balls so we stopped at the drugstore on Washington Street. It was usually pretty quiet in there but today it was crowded. And everyone was talking, strangers were talking to strangers and all of them upset and haunted-looking. In the drugstore we listened and we discovered that war was declared, that the United States had entered the war I'd been watching on the newsreels. We left the drugstore with our malt balls. Everything was so strange. The day was crisp and cloudy, people were still huddled or staring or running about. The breeze made branches rattle above me and it seemed ominous. The street seemed to have changed. Everything was recognizably in its place but the feeling was different. It was as though something hung over the street that made all of the things, the houses and the trees and the cars, look less solid. As if they might vanish or become dangerous. When I got home, Clara was having hysterics because she was afraid Pete might be shipped off to the South Pacific.

The next day was the same, all the world was still different. I turned on the radio for security, to get in touch with the afternoon radio shows and know or hope that things were really normal. But the radio shows weren't on. I was shocked, horrified. The President was making a speech. "This day will live in infamy," he said. "There is nothing to fear but fear itself." Then commentators talked. All the shows were gone. It was horrifying, it was the last straw. If one couldn't even count on the radio shows, then what was there left? Would they ever come back on again? Would there be bombs dropping on Denver?

The radio shows did come back on the air, bombs didn't drop on Denver, and life went on more or less as it had. Except that from that cool and cloudy day in December, people were looser, they could talk to each other. There was something of kinship in the air, a common purpose or a common fear. Men dribbled away into the draft but no one I knew well.

Things were the same as they had been in choir and in school. I kept the bullies at bay with pockets bulging with stolen money and malt balls. I had stealing from Clara's purse down to a science now, a routine. I was still cleaning the apartment and finding coins on the dresser and on the table. When she'd leave the room I'd take some but not all of the coins at the bottom of her purse.

I suppose it was inevitable I'd be caught. The kids perhaps got to talking among themselves about how I always had money and where did I get it? Then someone took the question to the teacher.

One day the teacher asked me what I had in my pockets. I had the feeling she knew the answer. She started taking malt balls out of my pockets and then she found lots of money underneath. She was suspicious. She took my malt balls and my money, all of them, and left me with empty pockets. I was very worried that my system would be discovered and then what would I do?

When I got home from school that day, Clara was there. The teacher had called her at work and she had come home early. She had my malt balls and my money. Her face was red. When I came in the door she asked me, "Where did you get this money?

"I found it," I said.

"You're lying," she said.

"I saved it," I said.

"You're lying," she said.

I wondered if I told her the truth would she say I was lying then too?

Then she started beating me and screaming how much she'd done for me and how she'd been sick and how bad I was. She asked me about various things I had around the apartment. She asked about a pair of pirate guns I'd bought that were like those Errol Flynn had had in a movie. "Where did you get these?"

I told her I'd swapped a couple of my toys for them.

"You're lying," she said.

It was an ugly scene. I hoped she wouldn't tell Pete about it but she did and he looked very hurt. This, somehow, the betrayed look on his face, was more painful to me than her rage and her beatings.

It went on for several days. Christmas vacation was coming up at the end of the week. Clara talked with Pete and with other people and came to a decision. There were many working mothers now whose husbands were drafted, and their children would be put in other homes where someone would be there to supervise when the child came from school. The mother would pay the family a certain amount of money and the child would visit the mother when she had a day off work. Clara decided to put me in such a home. I had proved myself to be not enough of a man to bear her trust while she was at work or out with Pete.

I felt very bad. I couldn't stand being at fault. I had to steal to keep from being beat up, didn't I? Not to mention the problem of eating. I stole from her because she wasn't providing me with what I needed. I managed to persuade myself that my stealing wasn't that bad, that she just wanted to get rid of me so she could have Pete to herself. I still feel that way.

Christmas was awful that year, and before school started again, I moved to Ray's house.

13

At Ray's House

WAS THEIR NAME SPAULDING? That name jumps to my mind. Though I'm not at all sure it's right. They lived in a narrow house in a narrow lot a few blocks away. Their house was brick below and frame above, with a hallway past the living room to the kitchen in the back, and a narrow stair above the hall to the bedrooms upstairs. Ray and I slept in a double-decker bed. There was space in the bedroom to play.

I don't remember much about Ray's parents except that they were nice to me.

They were nice to me and they were there. Mrs. Spaulding was always there. I was never alone except on Sunday. I didn't want to be alone. I hated being alone.

These people were quiet and good. If anything, I shouldn't have fit in, with my dynamic naughtiness, but quietly, kindly, naturally, they brought me into the warmth of their family and I was warmed, touched, grateful.

For me, it was only Ray. His parents were vague and distant. There was a sort of a vague little girl running around. It was Ray I was living with and to me the others composed part of the environment.

Ray was a year ahead of me in school. He was older and taller. He was handsome and athletic. He was popular in school. He was, in fact, all the things I had learned to fear and hate. He was even quite bossy, guiding our play. But he was nice to me and he had a great sense of fairness. Fairness and generosity. He let me play with his toys and I therefore had to let him play with mine. He loved games, everything was a game, life was a game or a whole collection or complex of games. And he had learned the rules. He had learned fairness and honor, had enough confidence in himself that he could afford to allow the other guy to shine without yearning to knock him down. It was this, his honoring of my existence, that made me grateful beyond my expectations. This mixed with his fairness, the sense of self-assured equality, of trustful sharing that made me swear early on not to steal from the Spauldings and not to start a fire there. He even walked home with me from school so I didn't have to worry about bullies at all.

Ray had a wave in the front of his hair and in the back a tuft always stuck straight up. He played pretty rough for my taste, being older and athletic. They had a long narrow backyard of just grass where we sometimes played. The furniture in the house was plain and functional. The front porch was narrow, the front lawn tiny but green. The kitchen was modern with shiny chrome all around. We spent a lot of time there helping Mrs. Spaulding with various chores, for which we got paid. It was at this time that margarine was invented to help the war effort. It arrived in a big one-pound block of white stuff like lard only harder, and with it came a little packet of orange powder which we had to mix in for the color. The whole family took turns doing it and we all groaned about it because it was hard work and took a while but we groaned cheerfully because again it was fairly handled and because it was to help win the war. I could never mix the color in to my satisfaction, it always seemed to be a little streaky or there would be little spots that I'd miss and it would trouble me. We had to buy the margarine because of the war. Although butter was available it was very expensive. If anyone was the culprit in the question of mixing margarine it was the butter people because it was they who insisted that margarine be sold white to be sure to distinguish it from butter. Later they had to renege because people were so mad at them about that. But margarine was the first real thing that we could do for the war effort and everyone across the land was mixing in that coloring with a will. Everyone wanted to win the war and everyone did what they could to help.

In the bedroom we had our toys. Ray slept on the top bunk and I on the bottom usually, though sometimes we'd trade off and when I was on the top bunk, I could reach up my hands to touch the ceiling. I had brought just a few of my treasures along at first but then on days after church I'd walk by 930 Washington and dig up some more to show to Ray. Ray was my hero now, he was Jack Armstrong, the All-American Boy. He was a good person and I wanted to be like him, I wanted to be a good person.

Early on, we got into marbles. It was a game I could play since it didn't take much physical effort so it didn't give me asthma or mess up my truss or my glasses. It didn't cost much to get started either, a dime for a bag of ordinary marbles and a nickel or another dime for an agate. Suddenly everywhere it was marbles and you could see boys crouched in groups in alleys, vacant lots, schoolyards, wherever there was smooth dirt. You could tell how well they played by how big a circle they drew in the dirt. The idea was to knock the marbles out of the circle with your agate. The little kids could roll their agates but a real player shot with his thumb across a bent forefinger. Usually you had to shoot from outside the circle. Every time, the rules had to be decided. Like whether you got another turn if your agate hit a marble but didn't knock it out, whether agates were left in if they didn't leave the circle and thus could be taken, whether a marble on the line was in or out, whether you could shoot from inside the circle when you knocked out a marble, what was the penalty if you played out of turn or let your shadow fall on the circle when someone was trying to aim. But always if you knocked out a marble, it really truly belonged to you. Often there were fights over the rules and I was in constant dread to hear a bully say, "You went over the line," and then there was the nitpicking squabble of what constituted going over the line and whether I actually had. Weaker kids sided with the bullies for safety and bullies could slow down the play considerably. But a good player could win marbles in spite of the bullies and I got to be a really good player after a while. I went about then with my pockets bulging with marbles instead of malt balls.

Marbles became the obsession of many boys at this time. Perhaps it had something to do with the war. But always we could find a marble game going on somewhere or start one. We played after choir, we played in the school yard, and we played with the neighbor kids.

And it was amazing how good I was getting. I could calculate the angle, had good control over my agate, and could plan ahead. Whenever you shot a marble out of the circle, your turn continued and it was possible for the first player to take every marble in the circle before anyone else got to play. I didn't do that often but when I did, and then got up and stood in glory before the other kids, brushing some of the dust off the knee of my corduroy trousers, pushing my glasses back up my nose, it was grand.

I always liked the drama of marbles, especially when I got so good. It was essentially a cool game, quiet and tense, so that little things became very powerful. That's why there was a penalty for letting your shadow fall on the circle. But I found that if my shadow moved along the edge, if I moved my hands or waggled my head on the edge of my opponent's vision, it worked very well to distract his aim.

One day after choir I went to Clara's apartment to visit and found that Pete had given her a knickknack which was a little dish with swans sitting on clear blue marbles. They didn't look like the ones we used, they were made of glass and had a soft watery depth to them. Though I wasn't stealing from Ray's house, Clara was a different thing and I took one of these marbles to lay out in the circle and it was splendid, it looked strange and mysterious lying there in the dirt, one magic sea blue marble among the dime store rabble of the others. The blue marble was more fragile than the others and it broke after a few days. The next Sunday I got another and someone won that from me so I had to get a third. I hadn't taken more than five or six, sinking the swans deeper in their sea of blue marbles to hide the loss, when Clara noticed and I got a beating for it and had to stop taking them.

The best way to play was on one knee and all the good players went about with one knee dirty. Sometimes little kids would want to play or sometimes girls too. We always let them play, the little kids rolling their agates into the circle ineffectually, the girls having to sit sideways to keep their skirts over their knees, and this would spoil their shot and make them all dusty so they wouldn't want to play again. We'd let them play, they'd put in their marbles, we'd take them out, and that was that. Many of them thought we were very rough and mean to take their marbles but that was the rule, we took each other's marbles too.

After many months, I became the best marble player in the neighborhood. It was strange. I had begun like a little kid, a sure mark to get some new marbles from, and as the weeks and months went by, I became accepted as one of the boys, a respectable player who knew the rules and didn't cheat, didn't cry when I lost. Then came the great time, when I was allowed into the gang as though I wasn't different, when I was known to be a good player among other good players and we'd draw a big circle and we knew each other's play, knew the challenges and the subtleties, knew each other's little tricks and ways. I liked to not even look to see if the target marble had been knocked out of the circle. I could tell by the sound, the satisfying crack of the agate hitting its mark, that I'd won a marble and another shot. There was a joy in the skill, the surety of my power, of my place among these other boys standing around me in their corduroy trousers with one dusty knee, their pockets bulging. Some of them had their favorite agate which they occasionally had to pay many marbles to get back but I had several agates and didn't feel special about any one of them. I kept my agates in my shirt pocket where I had kept my farmer matches before.

When I became the best player, then nobody wanted to play with me anymore. Too often had I taken all their marbles and left them with the embarrassment of having to buy more. Too often had I played my turn and left nothing in the circle for them to shoot at. I became a monster then, wandering the streets gobbling up everyone's marbles. And the question arose in my mind, should I play less well so that I would still be allowed in the game? But I couldn't do that. This was a big decision in my life, to be as good as I was, to shoot with all the skill I had, even though in doing so I became ostracized. There was some sorrowful pride in it, I suppose. They'd let anyone in who couldn't shoot well but when they saw me coming they'd say, "You can't play, you'd just win all our marbles," and so in the end I was back to being alone, standing outside and watching the others enjoy themselves, walking alone, kicking stones down the sidewalk.

But my fascination with marbles lasted many months. It may even have begun before I went to Ray's, I'm not sure. But in the meantime, Ray and I did do other things.

For instance on Saturday we went to movies. It was very exciting to me that Ray liked to go to movies. We went every Saturday afternoon and saw almost the entire *Captain Marvel* serial in which there was all sorts of turmoil about a magical, mechanical scorpion which would be equipped with lenses. If the scorpion got into the wrong hands and if all the lenses were in place, it could destroy the freedom and safety of humanity. Each person of a group of anthropologists was given one of the lenses to guard. But one of the anthropologists was an evil traitor called "The Scorpion," who wore a robe with a hood and had henchmen who went around stealing lenses and tying people up. But Billy Batson, a frail little fellow with the heart of a hero, could turn into Captain Marvel whenever he wanted to. All he had to do was say, "Shazam!" and there he was, Captain Marvel, big and strong and able to fly and knock the bad guys into eternity. I was especially thrilled by the scene where the rays from the scorpion melted a mountain, and by the scene with the machine guns that appeared automatically in a slot in the wall and moved by themselves and fired seemingly inexorably at Billy Batson and his friend Betty.

We were also very excited by the movies of Tarzan played by Johnnie Weismuller. And his son Boy, handsome with curly blond hair, always getting into trouble and being rescued by Tarzan. There were people tied by their legs to trees and a splendid big fight with a crocodile, black blood all over, because the crocodile was eating natives. Tarzan could swim very fast, even tipping over boats, to rescue Boy. Ray and I acted the movies out afterwards, me as Boy and Ray as Tarzan. I thought Ray was a lot like Boy. I wanted to be like Ray and Boy, to be good and handsome and able and sunny.

Walt Disney's *Pinocchio* came back through town at this time and was another movie that fascinated me and every kid in the neighborhood. We acted that one out too. I recalled that three years earlier, when Clara and Adam and I were travelling across the country, they had bought me a rubber stamp set of the characters in *Pinocchio*. There was Jiminy Cricket and the cat and Cleo the fish, the old man, the fox, the weasel, everyone. The day after we saw the movie, I went to 930 Washington to look for that set. I looked all over the apartment but it wasn't there and Clara was busy and didn't want to dig into the locker in the basement. The next week I got her to look for it there and she found it. Then, oh, I had something fine and special which no one else had, and the kids gathered 'round me to play with my rubber stamp set.

Then there was the movie *Dumbo,* of the elephant who was a disgrace because of his big ears till he realized he could use them to fly with. That, like the fable *The Ugly Duckling,* gave me some hope for the future.

A couple of Hitchcock movies came out then which gave us a sense of what war might be like. One was *Saboteur,* about spies.There was one being chased up the Statue of Liberty, coming out on the little balcony at the top, getting knocked over the side and grabbing the edge. The hero got hold of his coat and there was a thrilling shot where the seams of the coat are ripping and then he falls down and down. Another was *Lifeboat,* where a ship gets torpedoed and people climb all bedraggled into a lifeboat, one of them a lady news correspondent who starts to take pictures of a baby bottle and a doll floating by. But a man knocks the camera out of her hand and into the sea.

The most memorable thing that happened that year was the freak show. Ray's father took us to it. There were garish signs all over town. It was shown in a storefront in downtown Denver. We went there and there was a real spooky feeling about it somehow. The freaks were on platforms mostly, some were behind curtains. We saw the fat woman and the thin man, we saw midgets and dwarfs, we saw everything. There was a woman who the barker said was turning into a crocodile. She was lying down staring off into space with a cape on. Then she threw off her cape and went on staring into space in a decent bathing suit while we all gaped at the skin on her legs and arms which was scaly like a crocodile's skin.

There was a man turning into stone too. His legs were hard as stone and everyone was allowed to pinch and poke at his legs, even poke them with pins and the pins couldn't go in. The barker said that the stone was creeping up him and when it reached his heart he'd die.

Ray and I had both saved up some of our housework allowance money and at the freak show there was a table full of magic tricks you could buy. I was very touched when Ray proposed we consult so we'd be sure to buy different things and therefore have twice as much. I got a deck of cards that were attached to each other in a long series of folds and a box with a secret compartment you could put something in and close it and when you'd open it the thing would be gone. There was a tiny Bible too I got that had to be read with a magnifying glass. Wonderful things. And Ray and I would trade off and play with each other's magic tricks. We were both very careful not to hurt them or break them. We traded off comic books too. Nothing like that had ever happened to me before. We really pooled our treasures and thus had twice as much. And it was great to have someone to talk with about a comic book, someone else who knew the secret of the box with the secret compartment. It was having a brother. I wasn't used to it and I really liked it.

It was during that time I began to collect pictures of the war to make a scrapbook. I drew pictures too of Pete as a soldier doing things I saw soldiers do in the newsreels. I made a picture of a pilot parachuting out of a burning plane.

Ration books started then and shopping and eating were complicated with points. There was much less meat, less sugar, and a knowledge that everyone shared that rhythm of scrimping and stretching the ration book to last until the end of the month. The war was on the radio and at the movies, it was in the grocery store, the drug store, the kitchen and the dining room table. Yet the Spauldings seemed unafraid of it. They cheerfully and patriotically did what they could and, like everyone else, they were more open and talkative with people. But they were not upset. This soothed me.

During those few months with the Spauldings I soaked up their security, their decency. I honored them very highly. They were good to me and I wanted to be good like that. I idolized Ray. Somehow from him I got a sense of how it was possible to transform from Billy Batson into Captain Marvel, from Boy into Tarzan, from the ugly duckling into a swan. His kindness, his fairness and his recognition of me gave me strength. My response to all this was that I never did steal from the Spauldings and always behaved well there.

But when the school year was coming to a close, Clara told me I was going to spend the whole summer at a camp in the mountains. I told her I didn't want to go, that I'd rather stay with Ray. Pete waxed enthusiastic about hiking and fishing and swimming and riding horseback. I thought of Ray's rare acceptance of me, his protection too, and how bad I would be at all those things Pete talked about. I thought of choir and how I'd miss singing at Saint John's. I'd heard of the summer camp the church had, one that lasted only two weeks. I asked if I couldn't go to that one instead. Some of the boys from the choir were going. I'd have some protection there. But Clara had decided on Harmony Hall for the whole summer and I was powerless. Ray and his family kept telling me what fun I'd have, how lucky I was, but I was filled with forebodings. However, there was nothing I could do to stop it from happening.

Clara told me I could take only two suitcases so I packed my treasures back into the locker at 930 Washington with bitter regret. My Pinocchio stamps, my marbles, my magic tricks, my war scrapbook, lead soldiers, some books, everything. Clara and Pete came to get me and I waved goodbye to the kindly home and the dear friend who had always been fair to me. I never saw them again.

14

Harmony Hall Summer

WE DROVE A LONG, LONG WAY. The further we drove, the more my heart sank. We went through a little mountain town, then beyond. The road curved around a lake and not far from that, a big white sign announced, HARMONY HALL, in black letters. We turned in to a dirt road. On the right was a horse shed and a pasture. Three horses were grazing there. In front of us was a clearing, and behind that a rustic log lodge with a big porch in front and a string of little cabins behind. It reminded me of those rustic motels we had stayed at when we were driving all over the country with Adam. There were boys here and there, playing ball and horseshoes. Pete parked the car by the woodpile, got out very enthusiastic, gesturing at the view of the mountains, at the horses, the boys, the rustic lodge and the woods behind.

We went up the steps, across the porch and entered the lodge. The living room was dominated by a huge stone fireplace, big enough for me to nearly stand up in and open in the back to the dining hall beyond. Beside it was an opening into the dining hall, a couple steps leading up to it, and a long table there. In the living room were dilapidated chairs and sofas, a piano, a pool table at the far end.

For a moment, with Pete's enthusiasm, the sun shining in the clearing, the sweet fresh smell of the air, the nice big porch and the magnificent fireplace, the boys playing quietly outside, the sight of a bookcase full of books there in the living room, I thought that it might be nice, that perhaps I could get along somehow. I might even be happy here.

Then Miss Johns came in and greeted us and my moment of hope evaporated. She was skinny, angular and energetic, and had dry wispy irregular hair, dry skin pinched around a tight heartless mouth. Her eyes were intense and squinted fiercely over rimless granny glasses. They seemed to say, "I'll get you." Her voice was clipped and buzzy. She talked amiably with Clara and Pete, then led us to my bedroom at the top of the stairs where I was encouraged to unpack. The room had three pairs of bunk beds with army blankets and coarse sheets, and one double bed. I got a lower bunk, one drawer in a bureau. "That's just the kind of blanket I sleep under," said Pete gaily. Pine trees glimmered outside screened windows. Gray painted floorboards, rustic wood walls. Clara talked at length about my hernia, my truss, my glasses, my asthma, how I mustn't drink milk or eat egg whites, all my physical problems.

I put my empty suitcases under my bed and we trailed back downstairs to Miss Johns's office in the corner of the living room, Miss Johns telling Clara they were prepared for that kind of thing, they had a boy there who was quite debilitated and got along just fine. "Jackie!" she called out the door, and a boy turned from his game and hobbled toward the house. He was the strangest-looking boy I'd ever seen. A long face with coarsened features, hairs sticking out here and there by his nose and on his cheeks, eyes going in two directions, narrow shoulders in a checkered shirt, big baggy pants, hip bones bulging crookedly huge, a club foot twisted inward, a big friendly smile.

Miss Evans came in from the kitchen. She was soft and placid-looking, pale and pliant. She had black tidy hair and a soothing voice. I knew Miss Johns to be a very bad thing on sight. It was on the surface.

Miss Evans was deeper. Miss Johns had worked many years as matron of the boys' reformatory in Golden. Miss Evans had been a nurse in Pueblo at the State Insane Asylum.

"In the evening," Miss Johns said, "we often have a fire in the fireplace and I'll read stories aloud. Or Miss Evans will play the piano and we'll all sing. On warm evenings we often sing around a campfire."

I didn't cry when Clara and Pete left. I was too numb. I stood morosely glowering as they told me how great it was going to be, how I'd see, I was going to have a wonderful time. I watched the dust rise as they drove away.

After they left, I was shown around and introduced to the other kids. The cabins held five or six boys each and were supervised by older boys who had been with Harmony Hall for some time. These older boys did dishes and chores too and got their summers free this way, plus a little spending money. They taught us younger kids horseback riding and swimming. They led us on hikes and exercise groups. At dinner they sat at the long table with the two ladies.

The lodge had a long hallway upstairs, bedrooms on each side with six or eight boys in each room. Miss Johns and Miss Evans shared a room and at the end of the hall were two bathrooms. The boys in the cabins used the outdoor privies. There were shower stalls in sheds out back. We were all expected to keep clean but there was no hot water.

There were two pairs of brothers. One pair slept in the double bed in my room. They were wards of the state, as was Jackie. These two were half Cherokee Indian and were extremely handsome but they were very shy and quiet. People hinted at a terrible tragedy in their lives. The older brother we all called Cherokee. He was taller than I by several inches. His little brother was only about five or six and very dependent on Cherokee so they were always together. It took weeks but I did eventually become friends with Cherokee, whose main concerns seemed to be the care of his brother and keeping out of trouble.

The other pair of brothers were of a different sort, Peewee and Len. Len was the older and he supervised one of the cabins where they both slept. They were small and wiry with round heads and pinched features, thin lips, sandy hair in crew cuts. I had already learned by then to beware of crew cuts as they usually seemed to go with a mean, nasty temperament, and these were no exception to the rule. They were, in fact, outrageous bullies.

Dick Waters slept in one of the lower bunks in my room. He was chubby although not fat like me. He had rosy cheeks and freckles on pale skin. He was the same age as I and the same height. He had been there a few days already when I arrived and was very unhappy. His home in Denver was catercorner across from Saint John's and he had often watched the choirboys going in and out, heard us singing. He knew, then, in some sense, who I was. He became my closest friend at Harmony Hall.

Most of the kids were there because their parents were working, but it was understood among us that we shouldn't ask, someone might be from the reformatory or have a history they would prefer to forget. Jackie, however, was kind of a showpiece. He had been sent to Harmony Hall from the state orphanage as a special favor for his good behavior. The orphanage was a musty old mansion on the edge of Denver with gables and pilasters, creaking floors, narrow wavery windows that let in a little, dim, dusty light, no place to play outside except a field to the south with nothing in it but stickers and thistles. A year or so later the orphanage got scandalously into the news for abusing the children and for vague horrors. Harmony Hall had gotten a special citation for their care of children. When I heard about the orphanage scandal, I remembered Jackie always telling us that he would rather have been left back in the orphanage though he'd never tell this to Miss Johns or Miss Evans. Jackie couldn't play most of the games. Nobody ever tried to teach him to ride or swim. He was "good old Jackie." Hobbling around, always available to the Misses Johns and Evans to carry messages or impress visitors, his only necessary skill was the big friendly smile and he did that very well indeed.

The day began early with the compulsory wash in cold water with scratchy soap — faces, ears and armpits. Then we'd make our beds, dress, and go down to the field in front of the lodge to do our exercises. Exercises were done in squads of eight boys, each squad run by one of the older boys. After all of Clara's talk about my asthma and whatnot, I was put in the misfit squad with Jackie and six other weak and clumsy boys. Our squad leader was an amiable older boy named Jim. Miss Johns announced early on that the best exercise squad would get to go to town and see a movie, and Jim, with admirable leadership and indomitable cheer and patience, led us through toe touches and squats, walking squats, jumping to touch our toes in the air, pushups, jumping jacks, and all the rest with his "We'll show those others!" or "We're gonna see that movie!" Miss Evens would come out onto the porch and ring the big triangle with a metal bar, knocking it 'round and 'round in the center of the triangle, making a tremendous noise. This was the call to breakfast. But Jim would say, "Let's do a little bit more! There'll be enough to eat!" So we'd go on awhile longer, squatting and pushing and jumping, panting and sweating. Jim didn't sneer at us. He seemed to like us. And because of that, the Misfit Squad worked hard, clumsily, even grotesquely, but with a will.

Breakfast was usually cereal. Never my toast and tomato juice with bacon, although Clara had helped by saying I couldn't drink milk and sometimes they gave me tomato juice to pour onto my cereal. Sometimes we got bread and butter and sometimes cooked cereal. I didn't mind the cooked cereal too much. My favorite cereals were Grape-Nuts Flakes and Shredded Wheat but they never served them. Sometimes I'd be served milk by mistake and then one of the boys would say, "Drink your milk," and I'd say, "I'm not supposed to drink milk," Then he'd drink it. Often, with a glass of milk and a bowl of Wheaties before me, there was nothing I could eat and often I'd sit there and simply wait, not eating, until it was possible for me to leave.

We sat in the dining hall, the two ladies and the big boys at the long table, us little kids at little tables with assigned seats. My place was at a round table in the northwest corner some distance away from the long table and there I sat two or three times a day all summer long.

After breakfast there was usually a planned outing of some sort. A hike, perhaps, or swimming or fishing. Or we would be taught how to ride horseback. Since there were only three horses, the riding had to be done in shifts. I hated the riding lessons. There was a resident dog at Harmony Hall, short-haired and black and white like Ritzy had been, but a nasty cringing type of dog who hated boys. His worst trait was his penchant for nipping at the legs of the horses when boys were on them. So when I was helped up onto a horse by one of the older boys, found myself too high off the ground to be attentive to the boy's instructions, the horse snorting and prancing under me, I'd be clinging to the saddle looking everywhere for that dog. "Don't be afraid!" the boy would be saying. I'd clutch the horse's mane or pull the reins till the horse reared. I did everything wrong. One time an older boy took me and another boy down the trail on horseback and my horse kept veering toward one low branch and the next trying to rub me off. I did badly then too. After a while they didn't make me ride anymore.

Swimming lessons were a worse nightmare. When swimming was the plan, we all had to pack up and make ready, our swimming trunks on under our trousers. I, of course, wore my truss under my trunks. We'd all walk in a line across the clearing and down the trail, over a terrifying rickety bridge across a rushing stream, then up a hill to a little lake. I'd arrive wheezing with asthma, unable to see properly for lack of oxygen, foggy, confused. There was a battered old pier on one side, a couple rowboats tied to it. This was where the lake was

shallow and where we were to get our lessons. Everyone would take off their clothes, get into the water, and start splashing each other. I'd delay as long as I could. I didn't want to be splashed. "Get into the water, Stanley," Miss Johns would say and I'd go down and stand in water up halfway to my knees wishing myself invisible. But an older boy would call me to come out where it was deeper. When the water came up to my waist I was always afraid because I became then so light that I felt I'd fall. The older boy would make me get down in it, he'd hold my head up, I'd gasp and flail, he'd tell me what to do and I'd be so frightened I'd do anything else but what he said. I didn't hear what he said. First he'd talk patiently then he'd start shouting at me angrily. I was always intensely grateful when it was over and we'd file in a long line back up the path, over the rickety and terrifying bridge across the rushing stream, and back through the clearing in front of the lodge to lunch.

Rowboating wasn't too bad. Since there were only two rowboats, we did that in shifts too and some of us would get to just sit by the lake and wait, slapping mosquitoes. When my turn came, I was scared. If the boat turned over, I would probably die. But I never had to row so the burden wasn't on me and I simply sat as still as possible and waited for it to be over, one way or the other.

Hiking was a misery of asthma and shame. We'd go along a path in a long line, up and up. No matter if I started in front, I'd very soon be at the end of the line with Jackie, he hobbling stolidly and I wheezing and staggering in the brainless, out-of-focus nightmare of asthma. "You're holding everyone up!" I'd hear shouted at us by some older boy. "Come on, you can do it!" I'd hear the others singing out of tune 'way ahead of us and realized they were roasting hot dogs and marshmallows already. They were sitting down. Finally Jackie and I would arrive exhausted. There would be a view, which I never cared about. Someone would hand us hot dogs and marshmallows. The chance to sit down was past. Gasping, exhausted, we would try to consume the food as the others were putting out the fire and heading down again. We'd finish eating and stagger after them back the way we came.

Then we had to take a shower. There were three shower stalls and again we had to take turns. The water was ice cold, the soap scratchy, the towels damp and threadbare. After the shower, we were inspected to see that we had washed our ears and hair thoroughly.

Everywhere there were inspections. Miss Johns's sharp eye glared into us constantly. It hushed our voices, deadened our play, and caused us to mistrust each other. It took the flavor out of the hot dogs and the warmth out of friendship. Laughter in Harmony Hall was not an expression of delight but a whip of discipline, a thing to dread. It would start with a glance from Miss Johns at the older boys and sweep hollowly through them and into the younger boys. Anyone who didn't laugh became laughed at. Anyone who didn't spy and tattle became spied and tattled upon.

Fishing was the one planned project I really didn't mind. For one thing, the walk was along the highway back to the lake I had seen when I first arrived at Harmony Hall. And since it was level and we could walk slowly, I didn't arrive at the lake with an asthma attack. We all had brought poles from home, it was required equipment. We had our worm jars too and the older boys would put the worms on our hooks. Then we'd put the line in the water and sit down. Dick Waters and I could sit together and talk. Everyone had a special spot. There were some big rocks that some boys chose as their places. Dick Waters and I sat under aspen trees and leaned against the trunks. We talked quietly, gazing across the water, watching when someone caught a fish. The fish in this lake were suckers, unappetizing creatures with big suction-cup mouths. The boys who caught fish cleaned them, dug a little hole in the ground to bury the guts, and took them to Miss Evans. She then would bread them and fry them and those kids could eat fried suckers instead of what we had normally for supper. Sometimes a boy would catch two or three fish and then he'd give fish to younger boys to take to Miss Evans. Once, an older boy caught an enormous sucker. When he held it up, it hung from the middle of his chest down all the way to the ground. That evening, everyone got a piece of it to eat. As every fisherman knows, suckers aren't very good food but in comparison to Miss Evans' usual cooking, they were quite a delicacy.

One morning as we were fishing, a soft rain started up and as Dick and I sat under the trees, two suckerfish came near us with their suckers open to the sky moving along the surface of the water. I pulled in my hook and carefully lowered it down directly into one of the suckers' mouths. Dick saw what I was doing and did the same with the other fish. The suckers swallowed our hooks and we pulled them onto shore. An older boy showed us how to clean them and we dug our little holes to bury the guts. Mine had eggs inside which were of a sickly yellow color. We brought our fish to the kitchen door where Miss Evans took them with noises of astonishment. There were noises of astonishment at supper that evening too. "Stanley caught a fish!" "Would you look at that!" "And Dick caught one too!" "What do you think of your fish?"

Afternoons, we were often told to go out and play games and the older boys would organize football or baseball. Some kids would play horseshoes or catch, some boys would be sawing firewood as a punishment for something, and Dick and I would wander off into the woods. We never went very far. We felt like Hansel and Gretel in the woods, fearing to get lost, fearing the possibility of a bear or who knew what.

The Misses Johns and Evans had told us never to eat red berries and never to drink any water except from the tap. The sense was that if we did these things, we might die. There was one little boy who got a bad case of diarrhea. He was pale, bent, and running constantly to the privy. "He had it coming," Miss Johns said, "He ate red berries."

Dick and I had a favorite place where we liked to sit and talk. It was on the hillside above the woodpile. One afternoon, we brought two other kids up there. We roamed, the four of us, a little further into a draw and there, from under a rock, a tiny rivulet dabbled out into a tiny basin of stones and mosses. The water caught the sun and shimmered in a smooth pattern, flashing subtle lights across the mosses. We all knelt around it in awed reverence. The sight and sound of the water made us all thirsty. At the same time, we had the idea that the water might be poison. But none of us was happy, we all felt unloved and contemptible. If the water killed us, who would care? Dick Waters had a neat little gadget which telescoped open into a cup. He pulled it out of his pocket and opened it, dipped it into the basin, and drank. I took it from him then plunged into the water. I felt the water cold on my fingers as I filled the cup. I drank. It was wonderful water, delicious. One of the other boys took the cup from my hand and drank, then the other one.

And there we knelt, the four of us. Possibly we had all drunk poison together. Perhaps we would all die. Assuredly, we had disobeyed. Still kneeling around the spring, we swore to keep our deed and our spring a secret, no matter what happened.

None of us got sick. All of us kept the secret. And often throughout the rest of the summer, we'd go back to the spring to drink. The thought came to our minds that perhaps it would kill us gradually as we kept on drinking it. But we didn't care. We had a precious and beautiful secret.

Supper, back to my assigned seat, was usually some watery soup. Sometimes it was spaghetti or macaroni and cheese and those things I liked pretty well but the watery soup was hard to take, even on an empty stomach. We had tin plates and tin cups. The plates had high rims and the soup lay in them like muddy water. I did lose weight there. Everything tasted so bad. It was fairly quiet at supper as it was at breakfast. The two ladies sat in state in the middle of the long table with their older boys to either side. Under their eye, there was very little to say. There seemed little to say at any time. It felt like the fairy tale of the Snow Queen in which little Kai gets a piece of glass in his eye which rearranges the light so that he sees everything as ugly, grotesque, hideous, and he is inexorably attracted to evil. So we forty boys sat over our foul dinner, all of us quiet, the clank of spoons on tin plates the predominant sound.

Or supper around the campfire — at least then I could count on hot dogs. The worst problem about the campfire was not the mosquitoes, it was the enforced caterwauling. "Row, Row, Row Your Boat" was to me a horror. We were divided into four sections with a couple of older boys in each and Miss Johns would point to each section in turn, her face under-lit, flickering in firelight demoniacal, and at each gesture of her hand the ghastly yowling would double, triple, quadruple on my sensitive ears, my perfect pitch which had been honed by the nuns in Bisbee and by Mr.Pew with Bach *Cantatas,* with Handel's *Messiah.* My voice had joined in the choir and rung prayers to God as fitting as any harmony of voices calling out their gratitude for the blessings of life. "Come on, Stanley, sing! Row, row, row your boat, gently down the stream! You must sing, we all have to sing! Louder! Louder!"

If supper was in the dining room, we would spend the evening variously. Sometimes Miss Evans would play the piano and the caterwauling would go on indoors. Sometimes Miss Johns would read to us and we'd have to sit and listen to her dry buzzy clipped voice. Whether it was her style or reading, her choice of stories or simply my rebellious hatred of her, I don't know. But the fact is that I disliked every story she read to us beside the crackling fire in the huge stone fireplace.

Sometimes we'd play games, word games or things like Simon Says. Or we'd learn to tie knots. Sometimes we were left to ourselves. Then the older boys would play pool or throw darts and we younger boys would play paddle-ball or checkers. I had learned checkers already from arriving early at choir on occasion. I didn't like checkers very much but it was the best possible thing to do in the evening at Harmony Hall.

Getting ready for bed included a nightly tick inspection ritual which I hated mightily. What it consisted of was I would stand naked in front of another boy while he looked me over. Then he'd stand naked while I looked him over. The comparison was a bitter thing to me. Plus the embarrassment. There was my bulging fat, my small penis, the folds and creases left by my truss. And there was his body, whoever he was, slim and graceful with a bigger penis than mine. Harmony Hall was a gym class all day every day. Nevertheless, from the stories I had heard, I was deathly afraid of ticks. Ticks crawl over you for hours with eight legs like a spider. Then they bury their heads in you, suck your blood and swell up like a balloon. Then you get a horrible fever and some people die from it. I was sure I'd be one of those. We couldn't pull the tick out when it got in either, we were supposed to go to Miss Evans and she'd draw a circle around it and leave it in. We never understood why.

Sometimes the boys were lax about doing the tick inspection and I'd go to bed without it, wondering if that night I'd get the tick that would kill me. One night I was standing naked alone in my room and Miss Evans came in. "What are you doing with no clothes on and out of bed?" she said. "I need a tick inspection," I said. She slapped me hard on the butt. "You don't have any ticks," she said. I got into bed and lay there in a rage with my butt smarting. I never did get any ticks.

I had brought my bottle of constipation medicine with me to Harmony Hall. It was the only thing I had that I valued. Constipation was something I didn't need here. I kept my big square white bottle of medicine under my bed and every night I went downstairs to the kitchen to get a spoon, went back upstairs, measured out the thick white gooey stuff and swallowed it down, put the medicine bottle back in the suitcase under the bed, took the spoon back downstairs and washed it, then climbed up again and to bed.

We weren't supposed to talk or laugh after we got to bed. If we did we'd have to stand in the hall for an hour, our bare feet chilling us on the cold floor, weariness swaying us, shame making us want to weep, making us afraid to weep. Maybe, as we were in our beds going to sleep, someone would say a few words. Then we'd hear a creaking floorboard and we'd lie in a heart-sinking terror waiting for the voice of one of the ladies, "Who's that talking?" Then the electric silence as we waited for the boy to speak up. "It's me, Miss Johns." Then, eyes wide in bed, we'd wait to hear the inevitable, "Well you'd better come out in the hall." And we'd watch or listen to him crawl out of bed and pad along the floor to stand in front of the Misses Johns's and Evans' door, our hero for the night. Because if the culprit didn't answer, if no one answered, we all had to get up and stand, cold, tired and silent, twenty or more of us, huddled together in the hall, waiting for the word from the ladies' bedroom to release us.

I hated those two women, we all did, I think. Even now I hate them more than I hate anyone. They stuffed us with false jollities woven in a net of terror and self-disgust. Although Miss Evans was feminine, there was no going to her, no way to appeal to her. She was part of it. It may have been that she was the Snow Queen herself, breathing ugliness and grotesqueness and ghastliness into everything, making everyone suspect to everyone else, and rightly so because she suffused disgust into everything and everyone around her. No one was together with anyone or anything, all was separate, shattered like a broken mirror, each piece grating on every other piece. Nobody could be trusted. Anyone might turn on anyone, might tell on anyone or laugh at him.

Ever since I had left Macomb, I had been alone. Alone, and for that reason, and for other reasons, like my good mind, my beautiful voice, my adult ways, my multitude of sicknesses, I had been special and everyone around me knew it, looked at me and responded in one way or the other to my specialness. I stood out. But here I knew better than to stand out. The more one stood out here the more he was jeered at, the less recognized. If one stood out here, one was cut down, everything admirable became degraded. I didn't want that. I never got a tick, I never got sick, I never wet my bed or talked after lights out. As much as I could, I kept out of the way, did as little as possible, rebelled by failing, failing at swimming and horseback riding as I had failed in gym class. Although I have always loved to learn, I have always hated to be taught. And the contemptuous attitude of Harmony Hall only fixed this more firmly.

I had a lot of trouble getting to sleep there. The window was always open and the cold mountain air swept across my bed. The bed itself was hard and sagged in the middle. And I was usually hungry so I would lie there, alone because we were not allowed to talk. Tucking my pillow against my head like a teddy bear, I would lie on my stomach with my blanket wrapped around my feet. I would lie still and uncomfortable, black thoughts whirling through my mind, thoughts of revenge on the Misses Johns and Evans. Sometimes I would think how I would become powerful someday and be able to put such people in their place. I thought how nice it would be to watch their agony in the fires of Hell.

15

The Adventures of Harmony Hall

ONE DAY WE WERE ALL GATHERED in the meadow in front of the lodge waiting to line up and go swimming. It was a sunny day with no breeze and we stood around there, each of us separate, waiting without anticipation, with only, in me at least, a considerable dread. I suppose birds were twittering in the treetops but we didn't notice. We slapped at mosquitoes and felt the sweat running down our backs.

As we were standing there, a group of boy scouts marched by on the highway, left, right, left, right. They saw the big sign in front of us, "Harmony Hall" and they began to chant, first one, then a few, then all of them in rhythm with their marching: "Harmony Hell! Harmony Hell! Harmony Hell!" They were clearly taunting us to fight. There were perhaps twenty of them and more than twice that many of us, but none of us, not even the older boys, contradicted them. We simply stood there watching them, each one of us thinking about what they said, all of us staring at them, watching them march by. After that, we'd whisper it sometimes to each other as an outreach of affection and trust. "Harmony Hell," we'd whisper, one to the other, and know that though we were separate, we were not alone.

Peewee and his big brother Len, small, wiry, thin-lipped, crew cut, were everywhere bullying, everywhere except where Miss Johns or Miss Evans could see them. Peewee, especially, was always lording it over the smaller boys, pushing them around and beating them up. I mostly avoided him, was obsequious to him when I met him. I didn't play the games unless I had to, so I mostly kept away from his meanness. But I saw a lot of it, how he'd knock the little kids about and make them bow to him. I felt a lot of sympathy for his victims. He was a nasty fellow.

Then one day Miss Johns overheard as he fought a little boy, yelling and hitting at him. And Miss Johns called a special gathering in the clearing. It was a bright sunny afternoon. She brought everyone to form a circle, some on the porch and others curved around on the grass. She brought out boxing gloves. "You want to fight?" she said, and picked out a kid a little bigger than him, sent the kid into the circle with Peewee, the boxing gloves on them, and they fought. Peewee didn't do too badly though everyone was yelling against him, partly because they knew it was what Miss Johns wanted and partly because he was so mean. I joined in myself. "Get Peewee, hit him!" Miss Johns took out the boy. "You've been fighting with everyone," she said, "so you should fight another boy." And she sent in another. "Hit him hard!" we shouted. Peewee held his own. She sent in another. Still Peewee was doing well. "You also think it's okay to beat up on little kids," said Miss Johns and she sent in an older boy. "Get him! Get him!" We were all screaming now, the spirit was high amongst all of us. Peewee was beginning to sag with fatigue and heat. He weaved and wavered. "Hit him! Hit him!" "You even pick on tiny kids," she said, and sent in an even bigger boy.

Peewee had a bloody nose now. He was crying. His thin arms hung down like strings with the big boxing gloves on the ends of them. Tree shadows were creeping across the clearing. I had had enough. The thought occurred to me that this could be done to anyone. It was wrong.

I began to wince when he was hit, to suffer with him. "Len," she said, "it's your turn to fight him." And Peewee's older brother put on the gloves and went into the ring. Len was crying already but the power of Miss Johns was such that he had to fight. Len's eyes fogged, he flailed his arms, hit Peewee and knocked him down. "Pick him up! Pick him up!" Miss Johns was insatiable. "Pick him up and hit him again!" The two of them, thin and distraught, faced each other weeping. Peewee was covered now with blood. It was all over his clothes. The boxing gloves flapped like tied balloons in a stiff breeze. It was ugly.

I don't remember how it ended but Peewee was never a bully again. His face changed and his manner. His eyes, which had been narrow before, were now wide. His lips were fuller. He was polite. The strangest thing was the wide eyes. I couldn't get over how his eyes got wide and stayed that way.

It wasn't long after that that Dick Waters and I and Peewee and Len started talking together about how to get out of Harmony Hall. There was no use writing to our parents because the ladies read our mail. There was no use giving them a sealed letter because they wouldn't accept it. Dick Waters was sure his parents would get him out of there if they knew he was unhappy. Peewee and Len and I were not at all sure that our parents would free us. But it was a moot point because there was no way to let them know. The only thing that could get us out of there was our own feet.

It was idle speculation at first. We tried to think how we could do it, could walk to Denver. It had been such a long drive. It would probably take days. Len had a Colorado road map and he and Peewee pored over it. He also had a compass. We should carry only a little bit of stuff, no more than one small suitcase each. We tried to think when would be the time to go and decided that swimming lessons would be best. We weren't watched and counted then, we could slip off into the woods. There was such a confusion on the way to swimming, it would be a while before we were missed. We discussed what clothes we should wear. We smuggled some canteens to carry water in. We didn't see how we could get food to take so we said we should simply eat a real good breakfast on the morning, we should be ready with everything packed that we were going to take and when swimming was announced after breakfast, we'd be ready. We'd walk separately along the path to the swimming lake, each of us step off the path as if to pee, cut back to the lodge through the woods, and gather on the porch.

When the time came, the next swimming day, there was no opportunity for us to communicate. Anyway we had planned beforehand not to, so as not to raise any suspicion in anyone's mind. I was toward the head of the line. I very much wanted reassurance but there was none. I kept walking. Would we really do it? How would I know? We were coming to the rickety bridge and I had to get out of the line before the stream. In a panic of confusion, I walked off the path, unzipped my pants behind a tree and watched as the long line of boys plodded by me. No Peewee, No Len, no Dick Waters. I was afraid to go back through the woods so waited till everyone had passed and went back on the path, feeling foolish. But there in the clearing were the three of them waiting for me.

At the last minute Dick Waters, remembering his parents' admonition to take good care of his suitcase and trunk and all their contents, felt he couldn't go unless he brought everything. The trunk was big and heavy. Peewee and Len each had a suitcase. I had nothing I cared to bring except of course my constipation medicine and a spoon I had lifted from the kitchen some days before. Anyway, I had been told never to carry because of my hernia.

The trunk was, for a trunk, small. But it was a real trunk, green metal with black metal corner studs and a silver metal bar around it, a bulbous leather handle attached to that. There seemed to be nothing we could do but take turns carrying the trunk and we headed down the long road.

It was a hot day, the sun beating on us hard. Dick and Len carried the trunk between them at first and the three suitcases were carried by their owners. I had to say that with my hernia and my asthma, there was no way I could help with the trunk. This caused me to feel very unmanly. Nonetheless, I managed to avoid carrying a suitcase which I thought could be just as bad although the trunk was much heavier.

We hadn't gone more than a quarter of a mile when we had to stop. They all took a swig of water and shook out their hands. Len complained bitterly about Dick's trunk. Another quarter of a mile and again we had to stop. What could be done? We couldn't leave Dick and his luggage in the road. Len, being the strongest, had to keep helping with the trunk. He was upset about it and he and Peewee complained as we stood sweating and tired, swigging water from our canteens.

By the time we got to the fishing lake, they were all really worn down. Our canteens were half empty and we looked at the lake and wondered if we should fill them there. Peewee and Len felt we should, didn't we eat the fish out of the lake? But Dick and I were both afraid of it. I had managed to go this far without carrying anything but my bottle, and the others attacked me for not doing my fair share. I pointed out that I had been told not to carry and that if I did, I might die. They, however, didn't believe me, said that I had to help, that we were all in this together. I didn't see that any of us were together with anything.

Angrily, I tucked my bottle of constipation medicine under my arm, picked up two suitcases, and started down the road. I was beginning to hate Dick. If I dropped my constipation medicine and the bottle broke, I would probably die. I walked fast, Dick and Len, staggering with the trunk, soon fell behind but Peewee, carrying only one suitcase, kept up with me. The road curved around the lake and soon we saw the others as tiny figures across the water. Peewee, nervous about separating from the others, pointed out that his brother had the compass and the road map, but I was angry and wanted to walk fast, show that I was a man, and get it over with.

We were approaching the end of the lake where there was a power house and culvert. We kids had all been warned to keep away from there, the water was deep and the suction from the culvert pulled everything down. I looked back across the lake. There, not halfway around yet, were Dick and Len with the trunk between them. And there, just emerging around the mountain at the far end of the lake, a shiny maroon convertible, Miss Johns's car, her nephew's truck behind it.

Peewee and I ran to the power house for cover. There was a three-foot ledge on the water side hidden from the road. We got on the ledge, put our suitcases down beside us, and stood, our hands pressed against the rough cement block wall, listening to Dick's and Len's cries, Miss Johns'S rasping shrieks of rage, all covered and made ominous by the deadly gurgling of the water underneath us going into the culvert. We stared down at the crosshatch of the grate across the culvert, made wavery by the depth of the water as it rushed into it, and listened to the agonizing sounds coming across the lake.

Then for some seconds there was no more to be heard except the suction below us, until the sound of the car honking on the other side of the power house told us that we were discovered. We peeked around the edge of the building, saw Dick and Len in the back seat of the convertible, abject, Miss Johns's face with fear on it. I realized she was afraid we'd drown in the water and spoil her reputation. She commanded us to come out of there and we did, sliding along the ledge with the suitcases.

She ordered Dick and Len out, made us each carry a suitcase, pointed to Dick's trunk and told him to carry it. "So," she rasped, "You want to walk to Denver?" We staggered on down the road, hot, exhausted, frustrated and miserable, Peewee and Len and I each leaning grimly with a suitcase in one hand, I with my bottle in the other.

Dick couldn't carry the trunk alone however, He tried lifting it on his foot, step by step. Miss Johns had her nephew drive the convertible and she sat up on top of the seat. "You'd better do better than that," she shouted at Dick. He took off his shirt then, threaded it through the handle of the trunk so he could drag it, his face in agony, tears streaming down through dust on his cheeks. Peewee tried to stop for a drink of water but she shouted, "Keep going, keep going!" her face red, her hair stringing wildly out around it, her skinny arms waving in command.

Dick's trunk broke open then, his clothes started falling out of it, and the convertible ran slowly over them.

After a while she stopped the farce, sent her nephew back for his truck saying, "We should go back for some lunch." She had us get into the truck with our suitcases and turn back to Harmony Hall. Dick walked behind, picking up all his clothes, sobbing and snuffling. The rest of us were silent as convicts. When Dick had picked up all his clothes, he got into the truck too.

We arrived back at Harmony Hall in time for lunch. Everyone was sitting in the dining hall in terrified silence. We weren't allowed to go in there. Miss Evans had set up a table in the living room with "special food," dry bread and one glass of water each. The other kids filed outside but we had to stay in the living room. Miss Johns said that Miss Evans had figured out how much energy it would take to walk to Denver in relation to how much wood we'd have to cut to match the trip, an enormous amount of wood. We were all saying then that we didn't want to go to Denver. We spent the afternoon chopping and sawing wood, occasionally crying out for water. Sometimes we'd see a kid and we'd tell him to bring us some water. He'd run into the kitchen and come out again, "I can't give you any water." There was a silence all around us, not from the lack of people but from many people keeping very quiet, and this silence went on all afternoon.

Just before dinner time, we were given some water. "Miss Evans has estimated the distance to Denver in relation to the distance around the pool table," Miss Johns said. "We will be kind and not ask you to carry your luggage as you walk. You will each keep your own count of times around the table."

And so while the other boys ate macaroni and cheese, we four walked around and around the pool table. After dinner the other boys played games, Miss Johns made jokes about us and they all laughed and jeered at us. "How many times have you gone around?" We started early on to lie about the number of times. Nonetheless she said, "Why you're not even to Estes Park yet!" So we lied the harder and she got all the kids to shout, "Liar!" At some time in the evening we were given a little cold macaroni to eat. "Since we're not cruel," she said, "though where you'd get food on the way to Denver, I don't know." Then back to circling the pool table. Bedtime came and all the boys went off to bed. Seemingly as an afterthought she said to us, "I guess you'd better go on to bed, although I assure you, you would find no beds on the way to Denver."

The next morning as soon as we were out of bed we were sent to the pool table as the other kids were doing their exercises and having breakfast. We were afraid to ask if we could go to the bathroom but finally Dick and I did ask. "If you take breaks all the time," she said, "you'll be all summer getting to Denver." After an hour or two, we were allowed to go the bathroom and given some cereal, "out of kindness," then sent back to our deadly circling.

About noon, Miss Johns said to us, "Miss Evans and I have been discussing it and we feel that you must realize by now that you'd never get to Denver." We would have kissed her feet if she had asked us to. She sent us to take a shower.

We didn't speak to each other. After the shower, we separated but none of us joined the kids playing. Each was dejected, haunted, isolated. It took days before we could actually play or even talk with the other boys, or even with each other. And Miss Johns would tease us sometimes if we didn't do what she wanted. "Maybe you need to go around the pool table again," she'd say, and a black horror would rush across my soul because it might all start up again.

Miss Evans called each of us into the office separately and asked us why we had tried to run away. I hadn't the courage to say that I hated Harmony Hall. I searched in my mind for what was the worst horror among our activities. "Swimming lessons," I said. "You won't have to try to swim any more," she said, and sent me away, not happy but with one nightmare removed.

Now, although I always arrived at the swimming lake in an asthmatic haze, at least I didn't have the lesson to fear. Instead, I was put with the tiny kids, little Cherokee and the others, in the wading area by the pier.

We weren't allowed to go under the pier but I liked to look under there. The posts were black and shiny, and green stuff clung to them in patches and dribbled down. Strange creatures lived under the pier. The best was the leech, a black ribbon with rounded ends undulating, not as a ribbon would, with the waves, but with a volition of its own, starting at one end and shuddering down its length to the other. It was mysterious and beautiful. I knew it would suck my blood if I let it but there was no big alarm about that, you could just pull it off and it wasn't even as bad as a mosquito bite. I like to wrap it around my finger and watch it move, then release it in the water and catch it again.

There was one thing I liked about cookouts aside from the two hot dogs and the three marshmallows. That was what we called foxfire. Whenever we saw a dead branch with red pine needles still on it, we were to burn it immediately because it burned so well that it was a big forest fire threat. And it burned wonderfully. Put in on the fire and whoosh, it was all flames, then crumbling sparks then ash. They called it foxfire and it looked like a fox, orange-red and calling out its power to set the forest on fire. When I see them even now I think of flame, they look like it already. I'd watch them burn and think what a magnificent fire it would be if the whole forest went up at once like that.

Then there was going to be a long hike and the preparations and anticipation went on for days. For me as well as for Jackie, it was a dread which colored everything, and Jackie, whenever he would catch my eye, would wink and smile. What I would have done without him there for the hikes, I can't imagine. We had to make backpacks out of towels and string and there were other preparations too.

Finally the day came and we all got up very early and, without exercises or any of our usual morning routines, we set off with something to eat as breakfast on the trail. We walked and walked and walked and my asthma swept over my mind like thick fog but I staggered on beside Jackie. We couldn't talk, though others ahead of us were talking, we could only struggle on. I found myself wishing I was a cripple like he was so I could be with him at the end of the line without shame. We climbed and clambered over boulders. Sometimes we'd see some boys sitting down ahead of us, resting, and they looked like pure happiness, angels in heaven, and we'd go a little faster to get to them and join them, but when they saw us they'd realize they'd rested too long and they'd get up and soon outstrip us and be out of sight again.

As we expected, we arrived at the top after lunch was over and had time only to snatch something to eat and stagger back down the long trail in silence again. We arrived at Harmony Hall after dark for a cold supper. I was so grateful that the day was over. Then Miss Johns stood up and the left side of her face wrinkled in a grimace which warned me that she was going to play one of her tricks. "That was a wonderful hike," she said. "How many of you would like to go on another?" I looked quickly around at the older boys who had been with her the longest. They had their hands up. I put my hand partway up. "All those with their hands up will bring in a piece of firewood and go to bed.

Those lazy bums who kept their hands down will go on a hike now with my nephew." Although I had known enough to put myself on the winning side, I was still shocked that she would so blatantly be training us to lie. I lay in bed, exhausted, unable to sleep, thinking of the poor fools out there in the woods in the dark who didn't know, as I knew, when to lie. But I was ashamed that I wasn't with them.

One evening we were all playing games in the living room and Miss Evans sent for me. This was very unusual and I was frightened. I went into the office. She was behind the desk writing letters and she went on writing for an age. Her hair was black and smooth. Her fountain pen scratched and her hand moved quickly. Her white arms encircled the page. There was a lamp on the desk beside her in the shape of an oil lamp and I stood looking at her white arms in the circle of light. Then she looked up and light glinted from her black eyes under her black eyebrows in her white face. She told me to sit down and I did. "I'm writing to your mother," she said. "I've decided not to tell her about you trying to run away." She looked at me very hard and it seemed the light gleamed from her eyes into my heart and froze it. "It'll just be a secret between us." She went on to say that because Clara had been sick, we shouldn't disturb her with my errant behavior. I knew what she was doing. She didn't want Clara to know how unhappy I was. But I sat shuddering on my chair like the little neighbor boy had shuddered on the toilet when I showed him the cat's-eye ring. She didn't need any ring. She had the power in herself and it was beyond mine. I told her "okay" in a whisper and she stretched her white arm out of the circle of light, patted me on the head and told me to go back and play.

A week or two later, Clara and Pete came to visit me. I so much wanted to tell them, "Take me away from here! It's terrible here! I tried to walk to Denver!" But I didn't say any of those things. I said everything was fine, the kids were fine, the ladies were fine, the food was fine, it was all just wonderful and they went away and with them went any hope of escape from the harsh domination of Miss Johns and the piercing possession of Miss Evans.

The routines of the days went on and I slipped through them with care of myself as my major concern. I had managed to get out of swimming and horseback riding, even the long hike was behind me. But there was little in the days that I did enjoy. The routine itself gave me security, simply knowing how the day was shaped, and what to do as it went along, gave me a semblance of knowing how to live.

There was one passion. That was the hope that our exercise group would win the competition and we would be taken to a movie. Jim worked us hard but it was a joy to do exercises for him. We were working on appearance by then, getting the angle of our arms and legs the same, being on the same foot, bending at the same angle and keeping the rhythm.

Finally the day of the competition came and we were incredibly keyed up, especially Jackie. Jim seemed calm and confident. The spectators were centered on the porch, the two ladies, being the judges, in the middle. Jim gave the order to march and we marched in tight formation then stopped and, with Jim calling out the routines and keeping the rhythm, we did what we had learned, spectacular things, especially considering we were the clumsies, the misfits. But not now. With solemn intensity we moved in perfect unison, doing things I can't imagine having done. When Miss Johns announced that we had won, we were not surprised. We weren't the athletes the other groups were but we did a better job. We received our congratulations with a great deal of satisfaction.

The next afternoon the misfit squad went to town in the truck. The other boys came up to us, pressed money on us, and begged that we'd buy them candy. "I want a Snickers bar," one boy said to me. "Please could you buy me a bag of red-hots?" I put their money in my pocket, nodded importantly, and we were off to Estes Park.

I rode in the cab with Jackie, Miss Evans driving. What a joy it was to see the town, the first town we'd seen in months. We were all very jolly. It was like a dream. The first stop was the grocery store, and while Miss Evans bought a few groceries, we boys crowded around the toys and the candies. I bought the Snickers bar and the red-hots for the two boys and some malt balls for myself. Then we went to the movie theatre and lined up behind Miss Evans for the matinee. She had a long string of tickets dangling from her hand. She bought us each a small bag of popcorn and we went in and sat down. I sat beside Dick. The climactic scene was in a ski-lift car in the Alps, wind howling, the ski-lift stuck, the rope fraying, the hero and the villain fighting, the villain hanging by his hands on the outside of the car, having to be rescued. I think everyone was saved in the end. We were completely satisfied.

When we got home it was getting dark. I gave the two boys their candy and then we had to tell everyone the story of the movie. From that day I gained stature among the boys and more rapport.

Not long after that, I saw some kids squatting in that way that meant they were doing something that fascinated them, so I went over and saw they were building little houses on each side of the trail. They had taken cartons and cereal boxes out of the trash and were cutting doors and windows in them with a knife. I went and got a box out of the trash too and began to build my own house. It became very exciting. I brought in Dick and Peewee and Len and they built houses too. It got so interesting that we went back to it day after day. We scouted the woods for useful objects. There was a neighbor not too far away who had an electric fence which we had all been warned about. We were very careful about his fence but he had a lot of trash stacked outside it and we rummaged through this and found things we could use for our project. There, I found roofing, several pieces of it, enough to keep every house safe from rain. Now ten kids were playing, so there were ten houses. And there was much to do. A kid found a bunch of nice pebbles in the stream which we could gravel our paths with. Very soon we felt the need of money and one boy cut up paper and marked it with dollar denominations. Then a bank had to be built and he became the banker. And so I began to be paid for my roofing, and I paid the window-cutter to cut my windows better and paid the kid with the pebbles for a gravel walkway. One Sunday we decided we needed a church and the whole village got together and built a beautiful church with a steeple made of a straight stick whittled to a point.

We had many occasions for village meetings. There were problems to solve. Early on, we had a problem of counterfeit money. I solved that one myself. I found a rock by the stream that was flat but had certain cracks in it so that when the paper was put just on the stone and we'd draw patterns on the paper, the cracks would show up on those patterns in a certain way that couldn't be copied. For this, I was elected mayor of the village and keeper of the stone. I kept it in my pocket wherever I went. Everyone turned in their old money and got new official money that had the mark of the stone.

Some of the other kids suggested that we should have a war to test our houses with slingshots. We had a meeting over that, discussed it, and voted against war, the reason being the village looked so splendid and the thought of the destruction that a war would bring upset us. Besides, there was much still to do in peacetime, many improvements yet to make. Someone had found some cloth for curtains and we all wanted curtains on all our windows. A theatre was being built and a general store. Multicolored broken glass had been found and at a meeting, we decided to put a stained-glass window in the church. Our yards needed to be fixed up. Trees were brought in and planted. Pieces of wood were found to reinforce the houses. Two kids became carpenters. Always we were searching in the woods and in the trash for things to use.

We dreaded any planned activities that would pull us away from the village. Such a community spirit built up over it that we were always talking about it, it was always in our minds and there was much to do there. Once or twice, other kids would come to the village when we weren't there and kick over a house or two and the whole village would work to help those kids whose houses were hurt. We decided it would be best if someone were always there to guard the village so that such a thing wouldn't happen again. It wasn't hard to recruit guards because so much needed to be done in the village. When it rained, a little streamlet came down through the village and we built bridges across it and roads. Rock walls had to be built to protect the houses from runoff.

Finally Miss Johns and Miss Evans heard about the village and wanted to see it. We had been worried about them, afraid they'd say we couldn't do it, but we had to bring them and show them and they were amused, they thought it was awfully cute. After that, we could get things out of the kitchen from Miss Evans. Burnt matchsticks, for instance, were very much wanted for fence posts and for sidewalks.

Occasionally a kid would get distracted from the village by other games and he wouldn't keep his house in good order. Then we'd have a meeting over that and vote on what to do. Although I was mayor because I had the stone, I had no more power than anyone else and the meetings were a model of the democratic process. Each boy had his say and everyone spoke and voted with equal strength.

Each house was different. So much material of so many different kinds were brought in that there was much scope for variety. Some walkways were of pebbles, some of matchsticks, some of broken glass. Some houses were tall and others were sprawling. Some yards were full of trees and others covered with gravel and glass. One kid had water in his yard and built a well. Another kid found a complicated piece of junk and put it up as a pump, but no one could recognize what it was and he finally removed it as a failure. Some houses had chimneys and others had carefully made ladders. One or two kids made lawn furniture. Painting became a big project. Everything had to be painted. There were watercolors and crayons for that. As the days and weeks wore on, the village became more and more wonderful and complex, more and more bright and pristine. One or two of us had seen Tiny Town down by Colorado Springs and felt that our village was far superior to it, partly because it was smaller but also it was more of a village, not so much a collection of houses. We felt ourselves strongly as a part of something that was great and wonderful. We were like gods making a world.

Remembering the village makes me feel disturbed and bitter. It was an exquisite thing. When we would go out there in the morning, the mist rising from the forest floor, the sunlight just touching the church steeple and the tops of one or two of the trees, the quiet streets, the well-cared-for houses and yards variously made by the unique mentalities in the group, each configuration intrinsically dramatic and all together forming an amazingly wondrous thing, an enchanted village, a jewel of human endeavor. It was an ideal civilization. Among the ten of us there was kindness and warmth, camaraderie and shared obsession. We were making incomparable loveliness out of trash. Everything in the village was there because of a natural need, either for the safety and comfort of the village or as a personal expression. Yet no individual kid was terribly important. The important thing was the village itself and the feeling of community we all had. What makes me bitter is the fact that this has never happened to me again. It seems to me that such a spirit of togetherness should be the norm, that people should naturally work together to make, in concert, the most wonderful community possible with what means are available, that the splendor, the attraction of such an endeavor should keep people from self-indulgence and destructiveness. Yet it's never happened to me again, I've never even seen it again. Was it, then, the result of the misery of the earlier part of the summer? I don't like to think that. Nor do I like to think that such a thing would necessarily be fleeting because many of the grubby realities of life are excluded from it.

You know the hand game adults like to show to children, "Here's the church and here's the steeple," closing their hands together, fingers inside, forefingers pointed for the steeple, the thumbs being the church doors? I've always hated the way they made that fat church and then opened the doors and there were all their fingers wiggling — hanging from the ceiling. Very unattractive. My church was always made slender with no people in it, my fingers kept outside as a roof. It was much more my sense of a church.

I don't know now exactly how I got the slivers under my fingernails. I know it had to do with the village because I felt I mustn't let anyone on the outside know about them. I think it was the mirror. I found a piece of a broken mirror and with great excitement made it into a goldfish pond in my yard, like the one I had had with Ryda Rue in Macomb and like the one my grandmother still had in Winfield. It glittered beautifully and when I looked into it, I could see myself. Although I tried to pick the slivers out with a pin, I didn't succeed and went for several days hiding them. But my fingers swelled up tremendously with a great deal of pain, especially the middle finger, and another boy saw it and told Miss Evans about it. She got a needle and told me to sit on the back steps. I watched with fascination as she sterilized the needle with a farmer match. Then she punctured the swollen middle finger and squeezed out an extraordinary amount of pus. I don't know if it was the pain or the horror of it but I passed out onto the ground and woke with her pale face bending over me. A kid raised me up and they told me to put my head between my knees as Miss Evans put iodine on my middle finger and started to work on the thumb. "This is just a tiny one," she said, "you don't have to faint." She pricked it and squeezed and I threw up on the ground. Miss Evans was angry. She made me get a shovel and bury my vomit after she'd put iodine on my thumb. I was very much relieved that she didn't blame the village for my slivers.

Now the time was coming near to leave and everyone in the village felt terrible about leaving it. "We'll come back next year," someone said, but we knew it would be lost over the winter. We asked Miss Evans if we could have a piece of canvas to cover it and protect it from the snow. She found a big black tin storage box with a hasp that we could put the village into and leave it out in the woods. We took days packing this box, uprooting houses, picking up pebbles and glass and matchsticks, labeling everything. The bridges had to go in the box, and the church, the general store, the well, even the rock walls were secured in there and labeled, and some things we had collected and hadn't used yet. Last of all, on top of everything else, I placed the money stone and we closed the lid. There wasn't a lock for the box so we got a piece of wood and shoved it tightly into the hasp. Then it was time to pack our clothes.

Early in the morning of the day we were all to leave for home, Dick Waters and I and the two other boys who knew about the secret spring went up the hill behind the woodpile one last time and, sitting in a circle around the gleaming water, each in turn dipped Dick's telescoping cup into it and drank in ritual solemnity.

16

Harmony Hall in Denver

IT TOOK SEVERAL DAYS to get moved to Denver. Dick Waters was one of the lucky ones whose parents came and took him away early on. He really did escape. I was to stay on with Harmony Hall in its house in Denver, with Jackie and Cherokee and some of the others. The end of the summer was not the end of Harmony Hall for me. However, I was eager to go to the city, and when I finally rode down in the car with Miss Evans and Cherokee and his brother I was excited. When the lights of the city shone out through the twilight, I was thrilled. And when we drove up to the big house on the corner and I could see my friends through the window, I was glad. Thus do we keep ourselves encouraged — a change of place for hope, and familiar faces for security and comfort.

It was a white frame house, two storeys, with a pillared porch, a white-painted fence, a sign saying Harmony Hall in script, and a well-kept lawn with a double swing in the middle of it. Behind the house was a stable with the hayloft made into a dormitory. There were lights on there too. I went in the stable. The ground floor was a big room with pillars, a pool table, a dart board, two puppies, a padlocked door, and beside it a steep narrow stair leading up to the hayloft where beds were three feet apart. The kids were unpacking, one drawer each and the rest under their beds.

Cherokee and his brother and I got a room in the house. It was a sun room over the front porch, two cots, a double bed for them. I don't remember who got the other cot. The room, all glass, faced east and, although there were curtains pulled over the windows, the light still came in and it was cold at night. There were three other bedrooms in the house, one for Miss Johns and Miss Evans, the other two with bunk beds for some of the boys.

Meals were in the dining hall, a room crowded with three long tables with benches. Miss Johns and Miss Evans didn't eat with us boys there. They had a separate dining room which was quite elegant with fine dishes in glassed-in cases, old framed photos and a lace cloth on the table.

Between the house and the dorm were a slide and a couple of swings. The whole front yard of mown grass with the double swing were out of bounds to us. In the back behind the dorm was the alley but we were not allowed to go into the alley. We were not allowed to cross the street, not allowed to walk around the block unless we were in the company of one or two other boys and got permission first. We were not allowed to run in the house or the dorm, not allowed upstairs in the dorm unless we had a bed there, not allowed to shout except at certain times. There was a vacant lot down the block but we were not allowed to go there. If anyone was late for a meal, he didn't get to eat.

Shortly after we arrived, there was a spate of crying among the little kids. There was a bunch of them sitting on the back steps crying together. Miss Johns came out, gathering the older kids around, "What is all this crybaby stuff?" she said, getting the older kids to razz them, "Crybaby! Crybaby! Crybaby!" Suddenly everyone was calling everyone else names. I was "Fatty," of course, although I had lost a lot of weight that summer.

An attempt was made to start up a village. We found a Spam can, a few bits of glass, toothpaste boxes, but there was no place where the village wouldn't be trampled and have balls fall into it, and there was no time to work on it anyway because of school starting.

We went to school in masses and clumps. We were the Harmony Hall kids. It was a fairly new grade school, not far from Harmony Hall. The art teacher liked me a lot. She gave us each a big sheet of construction paper and on mine I painted a gigantic sailing ship. White breakers, white sails, blue sky. She hung it on the wall and it was there almost the whole semester. It pleased me extremely that she left it up so long, and I looked at it a lot.

I painted other sailing ships, I painted horses too and other ancient things while the rest of the kids were painting images from the comics and the news. I was making a collection of pictures out of magazines of the war in Europe. As soon as we came to Denver, we found ourselves surrounded by signs of the war. One kid had a pin which he wore on his shirt with a little string you could pull and then a little doll of Hitler would come out and hang from a gallows, its head tipped to the side. New kids came to Harmony Hall with tales of their fathers fighting and heroic in the war.

We ate very little meat. Some of the older boys grumbled about this but Miss Johns would say, "There's a war on." "The soldiers need the meat." "Don't be selfish." "Eat up what there is, you get no more." "If we didn't eat anything at all, it would be the best for the war," we joked with each other. There was a certain camaraderie about the war all over the city.

I was doing well in school, I was even doing well in arithmetic. We were being drilled in the multiplication tables and I discovered a system for the nines. My teacher was very impressed at my speed with the nines so I told her my system. What you do, you subtract one from the number you're multiplying by nine and put that result in the tens place. Then you subtract that number from the nine and put the result in the ones. Take 9 times 7. 7 minus 1 puts 6 in the tens column; 9 minus 6 puts 3 in the ones column; and that makes 63. She was extremely impressed that I had invented that. Actually, Pete had taught it to me, but I never told anyone that.

In the mornings, I was bed inspector. I had to go to each bed and the kids would show me their sheets. If they weren't wet, they could make their bed. If they were, the kid would wash them in the bathtub, hang them up to dry, miss breakfast, and then be teased by the other boys. There was a new kid that came to Harmony Hall, a thin boy with a crew cut and great big eyes. He was pretty old but he was put with the little kids. Everyone wondered about that. When I went to check his bed, I found several brownish-yellowish spots on his sheets. It was certainly not piss so I told him to make his bed but then I went to Miss Johns and told her. "Well, we certainly know what that is, don't we?" she sneered. I hadn't the faintest idea what it was. She clomped up the stairs and soon we heard him howling, then he washed and hung up his sheets. The boys talked about it, they said he played with himself all night, that he was crazy, and that was why he was put with the little boys.

There was the time too when two of the older boys were made to sit on the forbidden swing all day dressed as women, a punishment for something, I didn't at the time know what.

Sometimes on weekends, Clara and Pete would take me home to visit. It was wonderful to get out of Harmony Hall, to play cowboys and Indians in the vacant lot with the neighbor kids — although they were distant from me now. There were the treasures too, things I couldn't take to Harmony Hall because they'd be stolen. My printing set, my growing collection of war pictures. Pete gave me things sometimes which I kept together in a shoebox — a khaki handkerchief, medals and ribbons, and a set of sergeant stripes which he told me I must never wear because it would be against the war. Some of the brightest and prettiest decorations he said were nothing much, and some of the dull-looking ones he said were great. I found them quite confusing. He got me a book that explained them all but I stuck to my own impressions. I knew what I liked. It was the articles themselves, not what they meant, that I cared for.

Very often Pete would have something planned — the zoo, a picnic in the park — or would drop me off at a double feature movie. So Saturday afternoons were usually pleasant if I managed to get home for them.

The big thing that happened was that I got back into choir. So Wednesday evenings and Sunday mornings I'd go to Saint John's and sing. Jon was still there. I told everyone how I'd been imprisoned in Harmony Hall and what an awful summer I'd had. And Jon was sympathetic and he spoke to me and we were friends again. We had a lot to talk about. Often he'd walk with me to the bus stop and we'd talk until the bus came. He was an endless source of sympathy and he listened to my stories with a great deal of interest. I talked with him on and on about Harmony Hall, telling him the same stories repeatedly, adding details. He was always duly horrified. He seemed truly interested. But no matter how often and how dramatically I told him about it, he didn't understand it, couldn't feel it. No matter how much I explained, he hadn't lived anything like it. The more I talked, the more wide I felt the gap between us. It was the first time I had ever recognized the impossibility of explaining. It simply didn't get across. The thought never occurred to me to talk about something else, to think and dream as we had before. For one thing, it was his sympathy for my hard life that had brought him again to my side, but the thinking and dreaming had come to an end when I had disgraced myself by drawing his hand on the blackboard. Neither of us brought it up. Besides, I was obsessed with Harmony Hall and was glad for an opportunity to go over and over the stories of it. Nonetheless, our relationship had changed. Before, we had been equals, with me struggling and aspiring to maintain that equality in spite of certain inequalities — most particularly the inequality of money. But now, it was all different. I had a tale to tell. He was my audience. I was in the spotlight. He was in the dark. I was eloquent, but he wouldn't come out of the dark into the spotlight where I could see him, see myself in him. This didn't frustrate me at all. It seemed right. He was kind, sympathetic, but shadowy. Although I was delighted to have him back as my friend, it seemed as though he had feelings but less substance. It was not the obsessive joy it had been before.

Dick Waters lived within a block of Saint John's and if I left early for choir, I could stop by there on the way. I couldn't be late after choir because I was expected, but I could be late getting there. David Pew would frown at me when I came in to practice late, but that was all. Sometimes I could go and visit Dick on Saturday morning instead of playing with the neighbor kids at 930 Washington. The neighbor kids were distant from me now anyway. It seemed there was no way for me to relate to anyone very closely unless they had been through Harmony Hall. So whenever I could, I'd visit Dick if only for half an hour, I would be sure of his understanding, because his perspective was very close to mine. With him, I could be comfortable. It was a great relief to visit him. It was the only time I was not alone.

No, there was one other time I was not alone, that was when I took Communion.

It took a long time in Saint John's for the hundreds of members of the congregation to take Communion. They would file in an endless-seeming line down the aisle to the altar and each member would kneel and receive the pressed wafer, the drink from the Communion cup, and a blessing. And the whole time that this was going on, the choir would sing and David Pew would play the organ. Then when all the rest of the congregation had received it, the choir would come out and receive Communion too.

When my turn came, I would kneel there and I would truly and deeply feel how I was partaking of the body and the blood of Christ, how I was then at one with God and the Angels. And I was pure. I'd rise from my knees and for a brief time, I'd be pure, I'd be truly part of the whole world and it was very sacred and solemn.

Clara was coming regularly to church now at Saint John's to bask in the glory of my little solos and to take part in the thing that was so important to me — my religion. But her presence there was no real satisfaction to me. I knew her too well to think that she had taken up religion with any real religious feeling.

Jon and I went often after church to visit his aunt at the Cosmopolitan Hotel and we would have lunch there with that lovely lady and then go to a movie at the Broadway Theatre. There were wonderful movies coming out then. The movies made during the War seemed to be a little more thoughtful. There was *Northwest Passage* with Spencer Tracy, there was the Marx Brothers' *Night at the Opera*, there were J. Arthur Rank movies. They dug out old movies to run, early sound movies, westerns. I saw the Korda brothers' *Four Feathers*.

But everywhere, I was set apart. In school, as a Harmony Hall boy, in church as a choir boy, in choir as a soloist, in the Washington Street neighborhood as the boy that didn't really live there anymore, in Harmony Hall now as the one who got away on weekends and Wednesday nights for choir.

Some of the kids at Harmony Hall were jealous of me because I got away. Others were simply wistful. They'd ask what it was like out there. I was like a soldier coming back on leave. I'd tell them about the movies I'd seen and they'd gather around me as though I was passing out candy. I felt sorry for them for not having any escape at all.

It was a cold and snowy winter. Wednesday nights for choir practice I'd take the bus but sometimes, because of the snow, the busses were late. I went in terror of the weather, worrying when it clouded up, or when a flake or two of snow would fall, wondering whether I'd get to choir practice on Wednesday or whether on a weekend I'd get away at all.

Sometimes Clara would pick me up on Friday night and that was by far the best. Other times I'd take the bus to Washington Street on Saturday morning — those were the worst times because often she was very late.

Any kid who was waiting to be picked up had to wait in a little anteroom near the front door. On Saturday mornings there were often several kids waiting there. We'd sit and fidget, trapped in silent anxiety. The doorbell would ring and all of us would listen to the voices of adult geniality and then one kid would be called and get away. Almost always, I was the last and I'd sit alone in the anteroom in misery. Would she come at all? I'd smell lunch cooking, then I'd hear the other kids eating lunch and still she hadn't come. I'd hear the kids clattering away from the lunchroom and maybe Miss Evans would come into the anteroom then and say I could have something to eat. Nothing left but a few crusts, maybe a bowl of something tepid, the dirty dishes and spilled ketchup on the table.

Harmony Hall was only a few blocks from the Bluebird Theatre and one time, approaching Christmas, the whole of Harmony Hall trouped along the snowy streets to see a movie. Miss Johns and Miss Evans had set it up beforehand so that we could all get in and we filed docilely into a block of seats reserved for us. The movie was Charlie Chaplin's *The Great Dictator*. I found the whole experience surprisingly unsatisfactory. I had no close friends now at Harmony Hall, therefore no one to sit with at the movie and it was no escape. Surrounded by the Harmony Hall kids, supervised by the Misses Johns and Evans, was not a movie, it was an irony.

I had been to the Bluebird Theatre once before, many years before, I don't know when. It was with Clara. Perhaps it was the opening of the theatre. There was a big neon bluebird on the end of the marquee and they were showing the movie of Maeterlinck's *The Bluebird* with Shirley Temple. All the torn tickets went into a big glass drum and at some time during the evening there was a drawing. The organ played, someone stuck his hand into the drum and pulled out a ticket, and it was Clara's and she won something, I don't remember what. That evening had had a special magic in it. Clara was so excited, the movie was mysterious with people in animal costumes. Not that *The Great Dictator* was a bad movie at all, but it was about the war and I compared the two evenings in my mind; the happy one with Clara and *The Bluebird* and the dismal one with all of Harmony Hall and *The Great Dictator.*

Christmas was a big deal everywhere. In Harmony Hall, there was a big tree that everyone was made to decorate under the strict supervision of Miss Johns. We were all told where to put what decorations. It was hollow and regimented. At 930 Washington, Pete made a real attempt to make a festive Christmas. He was extravagant and there were many presents under the tree, and a jolly atmosphere of excitement. In choir, there were new pieces to sing and I had many solos. There were several special occasions where the choir was needed at the church. On Christmas day, the choir went downtown and sang, then we were given lunch and our pay envelopes with an extra two dollars in them.

Jon and I had permission to go to a movie after that. On the way to the movie, we passed an alley and there was a woman in it with her back to us. She had her dress pulled up to her waist, she had no underpants on, and she was vomiting against a wall. Jon said we shouldn't look but I stopped and stared at her. I thought maybe we should help her, she was in trouble. But her dress was so very far up, it seemed that we shouldn't. We wandered around the streets for some time looking at all the Christmas decorations and haunted by the image of the woman in the alley. We were late for the movie.

I got to stay on Washington Street the whole time from Christmas through New Year's. It was heavenly. I worked a good deal on my war scrapbook after Christmas, pasting in magazine pictures, finding more pictures. This brought me closer to Pete. Clara and I were in constant fear that Pete would be sent to the front, that then he might be killed like other men were being killed.

Soon after I arrived back at Harmony Hall, we got our report cards and the Misses Johns and Evans made a big scene about them, giving us extra chores or extra cake. I did well in all my classes and got lots of cake. They were so pleased with my report card that they decided I was more grown up and could sleep in the dorm with the bigger kids. The room I'd been in was drafty and cold and the light often woke me early in the morning but I had grown accustomed to it. And in the dorm, I would be the youngest kid there and the only supervision was Miss Johns's nephew, who was about sixteen and had a special room of his own and was the enemy. However, I was given no choice in the matter and I moved to the dorm.

The two puppies had made the gaming room downstairs an awful place. Nobody had cared for them very much. Miss Johns had presented them as a rather disgusting duty. When they were taken out they had to be watched constantly; when they were kept in, they fouled the gaming room floor and the first kid in there had to clean it up. Therefore nobody wanted to go in first. They also yapped. They were, in coloring, reminiscent of Ritzy, white with brown spots, but their neglected and frantic personalities made them a grotesque parody of him. I avoided the gaming room and the puppies as much as I could and never had to clean up their messes.

The dorm was long, the cots were three feet apart and Miss Johns's nephew's room was at the far end. My cot was at the end nearest the stairs next to Jackie's, and so I got to know Jackie better. I couldn't help watching his tortuous efforts as he took off his clothes or put them on. It was agonizing. For Christmas they had made a big deal about giving him suspenders and now he had to wear them all the time. They were very bright suspenders, garish, and he hated them, but there was nothing he could do but wear them always. He even felt obliged to be very grateful for them. But he hated them.

He and I whispered together sometimes after lights out, conspiratorially. He compared the orphanage to Harmony Hall. The food at the orphanage was not as good, he said. I couldn't imagine food worse than Harmony Hall's, but so he said. Still, he preferred the orphanage. It was because of his position. At the orphanage, he had been one of the kids. He had equality. Here, he was The Cripple. The ladies showed him to everyone as though he was some sort of achievement on their part. And because of that and other things, he was not one of the kids. Rather, he felt useless and in the way.

Jackie had an awful time going down the steep, narrow stairs from the dorm. It took a long time. It was an insoluble problem because if he started down earlier than the others — which was hard to do because of the difficulty of putting on his clothes as fast as the others — they'd crowd impatiently behind him. If he didn't go till after the others had already gone, he'd be late for breakfast. "We can't spoil Jackie," Miss Johns would say, and so very often he wouldn't get any breakfast. Early on, I began to help him with this problem. I'd go down slowly in front of him. With me there in front, he'd be less scared and could go faster.

Jackie didn't remember his parents. I told him I didn't remember mine either. But no one would ever adopt him. He knew that.

For my birthday, Clara gave me a violin. She really wanted me to take piano lessons but there seemed no way to do it. And a violin class started up in school three times a week. It was a beautiful violin, a small one, in a nice black case. I still have it.

I was very upset when I realized that I had to take it to Harmony Hall. I had nothing I valued at Harmony Hall except my constipation medicine. If I couldn't have my sergeant stripes there because they'd be stolen, how could I keep a beautiful and expensive thing like a violin? I kept it under my bed with my two pieces of luggage. It didn't fit. Something had to stick out. I'd go and check on it now and again and try to rearrange things so it would fit better. The three mornings a week I took it to school, I left it in the room above the gymnasium where the violin teacher was. But of course she could leave the room and someone could steal it then. I worried about it when I went to choir too on Wednesday evenings. Weekends, I took it to Washington Street to practice. It was more than a little nerve-wracking.

There were five of us taking the lessons. When the time came, we'd be excused from class and we'd climb the stairs to the room above the gymnasium. We could hear the noises of gym class loud and clear, the echoing yells, the ball booming. The smells of lunch cooking wafted up to us, then we'd get to work. Twee-twee — twee — twee. There was no music in any of it, no beauty except the beauty of the violin itself and the remembrance of beautiful music that could be played on the violin. And this was how one began. Twee-twee — twee — twee.

Fairly often, the violin teacher would keep us a few minutes into lunchtime and I'd get to Harmony Hall late for lunch. Miss Johns and Miss Evans were always making nasty comments to me about it. I always had a good excuse. But I had so many special privileges. I was a lot of trouble. Choir practice, going home on weekends, and now violin lessons. They took every opportunity to tell me what a bother I was. They were really quite huffy about it.

I was becoming distraught with the stress and confusion and heavy responsibilities coming at me from all sides. The violin teacher, David Pew, Clara and Pete pushing me to struggle and achieve, to form music in the depths of me and bring it out. I had perfect pitch, and that was a rare thing, a precious gift that they were all excited about. It was my duty, my fate, my only escape to sing and to play the violin superbly. Maybe if I did, Clara would take me back and I would have my home again, such as it was. But where I actually lived, everyone was against it all. The ladies were irritated and the kids were jealous. Their lives were all but empty and mine was overfull. I had no one in Harmony Hall I could call a friend. Jackie was limited. Dick Waters I could see briefly on weekends at his home. I didn't have time for friends at Harmony Hall anyway. There was Cherokee but he was essentially devoted to his brother. He and Jackie could only swallow their envy and encourage me from outside. I was alone and I felt alone and I had much tension in my life and I was alone with that. I was ten years old and I knew how to feel sorry for myself.

One Saturday morning I was waiting in the anteroom with three other kids for our mothers to come and get us. I had my violin on the floor beside me. I was going to practice at home. Soon the other kids' mothers came and took them all away and I was alone with my violin. After a while the smell of lunch came and the sound of the other kids gathering in the lunchroom. Miss Johns opened the door and said I should come and have lunch too. I took my violin, fearing to leave it unguarded in the anteroom. But Miss Johns said, "I didn't invite your violin to lunch." As the other kids laughed and jeered obediently, I went back to the anteroom, put on my coat, took the violin up to the dorm and put it under my bed. Then, of course, I was late for lunch.

Every detail of that long and dismal day seemed to stretch it to weeks, years. After lunch I asked Miss Johns if I could go and get my violin again. Anyone waiting in the anteroom was to always ask permission to leave it. "What, do you think it will come down by itself?" she said. I put on my coat again and got the violin, set it beside my chair, and waited for Clara to come and take me away. A couple of hours went by and I had to pee. I took my violin into the kitchen and asked Miss Evans if I could go pee. She said I could. Then more hours in the anteroom. The smell of supper came and I began to cry. First I sat wiping my tears then I began to sob. There was pain in my chest and I hid my face against the wooden back of the chair. I thought my heart was breaking. The kids gathered for supper. Some of them heard me and peeked in, went and told Miss Johns. She came and got me and made me stand in the lunchroom for all to see me crying. "Where's your violin?" Miss Johns said. I went to the anteroom and got it and she made me stand in the lunchroom holding it, crying. She stirred the boys to jeer at me as I stood. "What're you crying for?" she said, "Your mother called this morning and said she'd come to get you for supper!" I thought of the afternoon I'd spent. "Go up and wash your face," she said. I started up the stairs, violin in hand. "Are you going to wash your violin too?" Everyone laughed obediently. I handed the violin to her. Then when I had washed and come down again, I had to ask her for my violin.

Clara arrived and there were the cheery adult greetings. I stood mute, then followed her to the car. "What's the matter with you?" she asked. I couldn't speak. I was afraid to tell her. I had seen what had happened to other kids who had told their parents about things like this. They didn't get out. They got teased and jeered at without letup; they got the short end of every stick; they suffered badly. "I'm sorry I'm late," she said. I didn't listen as she rattled off her excuses.

I couldn't sing in choir practice that evening. Jon walked me to my home, called his mother to pick him up there in her big car. I couldn't tell Jon either, he'd tell his mother and she'd tell Clara, then Clara would ask Miss Johns and Miss Evans and they would smooth it over, make it sound like nothing, and there I'd be trapped with their ire and their constant sneering.

The next week I got constipated even though I was still taking my medicine. For days I could get nothing out and it piled up inside me until I became sick and one night I threw up in bed. I covered it with the sheet but they could smell it. Miss Evans took my temperature but it was normal. She made me wash my sheets in the bathtub. The other kids had all gone to school so I had a lot of time. I went into the bathroom, put the sheets in the tub and filled it with water. There was the toilet. I knew I couldn't present Miss Johns and Miss Evans with this problem. I had to solve it by myself. I sat on the toilet and pushed and strained, my vomit-scented sheets soaking beside me in the tub. Finally a little turd came out. I strained some more but nothing more came out. But I could hardly move unless it did. I started clawing at it, digging bits of it out with my fingers, then pushing and straining some more. I had to get it out. I was sick. At last, a big turd came out, a huge one. I was thrilled. I pushed some more, dug some more with my fingers. Another huge turd came out. Ahhhhh. I got off the toilet. My hands were covered in filth. I flushed the toilet. The turds didn't go down, they were too big. I broke up the pieces with my hands, I flushed and flushed. There was filth on the seat, on the handle, on the sides of the toilet. I cleaned that up, washed my hands, got back on and shoved out some more, flushed again and again. "What's taking you so long?" Miss Evans called through the door. "I had to go to the bathroom," I said, knowing that that didn't explain the repeated flushings. I was so happy. I had solved my problem by myself.

I washed the sheets with the soap, rinsed them, and took them outside to hang them up. It was very cold out and I had no coat on. The line was almost out of reach. I had to pull it down to put the sheet on it. I had never failed bed inspection before. I had seen other kids hanging up their sheets. They were usually crying or grim. But I was happy. I had succeeded. By the time I got back into the dorm, I was shivering. I wrapped my blankets around me and lay on the bare mattress. I lay there happily all day, alone except that once or twice Miss Evans took my temperature. It was a new injustice to add to my list. I was making a collection of them. When I got enough, I would tell them all at once and then I would get out of Harmony Hall. It seemed as though it was impossible to get out of Harmony Hall but I was going to do it.

It wasn't more than a week or two after that, after school, a number of us were in the living room. We could smell supper cooking. I was talking with Cherokee. He was a good listener, his obsidian black eyes sparked me on to telling my thoughts and dreams. "Anything is possible," I said to him. I don't remember how the conversation got to that point. "Anything is possible." Some kid heard me. "You mean," the other kid said, "that if I cut off your head, it would grow wings and fly away?" "Well," I said, "it may never have happened but it could happen." Some of the other kids were gathering around. It was an intrusion on our conversation. Then came the call for supper and we all filed in to the lunchroom. I was just picking up my fork to eat — it was spaghetti, my favorite — when Miss Johns came in. "Stanley," she spoke over the clatter of supper, "I hear that you said it was possible that someone could cut off your head and it would grow wings and fly away." I was flustered. "I just said anything was possible," I said. Miss Johns made the face that was the order for everyone to giggle. Everyone giggled. "I'll show you," she said, "that there are some things that are impossible." She took me back into the living room, brought in the boy who had accused me. "Now you, Stanley, stand there and hold your hands above your head. I'll even help you out." She placed me a few inches away from the wall, pulled up my hands to the place she wanted them. Then she handed a ruler to the other kid. "If Stanley's hands touch the wall," she said to him, "you hit them. And if you don't I'll put you in the same position he's in."

The thought never occurred to me then or later in life that the other kid was being punished also.

While all the other kids were eating spaghetti in the next room, I could hold my arms up all right, but by the time the kids were dribbling back into the living room my arms were hurting more and more. Finally, my hands touched the wall.

The kid hit them with the ruler. It happened again. He hit them again. I began to cry. I tried letting my hands down then putting them up again quickly. "Keep your hands up," he said. He was looking around the room wildly. He hit me less and less hard every time. Miss Johns came into the room. She saw my tears and the haunted look of the other boy. "Maybe Stanley would do better," she said, "if I held the ruler." So for a while she'd hit my hands when my arms would fall. Then she must have seen in my face the despair that I felt. "Do you think some things are impossible?" she asked me, pulling the ruler back for a big walloping whack. "Yes," I whispered. "Louder," she said. "Yes," I said aloud.

She sent me to bed then. I lay there brimming with hatred and shame. "Anything is possible," I said to myself so that no one could hear. "Anything is possible." I said it over and over again as I lay there and I could hear my heart beating, beating, beating in my ears.

The violin teacher kept us late several times, and each time it would make me late for lunch, and each time I'd be late for lunch Miss Johns would say, "You get here on time or you get no lunch." And on the third or fourth time I was late, she said, "Okay, no lunch," and she sent me to my bed to wait till it was time to go back to school. It wasn't my fault I was late. It was Clara that had wanted me to take violin lessons. I was in a cold rage.

When I got back to school, I asked my teacher if I might be excused to call my mother. I knew where she worked, a real estate company. I went to the office to phone her. There were people in the office and they wouldn't let me call until I'd answered a lot of questions. They were kind, though, and sympathetic. Was I sick? No, I said. Why didn't I call Harmony Hall? Then I began to cry. My chance had come. They sat me down and I let them get it all out of me, the whole collection of Harmony Hall injustices. They were on my side. They brought me food. They talked about me and looked at me. They called Clara themselves. I was filled with hope. "Maybe," I thought, "she would come and get me after school and I'd never go back there again." But she couldn't get away. They told me I had to go back, that she would pick me up there, at Harmony Hall. I spent the afternoon in the office. They brought me books to read. I was frightened to go back to Harmony Hall but they kept assuring me that I'd be all right, that Clara would come for me after supper, that the Misses Johns and Evans couldn't keep me now.

After school I went to Harmony Hall and climbed the stairs to my bed. I sat on my bed till suppertime. I was afraid. Hope and fear are so close. I went to supper very silent. After supper Miss Johns said to me, "Go up and pack your things. Your mother is coming to get you." I went up, silent, and packed my things. I still thought it couldn't be. I thought I'd pack everything, and bring it to the door and then Miss Johns would come to me and say, "You thought you were getting away, didn't you?" And then everyone would obediently laugh because she would have that look on her face. I was packing everything neatly in my bags. Excitement was growing in me. Then I thought, "Clara won't come." Of course, I thought, she simply won't come. My hands were fumbling, I couldn't fold things properly. A kid came up the stairs, his eyes were wide, he said, "They want you to hurry up!" He stared at me in amazement. He helped me carry my bags down the stairs to the foyer. Clara was there, tight-lipped. She was writing a check. There was none of the usual cheery adult chatter. Miss Johns and Miss Evans were standing quietly. They seemed almost subdued. They shook my hand. Kids were peeping around doors and corners. It was like a dream. Clara and I walked out the door, down the steps. I walked stiffly, feeling I might be shot down like in the movies or even yet called back.

Clara and I put the two suitcases and the violin in the car and got in. "Why didn't you tell me?" she asked. "I was afraid to," I said. "Well," she said, "you're never going to have to go back to that place again." She was still tight-lipped. I sat in a dream still, wondering what she'd do with me now.

I had grown wings and flown away.

17

The Gang

I SPENT ABOUT A WEEK at 930 Washington Street. Clara, frantically eager to find a place for me, to get me away and settled, searched impatiently with a great deal of hysterical confusion for someone who would take me off her hands. Finally she found an ad in the paper and drove me to north Denver.

It was a block beyond the end of the trolley line, not far from Elitch's Amusement Park. A red brick house. In the back bedroom was a sick man. The woman had dark hair in tight spit curls and she was like that, very nervous and jumpy. I was told to be quiet all the time because of the sick man. But I was a quiet child. I could sit for hours alone and play, with very little to play with but my dreams. Clara was very irritable as she transferred my school papers to the new school nearby and paid the lady with the tight spit curls.

Somehow, though, I got on these people's nerves, and after two or three weeks the woman said I'd have to leave. She had spoken, however, to the people next door, the Russells, a retired couple in a white frame house, and they would take me. Clara was so relieved that it was going to be simple this time that she jumped at the chance and I was installed posthaste with the Russells.

Mrs. Russell was so bland that I have no memory of her face. Mr. Russell had a lot of wrinkles. He was not very well. His hair was completely white. I got the bedroom at the Russells with windows looking out on their big backyard. There was a drug store on the corner and a little grocery store across the street.

School was in easy walking distance. It was red brick with wavery glass on the windows. It reminded me of Emerson School, the first school I went to in Denver, because of the dreamlike quality of the wavery glass. It was a three-story building and had a large dirt playground with the inevitable chain-link fence.

It was early in February when I entered the school in north Denver and I arrived with an intense determination to make good this time. Being alone now, really alone, without the security of the other Harmony Hall kids or anyone else, I had to make my own place, my own security. I was in the fourth grade now and I knew a few things. I knew that the kids would start calling me "Fatty" and I knew how to hire bullies. I looked over the class and very soon picked out two of the toughest. I spoke to them at recess, offered them each a quarter a week to protect me and to keep kids from calling me "Fatty."

I knew also that a quarter a week would not be enough to hold their attention on me. I wanted their attention, I wanted everyone's attention. I wanted to be somebody special. I remembered the malt ball fiasco and how I'd been caught. I didn't want to be caught this time. It had to be something different, something that wouldn't jeopardize me.

It was hard to steal from these people I was staying with. Unlike Clara, they didn't leave their money around. I was, of course, adept at stealing from stores. I knew a lot about stealing, had learned to see everything, see the faces of store clerks and where they were looking, learned to buy one thing and slip another in my pocket, look at comics till another customer came and distracted the clerk, then stuff something in my pocket or under my shirt. Sometimes the other customer didn't come for half an hour or more. I couldn't hang around for that length of time. In frustration, I'd tuck one comic into another, pay for one, and leave. Or the customer would come but wouldn't distract the clerk enough or would have the clerk looking too much in my direction. I had gotten to hating those people who looked in the window then walked on by, hating those who came in but still didn't act in a way that left me free to take what I wanted, hating the clerk who was alert and noticing and hard to distract. And hating the fate that left me alone when what I needed was accomplices. I had been reading steadily and with fascination the comic called *Crime Does Not Pay,* true stories from the annals of crime, biographies of criminals, big-time gang leaders and how they worked. How they worked was with accomplices. The leader would "case the joint," draw a picture of the "layout," then direct the accomplices as to where to go and what to do. The gang leader wouldn't even be there when the "job" was performed but he'd get a large amount of the take for doing the brainwork. It was a very attractive system to me. And there were all those kids in the school. Potential accomplices. But I needed their attention. I needed for them to be drawn to me. To get their help, I had to be attractive in some way.

Just about the time I arrived in north Denver, a new story began in the Dick Tracy comic strip. Dick Tracy was walking down the street. Behind him on the sidewalk was a huge fat buxom woman with a bandana over her head so I couldn't see her face. Mrs. Pruneface. Under her arm, she was carrying a basket with a cloth over it. There were several frames of him and her walking along the sidewalk. It was ominous. And Dick Tracy paid no attention to her at all. I wanted to shout at him to run away. Then, out of the basket, the woman took a bullwhip, snaked it out and whipped it neatly around his neck, pulling him off his feet. Quickly, she knocked him over the head with the handgrip, picked him up, and carried his now unconscious form away. Not a word was said. It was magnificent, it was thrilling. I was very excited.

I started making comic strips, a single strip on a sheet of a Big Chief tablet turned sideways, six or eight pictures, and I'd sell them to the kids for a penny each. I enjoyed doing it tremendously. I found myself able to create them in an exciting way, to draw them well enough for faces to be recognizable, to make the story interesting, as interesting as any comic in the papers. Except for the crime comics. It was a really exciting thing and I worked hard on it. A penny a sheet was poor pay for the amount of work I did on them, but it was a delight to have a way I could pass them around, have them received and read and enjoyed by kids. And I got a lot of positive attention for it.

I made several kinds of comics. There was the *Pirate* series, with the man with an eye patch as the evil hero. In those I got to draw my wonderful ship that I still loved to draw. In the *Cowboy* series, the cowboys were, of course, chasing bandits. Sometimes I'd do a cartoon modeled after those on the Double Bubble gum wrapper cartoons. Those were the best cartoons I'd ever encountered. I found it very hard to tell jokes in one or two frames. On the Double Bubble wrappers they seemed able to do so, sometimes even without words. I found that awesome and never did achieve it. Then there was the war series I called *Pete,* modeled, of course, after Clara's lover, still my hero. Sometimes he'd be a pilot, sometimes a tank commander. That was one of my favorites.

But my very favorite comic to make was *Demono.* In *Demono,* I really invented something out of my own heart, a monster, miserable and misunderstood, shaggy-haired and crippled, fugitive, homeless, unloved and unlovable. He shambled through the world, fleeing from his oppressors, one hand always reaching out before him in a blind hunger for something meaningful and sympathetic, encountering only harshness and cruelty, strangling, strangling people who were mean to him or who got in his way. Practically every strip, he strangled someone. When I felt particularly down and lonesome, I would make a strip or two of *Demono*. It was wonderful how much it soothed me.

Of these strips, I seldom made any copies but simply sold the original creation. Some evenings I would work on them for hours and make several. And the next day, the kids would buy them from me for a penny each and read them. But although I read the crime comics with the most interest of all, I did not make any crime strips. I was saving that for real life.

Mrs. Pruneface had Dick Tracy chained to a wall in an empty building and every day she would give him the tiniest taste of turnip juice, only as much as would cling to a fork. Dick Tracy was getting very thin, lines were developing on his face and his clothes hung on him more and more loosely. It turned out that Mrs. Pruneface had a very good reason to torture Dick Tracy because Dick Tracy had, in the pursuit of justice, caused the death of her husband, Pruneface. I was fascinated with this reference to the history of Dick Tracy and started searching for every item I could find of his past. I discovered much later that Chester Gould, who wrote the Dick Tracy comic strip, had a little graveyard in his garden in which he memorialized all the villains that he had created and that Dick Tracy had in one way or another killed.

I felt sympathy for Mrs. Pruneface. She had had her family taken from her and killed. This had happened to me too. They had even killed Ritzy. And although I did generally identify with Dick Tracy, in this case I felt strongly the enjoyment of revenge. Some people should die, I thought, and torturing people would be a glorious luxury.

It began on a small scale. Sometimes a kid would owe me a penny for one of my comic strips. Or I'd ask a kid to let me use his eraser or to give me a piece of paper. Or let me play with a toy he'd brought to school. If the kid balked, I'd send my bullies after him at recess. If anyone called me "Fatty" or made any nasty comments about me, they'd get beat up. With my bullies, I made my place, I became feared and respected by everyone. They might have homes and be loved, which I

UNION RAILWAY
CHAPTER I
THE BRIDGE OF PERIL
JOSE I'll give you 6 mounthes to finish a railroad from Central city to Argintia conecting South America with the United States
with the help of Bill you should be able to do it
It will be done as you wish sinior
Men were put to work to build the railway
Argintia
Border line
central city
Meanwhile
boys we've got to stop the railroad. we've been pulling easy robbries hear in South America but if the railroad goes through the United States will put a stop to crime
Jose got olny 6 mounthes to get the railroad through and if we can delay them long enough the rail-road will never be finished
the gansters place some T.N.T. at a cross-ing in the Track and
Some of the track has been blown up
Wha. Bill Someone must be trying to wreck the railroad
again the gang stricks
send out orders that no T.N.T. to be sold
gang Bill
No more T.N.T is to be sold
Hay boss I can't sell you any more TNT Government orders
WAREHOUSE
then we'll rob the railway warehouse come on boys
But it so happened that Jose and Bill were at the warehouse whe the crook attacked
The crooks are attack

Meanwhile another crook climbs on the balcony and begains to fight with Bill
THE CROOK BEGAINS TO STAMP ON BILLS HANDS
BUT JOSE SEES WHATS HAPPENG
I must Hurry
AAAAAA
Meanwhile the CHIFE RECOVERED CONISNESS AND GOT SOME T.N.T. AND ROAD TOWARD A BRIDGE THAT THE RAILROAD WOULD CROSS
THEN HE SET T.N.T IN THE PILLERS
JUST AS I THOUGH HEAR COMES JOSE AFTER ME JUST WAIT TELL HE CROSSES THE BRIDGE
T.N.T CHARGE
THE BOSS MUST BE AROUND HEAR
NOW
T.N.T CHARGE
THE END of CHAPTER I

wanted more than anything and didn't have, but I had found a way to force their respect. I had something special. I was different, I was as different as Demono and I was dangerous. There was some pleasure in that. I hated them, they had mothers and fathers who cared what their feelings were and gave them what they needed. But I was hammering out a place for myself, a special place for a special person.

It took a lot of money to keep up. I had to steal regularly from Clara's purse on weekends. But I had a lot of experience doing that. I could sometimes steal coins or even bills from stores if the clerk would leave the cash register open and be distracted for just a few seconds. But I was afraid some day I'd get caught. I thought of the safety of being a gang leader, sending in other kids to steal and having them bring some of what they got to me. The more I thought about it, the more attractive it became. Stealing was a very tense thing to do and if I ever got caught again, I'd lose my position of power in the school.

There were the comic books and there were Big Little Books, but to be up with the very latest one had to subscribe to the newspaper. The Russells took the Sunday paper only. It had a half page of color for each strip, which gave me the basic story, but the black and white strips during the week carried a lot of details that I urgently wanted to see. The lady with the spit curls next door took the paper every day and sometimes I could get her to give me her paper after she and her husband were through with it. Sometimes Clara would save the comics out of her daily paper and I could pick them up on the weekend. I collected as many as I could from these two sources but sometimes they would have forgotten about me and my urgent desire for comic strips. I cut out the Dick Tracy strips and saved them separate from my ever-growing collection of war pictures, but some of the strips I never got. This was very upsetting to me, partly because it showed me clearly how little Clara or anyone cared about me, and also because there was little in my life besides the comics and they had for me an immense importance which no one seemed able to understand. "I must have wrapped the garbage in it," they'd say, "started a fire with it," "forgot."

I realized that the only way I could get every paper was if I got it myself. There were all those newspapers lying on people's yards and stacked up in the drug stores. Every day, I'd take one from a different place. I'd come into the house with it and Mr. Russell would ask, "Where did you get that newspaper?" "I bought it," I'd say . Pretty soon I felt it would be wiser to tuck the newspaper under my shirt so he wouldn't see it. I was getting fatter again. I started stealing food from the refrigerator but I got caught at it. "You're to eat only at meals," they said. "You're too fat. We'll give you enough to eat." But I wanted more to eat. On weekends, I'd steal money from Clara to buy candy and newspapers. The need for the daily newspapers became intense. And it was an agonizing difficulty. I could, at great expense, have bought the noon edition from the drug store after school, but I couldn't very well do that and take the paper to the Russells' house every day. Mr. Russell would have frowned on it and eventually asked me where I had gotten all that money to spend on daily papers. There were two editions every day, the noon edition which came to the stores and the home edition which was thrown on the lawns in late afternoon. There were never very many papers printed in either edition; the war limited the amount of paper that could be used. And there were constant paper drives to pick up old newspapers and use them over again. After school, very often there were no papers left at the drug store and I would wander along the street looking for the home edition lying on people's lawns. I couldn't ask my neighbors for their papers because by now I had stolen so many and I didn't feel it was safe to call attention to myself. After a snow it was especially excruciating. A paper could be lying on the ground only a few feet from me and I didn't dare pick it up because, if I did, I'd leave my footprints and then I would be caught for sure.

I worked on ways to steal more food from the icebox so the Russells wouldn't know. A big dollop of stew could be taken if the remaining food was heaped up again. Water could be put into the fruit juice to replace what I had drunk. I'll never forget the divinity fudge Mrs. Russell made and how I trimmed the edges of it. Pies could be pressed down and the filling would squeeze out and I could scoop it up. "You must eat only at meals," the Russells said, "You should lose weight, you're too fat." "You mustn't eat too much, we need the food for the soldiers." That always enraged me when they said that. What about me?

I started teaching the other kids at school how to steal. I'd go in to a place, a drug store, or a five and dime, and I'd case the joint. There was a vacant lot behind the drug store on the corner of my street. It had a kind of a hole in it like a foxhole, five or six feet across, three feet deep, and that was my headquarters. I'd meet with the kids there. I'd draw a diagram of the store, where the candy was, the toys, the comics, where the door was, the cash register, any mirrors. I knew that mirrors were something to be feared and I paid a lot of attention to them and to how to distract the clerk. I always sent the kids in in pairs. I'd draw the diagram and show it to the kids. I'd tell them then how they must move. It was a choreography of sorts. We'd practice there in the vacant lot. The safest way to steal was to buy something. One kid could buy something while the other was slyly snitching toys or crawling behind the counter to steal candy. We'd practice a few times, discuss the problems of that particular store and of the particular clerk. Different clerks had different habits, where they'd look and how they'd move. The main things to keep in mind were how to distract the clerk away from being able to see the kid who was actually doing the stealing, and then for that kid to do his job with enough discretion that he wouldn't call attention to himself. It was like doing magic tricks where the hand of the magician is faster than the eye of the audience mainly because the audience isn't looking in the right direction.

The distractor would discuss with the clerk the possibilities of a present for his mother's birthday or ask which comic would be the best to buy. He would ask the clerk how old he was or tell him a funny thing that happened at school, even talk about the weather. In a grocery store, the best ploy was to knock something over, like a stack of cans, and the clerk would come and help pick them up while the other kid got away with candy and gum.

The kid doing the actual stealing was never to put things in his pockets. The stolen goods were always to go inside the clothes, and into the underwear, sometimes into the shoes. Comics slipped in very nicely under the shirt and tucked halfway into the pants. We had marble bags for small stuff pinned to the inside of the pants. Two bullies always went along, as lookouts and messengers for the kids doing the job, and to see that what was stolen was all brought back to be divided up.

After the job was done, they'd all come to the vacant lot behind the drug store and I'd be waiting there in the hole. They'd pull out from their clothes everything they'd got and spread it in front of me. Then we'd divvy it up. I took a third and I took first choice. The two bullies took the next third and the two kids that did the job got what was left. Sometimes there were difficulties about this. One of the bullies, for instance, would want something I wanted. I usually conceded. I kept a good relationship with my bullies. Sometimes there were arguments, not serious ones, about the large percentage I got of the goods. But that was how it always worked. We were in a tradition of thievery that was being again and again shown to the children of America in comic books, movies and radio shows. The Brain, the central person, the organizer, was the most important member of any gang. Once, one of the bullies said he could shove me out, take my place and get the largest portion of the goods. I told him if he tried that, I'd just hire other bullies to beat him up and get my place back. He didn't mention it again.

It was a delightful scene there in my headquarters in the hole in the vacant lot behind the drug store on the corner. Often there were half a dozen kids gathered around me, hanging on every word I said. There were girls as well as boys. Sometimes there were so many of us we didn't all fit into the hole and one or two would have to lie on the ground above and listen to me with their heads at the edge of the hole.

I told them in detail how to steal, how to steal from their parents at home, too. If your mother has a big purse and drops her coins into the bottom, you can take up to half, leave the pennies and some others. Not so much from coin purses, they're looked at. Be very careful with a pile of money. The shape should be the same as it was after you've taken a few coins. It's the same with cake. If you want another piece of cake, keep the cake the same shape it was too. If there's one coin on a table, don't take it.

Mrs. Pruneface and her assistant Emil chained Dick Tracy to the floor and put two giant ice blocks, one on either side of him, a plank across the top of them with a spike driven through it pointed down at him, its sharp point aimed at his heart. The plank was weighted with an icebox. And then they turned on the heat. That was shown by wavery black lines. And they left him to his inevitable fate. It was the worst pickle Dick Tracy had ever been in. As the ice melted, the spike went ever closer and closer to pierce his heart. It was so much like little Kai in "The Snow Queen," but there was no Gerda to come and save Dick Tracy. He was chained to the floor and entirely on his own.

President Roosevelt was crippled with polio and a big push was made to develop a vaccine for polio. Jars were put by cash registers in all the stores with signs on them, the March of Dimes, and people would put some of their change in the jars. Many people every year were coming down with polio and they would die or be crippled for life and the March of Dimes was going to end that misery. There was a great feeling of goodness about the March of Dimes. It felt like patriotism. It was a war we were fighting that was like the other war and everyone's dimes were bullets to kill the enemy.

The drug store on the corner behind which I had my headquarters had such a jar. The store was run by a fat, bald old man with a black moustache that hung down. He wheezed all the time with asthma and mostly stood behind the prescription counter. He was easy to steal from. Being fat and asthmatic myself, I knew that even if he saw my gang members steal from him, he couldn't move fast enough to do anything about it. And the March of Dimes jar on his counter was nearly full of money. There was really a lot of money in that jar. And so one Saturday, we took it. It was no problem at all. I had taught my people well, the job went without a hitch, and soon we were counting it out in the hole in the vacant lot. There must have been nearly thirty dollars in that jar, maybe more, ten for me and a five for each of them, the two bullies and the two kids who did the job. It was incredible, the feeling of glorious victory we all felt. But there was something that troubled me about it. It was, for one thing, a stroke in favor of the wrong side in the war against polio. It felt a good deal like being a traitor. But what really terrified me was that now we had stolen a real amount of money and I couldn't possibly keep the gang content with candy, toys and comic books. From now on, we had to go for the money.

I was too successful. I had a place now in Society. I was the Enemy. I had now turned eleven years old and was the uncontested leader of a gang of thieves. It felt as though we had robbed the soldiers and didn't deserve their protection. I sat in that hole in the vacant lot surrounded by my exultant students in theft. My hands were sweating, my eyes rolled up to the sky to look for the planes with the swastika or the red circle of the Japs to fly over and destroy us. One of my bullies threw a coke bottle up into the air. When it fell, it broke, and a piece of it hit my leg. I was surprised and relieved to see that it hadn't torn my pants, then watched in horror as my blood started oozing through and dripping down onto the pile of money I had there beside me. I put my hand on the place and my hand became covered with my own blood. I rolled up my pants to see and there was a cut. I was astonished. I couldn't believe it. There was no tear on my pants. I didn't know how that could be. It was like years before when I had felt the soft silky edge of the razor blade on my finger and then it bled.

A new boy moved in next door to the Russells' house, a very nice boy, not the sort I had in my gang but a good boy like Ray had been. Very quickly he got in with the best kids at school, the all-American crowd that I could never join. One day I stole the newspaper from his yard, tucked it under my shirt as was my custom and went into the house. Mr. Russell stopped me in the living room as I was passing through. "What have you got under your shirt?" "A newspaper," I said. "Where did you get it?" "I bought it," I said. "No," he said, "you didn't. It's the home edition, isn't it." And of course it was.

There had been complaints all up and down the street. Someone had been stealing newspapers. Mr. Russell told everyone it was me. He told Clara and she was angry. He told the people next door and they told their son he mustn't play with me because I was a bad boy. It was a deep disgrace. Mr. Russell had no sympathy for me. No one had any sympathy for me.

Then, during the next week after the March of Dimes coup, I was sitting at my desk in school and suddenly a cascade of what I thought at first was gravel splattered all over me and my desk. It was vomit. The kid behind me had thrown up all over me. We were both sent to the lavatory to clean ourselves up as best we could. I was really disgusted and let him know it in no uncertain terms. I was mean and threatening. But then I looked at his face and saw how sick he was, very pale with a greenish tinge, and I said it was all right.

In the comic strip, the empty building had become very hot and the huge blocks of ice had shrunk considerably, bringing the spike within a foot of Dick Tracy's heart. Dick Tracy saw that the water was always trickling toward his right and realized that the floor was slanted. He was chained hand and foot to the floor and was very weak from many days of starvation. His only hope, however, was to do something and do it now. He started beating on the floor with his buttocks as hard as he could and for as long as it took, which was a very long time, but gradually the ice shifted, and at last when the spike descended, it missed his body.

He had survived. His friends, who had been looking for him everywhere, heard the thumping and found him there and released him. I don't remember if Mrs. Pruneface was brought to justice or not. I suppose she was.

Shortly after the episode with the vomit all over me, it was beginning to be spring. I can remember seeing the tiny leaves popping out on the trees. I went to the drug store on the corner, the fat wheezing old man's drug store and I bought a comic book having, naturally, tucked another comic book inside it. By this time, I didn't even think of that as stealing. I was on my way back from choir practice. It was Wednesday evening. The fat old man wasn't there. A teenage boy was behind the counter. As I headed down the street, I heard footsteps behind me and I knew they were his, that teenage boy's. I wanted to run away but it was hopeless to run. There was nothing I could do to escape. His footsteps were going faster than mine. My back crawled with fear. I expected him to grab the collar of my shirt, to hit me over the head, or to whip a bullwhip around my neck. The sky was still light and the tiny new leaves quivered against it in a breeze that chilled the sweat that was running down my chest and back. He caught up with me and around the side of my glasses I could see his outline, tall and gangly, his white jacket and white soda jerk hat gleaming in the twilight. I couldn't see his face. For a few steps he walked beside me in silence. Then he spoke. "Yesterday," he said, "the old man caught a kid stealing in there. He hit that kid in the middle of the face and broke his nose. There was blood all over the floor and I had to clean it up. So you give me that comic book you stole and don't ever steal anything from that drug store again." We were still walking. We never looked at each other. I didn't say anything. I handed him one of the two comic books and he turned and walked back to the store. My knees were shaking as I crossed the street and went in to the Russells' house. I went to my room and stared out the window at the little leaves still trembling against the purple sky. I swore then never to steal again.

I told my two bullies the next day on the playground that I was through stealing. They didn't believe me. One after another my gang members came up to me and I told them too. I didn't speak against stealing, I just said I was through. For several days it was like that, they kept coming up to me, asking when we would meet to pull the next job and again and again I said I was through stealing. Then they started calling me names. They called me "Dirty Thief." I thought that was very strange. Then they told the teacher I was a thief, they called me "Fatty" again. They punched me and kicked me on the playground and in the halls. My own bullies were the worst. Whenever either of them saw me, they'd punch me. I had to find new ways to walk home, down side streets and alleys. I was afraid some day the y'd trap me and give me a severe beating. I pretended to be sick a lot, staying home or asking to be excused early. I was afraid to go to school, afraid to walk or play outside, afraid to wait for a bus or go into a store. Mr. and Mrs. Russell didn't speak to me at all except to call me to supper. And at supper we mostly ate in silence.

18

Cub Scout Summer

THERE WAS ONE KID IN MY CLASS who befriended me after all of this. He said his father was a den master of the Cub Scouts and that I could join the Cub Scouts and, although the thought of Cub Scouts appalled me, I very much felt the need for protection, people around me, so that I could go out on the streets and not be trapped and beaten. So I joined the Cub Scouts.

Mr. and Mrs. Russell were very distant to me. To them, I was simply a boarder, age eleven. There was no relationship there, no sense of family. I had my room overlooking the yard and I had meals with them and I had the street which was now full of dangers.

I usually slept Saturday night at Clara's place on Washington Street, and Sunday was full with church and afternoon movies with Jon. Wednesday evenings I'd take the long trolley and bus ride with transfers to choir practice and get back to the Russells' house quite late.

Then there was the rest of the week. The Russells weren't interested in me nor was anyone else. The streets were quiet. There were hardly any cars because gas was rationed. Very often there was no sound on the street except the hiss of lawn sprinklers. The war effort was now in full force, people were working in factories around the clock. Lockheed Aircraft was a big one that many people worked for, filling metal shells with explosives to make bombs. And on the sides of the bombs they'd put pictures of Mickey Mouse or girls in bathing suits or Hitler being blown up, for good luck. Women were doing work they'd never done before, like welding. I saw it on the newsreels, women wearing helmets with glass over their faces, sparks flying up, making airplanes. The few cars on the streets were all carpooling to work, many of them at odd hours like early afternoon or the middle of the night. Before the war, Denver had ended its day by nine o'clock and a child could be noisy till then. Now, the day was never ended and by the same token, never began. People with night shifts slept all day. You could tell their houses by their lawns, neatly trimmed but with the grass under the sprinkler sodden, puddles in the sidewalk, and most of the lawn yellow and dry.

Then there were the stars in the windows, quite a few now. A gold star on a blue background meant that someone in the family had died in the war. A silver star on a blue background meant someone had been wounded and might be there in the house. Either way, one was expected to be quiet.

There was no way I could fit into Cub Scouts. Somehow I couldn't tie those knots. There was a system of points which led to advancement and I kept failing on those knots. The only thing I could accomplish was that I did manage to carve a wooden knife and got some points from that. But it was very badly carved. It was awful. I was profoundly disgusted with that knife. Some of the guys had uniforms and I asked Clara to buy me a uniform. She didn't want to pay for it. She had bought me that violin, she said, and I wasn't using it. Everyone knew that Scouts was training for becoming soldiers and I wanted a uniform. I liked to stand at attention and salute. I was a little soldier. I had become patriotic, I didn't want to be the Enemy.

There was one more thing I stole. I still feel very bad about it. I felt now that I had fought and been wounded and had won for the side of right. I felt I deserved honor. I had gone from being the Enemy to being a soldier for America. But no one seemed to know what I had been through, no one honored me for the sacrifice I had made.

There was a medal that President Roosevelt gave to soldiers who were great heroes and were wounded fighting heroically for our country. It was one of the greatest wartime honors anyone could have. It was the Purple Heart. Anyone who had the Purple Heart had something beyond price, they had one of the highest honors in the land. It showed you had really shed blood fighting for your country. I saw a Purple Heart pinned to the cloth lining of the ceiling of a car. The car was parked on the street and no one was around. I wanted the Purple Heart, wanted honor and glory, and I took that Purple Heart out of that car.

Immediately, I started feeling bad. What could I ever do with it? I couldn't show it to anyone. If anyone caught me with it, I couldn't make any excuse for having it. I was afraid to keep it, afraid to try to sneak it back to that car. It was the worst thing I had ever done. In my hands, it was the worst dishonor. After a day or two, I threw it away on the street. It troubled me quite a bit.

Before school was out, the Cub Scouts began playing baseball after school. I always played the outfield. I hated baseball. But it was better than being kicked and punched by my old gang. My turn at bat was always a shameful disgrace. Strike one, strike two, strike three, you're out. I couldn't imagine how anyone could hit a ball with a bat while the ball was flying by like that. One day, the den master said, "We've got to get Stanley to hit the ball." He brought the pitcher up closer and had him throw slow. Didn't work. Then the den master showed me how to hold and swing the bat. Nothing. The kids in the field sat down. The pitcher tried coming even closer. Even the basemen were now sitting down. At last I hit the ball and ran to first base but I hadn't hit it very hard nor, of course, did I run very fast and the ball was thrown to first base before I arrived and I was out. It was grotesque.

One real advantage to being in the Cub Scouts was the free tickets we sometimes got to Lakeside Amusement Park. There were two amusement parks in Denver, Lakeside and Elitch Gardens. They were very much the same in many ways, with merry-go-rounds and bumper cars and roller-coasters. Lakeside had a bigger, scarier roller-coaster and was more garish, with crazy mirrors and loud noises, the endless canned laughter coming out of the Fun House and the big painted woman's face rolling and jerking with the laughter sound above the entrance. Elitch Gardens was higher class. It had a theatre and there were picnic tables. It was more family-oriented. Pete took us there now and again. But Lakeside was rowdy and wild and bright. The soldiers would go there on leave to pick up girls. The girls were all wearing short dresses then to save on cloth. They were ostensibly being patriotic. They couldn't buy stockings because all the rayon and silk was being used for parachutes so they all painted their legs dark flesh color as if they had stockings on. It was a freakish, sexy atmosphere.

I went with the Cub Scouts to Lakeside for the Fourth of July. We kids weren't allowed to have any firecrackers because of the war but Lakeside had a wonderful big show that year, with simulated battle scenes and rockets shooting up into the sky and images of soldiers and sailors and of the flag of the United States, all of it reflected in the water of the lake, and all around us the bare painted legs of the young women and then all the servicemen flirting with them and picking them up.

One Sunday, Jon and I saw the movie *Wake Island* with William Bendix and Brian Donnely, in which American soldiers were trapped on the island without any hope of rescue or of winning, with the enemy attacking them for weeks. The audience hissed and booed at the enemy. The island was all sand with no vegetation or any shelter. The Americans fought valiantly, dying one at a time. I realized halfway through that they knew they were all going to die and they were simply holding out against all odds. I was shocked. Was this, then, what heroism was? Then they ran out of ammunition and the movie ended when the last one died. There was the stunned silence in the movie house when the lights came on. A lot of war movies were coming out now. Haunting images. You would see someone in a cockpit, then a little row of black dots the length of the airplane, a little stream of black from the man's mouth. Then the smoke would billow from the airplane as it fell out of the sky and into the sea.

Then I started going a lot to the lake at Elitch Gardens. I would have preferred to go to Lakeside but it was far away and Elitch Gardens was close. I'd throw stones and sticks into the water, try to sink things in the water. I began imagining the war in my mind, walked the streets saying both sides of conversations aloud, making the sounds of war. There was one noise between a bark and a shot that I practiced a lot, there were machine-gun noises, and there was one I did that began with a whistle. I was glad I'd learned to whistle in McComb. There were noises I could make with a certain amount of spit in my mouth and a certain looseness of jowls. I practiced these sounds, walking along the streets, interspersed with conversation. "Japs on my tail!" "I'm hit!" "Mayday! Mayday!" "Help me! Help me! Oh, my God!" Passersby looked at me askance. I ostensibly didn't want to make a scene. I'd see someone coming on my side of the street and I'd cross over to the other side so that I could go on with my war uninterrupted. The noises I made weren't very loud. I had been told very strictly not to be noisy, to play quietly, as all the kids had been told across the whole nation, because of people sleeping who worked the night shift in war factories and because of the sick and the wounded who were there in the houses.

I wanted to be an American soldier. I wanted to shoot and kill people. I wanted to fly in airplanes and swoop and roar. Every cereal box had a model airplane in it of balsa wood. They were easy to build and

I built them and played with them in my room, making engine noises and shooting noises and dying noises and victorious noises.

Mr. and Mrs. Russell kept their radio on much of the time, everyone did, to hear the news of the war. One story we heard one morning at breakfast, an American Red Cross ship, clearly marked, had been bombed and had sunk. The wounded, hundreds of them, were in life jackets floating together in the sea all night. Sharks came and fed on them and those in the middle of the mass of wounded soldiers heard the screams of those on the outside in the night, all night long. In the morning, when they were rescued, there were only a few men left out of several hundred. I looked at Mr. Russell's face when we heard about it. He looked like he could kill. Everyone was enraged about it because the ship had been clearly marked with a big red cross.

I did a lot of reading that summer. There were a lot of war magazines about, mostly pictures of tanks and airplanes and soldiers fighting and explosions. I'd read the text too. I wanted to know as much as I could. I also got very involved in the Big Little Books, small but very thick books with a whole long story compiled from the comics from several years back, with all the pictures and dialog on the right hand page and a written text on the left. There were Flash Gordon in his starships; my old friend, the Green Hornet; and Tarzan — I had gone to Tarzan movies with Ray. There was *Terry and the Pirates,* about an American who got a gang of Chinese pirates to help him fight the Japanese in the war. There were the stupid ones too, *Donald Duck* and *Mickey Mouse* and *Nancy*. I didn't read those.

Buying food was now a complicated business. It took both money and points, points being stamps out of a ration book that everyone got once a month. Different kinds of food took different amounts of points and meat took the most. Once I was going to pick up some groceries for the Russells and there was a little kid there, and he pointed to the meat at the meat counter and said, "Points." "That's right, Honey," said his mother. I found that very interesting. I could remember when meat was meat, something to eat, but this kid was younger than I and only knew it as points, too many points to be able to buy it and take it home to eat. If you ate meat for every meal, you wouldn't have enough points to survive, you'd starve before the end of the month.

And I was fat, I couldn't hide that from anyone. It was unpatriotic to be fat. The Russells, getting me, got my ration book too, as well as extra money, to buy more food. But I ate it, I ate what was mine. They gave me nothing and I gave them nothing in return. But it was disturbing to be fat. When the kids called me "Fatty," they were calling me "unpatriotic" too. I didn't feel wrong about eating what was mine but I did feel guilty that, in the same act, I was being unpatriotic.

I feared the war. Always in the news were stories of women and children being bombed, refugees being strafed. I was always looking up into the sky to see if there were airplanes that were going to bomb Denver. I knew what to look for, the red circle for the Japs or the black swastika for the Germans. I had seen them in the newsreels, and I had seen pictures of children dead in the rubble and ruins of their towns. I had seen smoke and flames in city streets in those newsreels and I wondered when the war would come to Denver. No one would tell me if it would come or not. No one told me it was all happening very far away. I only saw the streets very quiet as though waiting for the inevitable, the sprinklers hissing on the lawns, and more and more stars in the windows.

The whole boys choir was very excited because we were all to go to a two-day outing in the mountains. I, of course, was dreading it. The drive up was okay, it was jolly, several kids in the car. They were all so excited that they were warm and witty. But when we got there, there it all was, frame houses, the army cots with not enough blankets, the bad food, the campfire and the campfire songs. I felt obliged to pretend enthusiasm. None of us slept well because of the cold. I wandered aimlessly through scattered trees, within sight of the camp in the meadow, worrying that perhaps no one would save the Sunday funnies for me.

And when I got back, I found that it was so. That Sunday's comic strips were gone and I had no way to get them. How could I make these people realize the importance of those comic strips to me? I'd tell them again and again but no one cared enough about me to even save the funnies.

Mr. Russell paid me a little money for helping with the lawn. Also, a neighbor lady paid me for helping with her lawn. The lawnmower was too hard for me to push but I could weed and trim and do other little things. The neighbor lady made the best lemonade I've ever tasted and always gave me a glass of it after I'd finished work on her yard.

I wanted more comic strips, more, there were never enough, even if I got all the newspapers I needed. I went back to making comics on a Big Chief tablet. This time, I made whole comic books and they were all war comics. I called my comic book *WAR*, drew a separate picture on the cover and folded it over so it was a book. I did it like the others, frames with people talking in balloons, action, a story in pictures. I worked very hard on it this time and made several copies of each one. It was long and laborious work and when I was done, I'd peddle them from door to door.

It was hard to be sure which doors I could knock on. I didn't want to wake up the factory workers who had to sleep during the day. Some of those people had a sign on their doors. Others I could recognize by the puddles under the sprinklers and the rest of the lawn dry. But at some places there was no way to tell and I'd wake them up. Some people seemed to be charmed and bought my comic books and that delighted me to no end.

Then as I was peddling my newest issue, I went down a side street and knocked on a door. "Would you like to buy a copy of my *WAR* comic?" I asked. "We've had enough of war here," the lady said, and slammed the door in my face. It was then that I saw the gold star in the window. She had loved her son and he had died in the war. I felt very guilty. I felt like I had killed him. I had so much wanted to kill those kids who were loved. "It wasn't my fault," I said to myself over and over. There was a puddle at the end of the alley with oil on top making a multiple tangle of rainbows. I stood looking at the rainbows for a long time, poking them occasionally with a stick to make them move. "It wasn't my fault," I said, but I knew I should have seen the star and kept away. The business of peddling my comics was suddenly repulsive to me and I decided to give up making them.

I found a caterpillar and I put it in a matchbox. I stuck a match into the box like a fuse and lit it. Then I watched the caterpillar writhe in agony and struggle to get out. I watched it die. I was evil.

Another thing the Cub Scouts did besides baseball was playing tag. They never wanted to tag me because I ran the slowest of all of them and if I was "It," the game was destroyed. But one kid was chasing me and I fell over a lawn sprinkler and my ankle really hurt. I couldn't get up. They carried me home with the crossed-hands technique. Mr. Russell put my foot in ice water and said it'd be all right in the morning. But in the morning, it was hugely swollen. He said I should stay in bed for a day or two. Somehow, I got to the phone and called Clara and she came and took me to Dr. Best. Some ligaments were torn. He wrapped it in elastic bandages and put me on a crutch.

My opportunity had arrived. The imminent beginning of school horrified me. Cub Scouts was appalling. My reputation in the neighborhood had me wandering alone, crossing streets to avoid people so I could go on making weird noises. I couldn't even face making my comics anymore. I told Clara how little the Russells took care of me. I didn't have to exaggerate. She set out to look for another place for me right away.

19

Interlude

CLARA FOUND A WOMAN for me to live with in South Denver, I don't remember her name. Her husband was in the war. She was young but her shoulders were stooped. She had brown hair which she always wore in a bun. She was very thin and she wore print dresses that looked faded and hung on her thin frame as though she were a stick. She wore slippers on her feet that shushed when she walked. She had a baby crawling about that her husband had never seen. The woman always looked sad. She seemed to do everything by rote. She played with the baby by rote, and when someone came to the door she would smile by rote. The baby was very placid and quiet. It was a ghostly atmosphere, ghostly. It was like living in a house with a star in the window.

It was a tiny house and the lawn sloped steeply down with cement steps to the sidewalk. There was the living room and the woman's bedroom, a tiny kitchen, and the bedroom in back, which had been a back porch but had been enclosed and made into the baby's room. It had yellow walls and linoleum on the floor printed with Porky Pig and Donald Duck. When the woman decided to take me in, she moved the baby into her own bedroom and I got the baby's room in the back.

The woman would bring the baby into my room to play. The baby had bright toys and blocks. I would build up the blocks and the baby would knock them down. That was the entertainment provided for me and my usefulness in the house combined. I was to play with the baby. And I was so relieved to be out of north Denver that at first I accepted it with gratitude.

I enrolled in a school on Evans Street where nobody knew me. I determined to present them with a new image of me. I wanted to be a good boy, to blend in quietly, and I was so weary from months of drama and nerves that nobody paid much attention to me.

I'd always had a lot of asthma, always been restricted by it, couldn't do things that little boys were supposed to do, like run and play and climb trees because if I did, the wheezing would come over me and my brain would fog up. Breath would become the one thing I'd want and it would be denied me. It was so basic, so common, so much a law of nature that I couldn't understand why other children were so interested in physical activity, felt that they only did it to reject me. I don't remember ever yearning to do those active things. I only remember feeling repulsed by them, haunted and horrified at the constant and inescapable taunting, of the great gap between what children were supposed to do and what I was able to do.

But now I was having asthma sitting quietly and reading or listening to the radio or going to sleep at night. So one Saturday Clara took me to the Republic Building for a few tests. They sat me down in the office and drew blood from my arm. I immediately passed out. But when I woke up, Clara took me to a movie as a reward.

The next Saturday, I took the bus to the real estate company where Clara worked. Everyone greeted me pleasantly and I went to Clara's desk feeling welcome. She showed me around the office then took me to the Republic Building where I was told to take my shirt off and then the people spent a lot of time scratching and scratching on my back, putting drops of stuff on the scratches and then looking at them. It was irritating. When we left, Clara said to me that I was allergic to absolutely everything, even my own hair and skin. She was exasperated and I was ashamed. I wondered if I mightn't be meant for some other planet.

But then she took me to the Blue Parrot, a restaurant we had gone to long ago several times with Lou when we were all together and would come to Denver for summers. It was a really nice place and it had a real blue parrot in it. That parrot had been there years ago and it was there still, the same parrot. Everyone always commented about how that restaurant was recommended by Duncan Hines. I had, as I had always had before, a plate of their wonderful cinnamon rolls, tiny things filled with butter and raisins. I had always liked cinnamon rolls since I was a baby and my grandmother had made them, but hers were bigger and more bready with not near so much butter in them nor so many raisins. These, at the Blue Parrot, were the ultimate in cinnamon rolls.

We went several times to the Republic Building and each time it was like that, the welcome at the real estate company, something awful at the doctors, then cinnamon rolls at the Blue Parrot. And afterward, a movie. Then Clara wanted Dr. Best to check me over too and I had to go to his office which was much more difficult to get to, with bus transfers and long waits on street corners and no Blue Parrot, no movie nearby to go to. But over the years, I'd been to his office often. He had a deep voice and a blank, knowing face behind thick glasses like Lou's glasses. Like mine. The fact that he had saved Clara's life gave him an all-pervading aura of solemn, almost religious authority.

Dr. Best put me on a diet. There were certain foods I could eat and others I couldn't. And I was supposed to lose weight. He put me on thyroid medicine too, to help me lose weight. Just as I had come to look forward to the cinnamon rolls at the Blue Parrot, they were taken away from me. The woman I lived with groused about the diet. It made things difficult for her, those things I must not eat and things I must eat too. Clara gave her more money for her trouble.

For a couple of weeks, I stuck with the diet pretty well, I thought. At least I was hungry all the time and grumpy and sour about it. That year, the kids at school had discovered that they could buy cinnamon oil and dip toothpicks into it and suck on the toothpicks in class. Well, it was a far cry from the cinnamon rolls at the Blue Parrot but I invested in a bottle of cinnamon oil and some toothpicks. It didn't seem like it would add to my weight to do that. It very quickly became an all-pervasive fad in the school and the teachers went to the drugstore by the school and asked them not to sell cinnamon oil to the children anymore. There were, of course, other drug stores and I and many of the other kids went on buying the oil. But then we could only suck on it during recess and at home, we had to be secretive and hide the little bottles, and soon the fad was over.

After two weeks on the diet and the thyroid medicine, I went back to Dr. Best and found that I had gained weight. He accused me of not sticking with my diet but to the best of my knowledge I had, except for the cinnamon oil, of course. Dr. Best took me off the thyroid medicine then and told me to do better on my diet. I was horrified. He didn't believe me. He had failed besides. He wasn't God Almighty after all. And the thyroid medicine had been a mistake too.

From then on, I went back to my old ways of eating, stuffing myself as full as I could, buying candy, asking for seconds, and raiding the icebox. The woman who was feeding me kept giving me tiny portions and refusing me seconds. "You're not supposed to eat a lot," she kept saying. I knew she was just trying to save money. She kept the leftovers in little containers in the icebox and it was very difficult to get anything from there without being caught.

Once, a friend of hers came to visit and they split an avocado.

She gave a tiny sliver to her baby. I asked for my piece too but she said, "Avocados are not permitted." But I knew they were permitted. I watched her and her friend and the baby eat their avocado and I began to hate her.

My eyesight was getting worse and Clara took me on a Saturday to the Republic Building again, although to a different office, where they put drops in my eyes and told me to look at a chart. The drops made my eyes oversensitive to the light and so I was told to go straight home, wearing dark glasses, and then stay inside. It was a terrible, woeful day.

I hadn't been in the house very long when I heard a woman screaming. I looked out the window and I saw a huge billow of smoke with flames underneath, maybe a mile away. People were running down the streets toward it. Someone shouted, "I heard the crash!" But I had been told to stay indoors so I didn't go. After a while, people were running back with the news. An airplane had crashed in a nearby field. It was a bomber, an American bomber full of American GIs. It had crashed and burned and everyone had been killed. I kept indoors, looked and listened out the window. I could see the smoke billowing up from the field and occasionally flames would lick up above the houses. And people would walk back from it and talk about it in the street.

The next morning, Sunday, I was allowed to walk to the crash site after church. Most of the field was black where the fire had burned the weeds and grass. Some of the weeds still stood but they were black and they crunched when my foot touched them. An area of the field was roped off and within the roped-off area were big hunks of blackened wreckage and there were trucks and workmen and they were dismantling the wreckage and hauling it away. But outside the rope there were little pieces of bent, blackened airplane and other little things from the crash and there were kids and grownups too hunting through the weeds with great excitement for something, anything, a souvenir. This was repugnant to me. Someone found a piece of thick glass and I was arguing with him, "How do you know," I asked him, "that it's from the crash?" Someone else found a smashed watch and was very excited about it. This really offended me. Some serviceman had died and this kid was thrilled to snatch up his watch. I went about among the kids who were searching and finding things and I argued and moralized with them. This crash was a tragedy, I told them, and people shouldn't be stealing from a tragedy. I was very self-righteous and I went home empty-handed. But it was the big thing going on for weeks. After a while, the ropes were removed and everyone went back and searched there for stuff, but after that one time I kept away.

One really nice thing about this woman I was living with was that she took the newspaper every day. For once, Dick Tracy came to me without any trouble, without my having to scheme and lie and steal. This gave a patina of much-needed relaxation to this period of my life.

Sometimes she would get letters from her husband. These were strange to me because she'd open the envelope and the letter would be on thin, thin paper like tissue, and covered with tiny writing. Sometimes she would read bits of a letter aloud to me. At such times I did feel sorry for her. It seemed he was constantly in terrible danger and she was worried sick about it. But I never stopped hating her because she had lied to me about the avocado.

Ever since I got to this woman's house, there was trouble and confusion about my ration book because it was missing. Everyone in the country got a ration book every six months and that ration book was valuable because you couldn't buy groceries without it. When I was at the Russell's house, sometimes they would send me to get groceries and then I would have to take the ration book with me to the store, but then when I'd get back with the groceries, I'd give it back to them and they'd take care of it.

So when I first moved to this woman's house and had no ration book, it was a pretty terrible thing. Clara had to give the woman some of her own ration points and go without meat, assuring the woman that it would be all straightened out soon. The Russells had told her they had given me my ration book when I had left, but they hadn't and I told her so. "Are you sure?" she asked me, over and over. I found this very irritating.

Since rationing was a strictly federal matter, it was finally the FBI that called on the Russells and, according to the story Clara told us, Mr. Russell was talking with the FBI men as Mrs. Russell was trying to burn what was left of my ration book in the incinerator in the backyard. I was terribly pleased that the Russells were proved to be villains. And I got a full ration book with a six-months supply of points. So for the next few months, I could really eat.

The pallid woman I lived with, however, had had enough adventure. She said it was too much for her to take care of me and I would have to leave. She gave us a couple of weeks to find a place, and on a Sunday afternoon Clara took me to visit a family that lived not very far away from 930 Washington. Clara was happy about this because they lived within the same school district and she wouldn't have to go to the trouble of changing my school. But I was suspicious of them, as I was of everyone now. They had two kids of their own, adopted kids, as they proudly and pleasantly told us, kids older than I. Everyone was very pleasant about it except me, and I couldn't believe all the pleasantness. At a lull in the conversation, the woman said, "Let me show you his room," and she opened the door to the front bedroom, the master bedroom, with the windows on two sides, cheerful light tan paper on the walls, pretty curtains, a closet, a dresser, room for all my stuff without the usual suitcase under the bed. "He'll have to keep it clean and make his own bed," she said, "but it'll be totally private, his very own room." I looked at it. It was heaven. "Totally private," I thought, "No more baby crawling around on the Porky Pig-Donald Duck linoleum of the place where I now was, but a dark tan rug of my very own." I was starting to cheer up. “He can bring whatever he wants,” she said, and I thought of all my toys that had been stored in the cage in the basement of 930 Washington for over two years. “I could bring them all here to this room,” I thought. I got quite excited. Clara and I went and got all my stuff from the woman’s house and I moved into that bright and lovely room that very evening. I never saw that woman or her baby again.

20

The Hultmans

THE HULTMANS WERE SWEDISH. Mr. Hultman was tall and bony with a long bony face and glasses and he smoked a pipe. He worked in an auto repair shop and his specialty was body and fender work. Mrs. Hultman was rosy and plump with a round face and a bustling, cheerful manner. She always seemed to be happy and straightforward. The two adopted children were Steve, who was several years older than I was and in high school, and Sally, who was two years ahead of me in school.

It didn't take long for me to see that the Hultmans were the best thing that had happened to me for a long time, maybe ever. They were a truly happy family. They had a great sense of working together, not only on chores but on problems. At breakfast and lunch, we ate in a little nook in the kitchen, Mr. and Mrs. Hultman on one side, Sally and I on the other, and Steve on a chair at the end. And everything was discussed openly among us in this nook. The first thing we really talked about was the fact that Steve and Sally resented having to sleep in the basement now that I was there. Mr. and Mrs. Hultman had given me their own bedroom, the best in the house, had moved themselves into Steve and Sally's room in the back of the house, and had moved Steve and Sally into the basement where they slept on either side of the furnace. And so in the breakfast nook one morning, right in front of me, they asked their parents why? What was the justice of this arrangement? "For one thing," Mrs. Hultman said, Stanley is our guest, and guests should always be given the best of everything. For another," she said, "you two are getting big enough now that you each need more space and more distance from each other." The problem was discussed openly from every angle to avoid any undercurrent of resentment.

"Why does Stanley always get the biggest piece of cake?" It was true, I always did get the biggest piece, which amazed and delighted me no end. "We want to be sure that Stanley feels welcome," she said. But I began to see glimmers of the importance of justice and equality in this household. And one day, with some regret and courage, I said, "I think it's time Steve gets the biggest piece," and I gave it to him and took the smaller piece that was meant for him. And then everyone was pleased and they beamed at me and at each other across the table because now I understood something that was basic to their family.

It was amazing. I could eat whatever and however much I wanted. They never reminded me of those foods I wasn't supposed to eat. If I had wanted to stick to my diet, I would have had to do it myself somehow, and I chose not to. Food was there on the table, and I could eat all I wanted of anything I wanted and I did so, I ate it, lots of it, with a hearty appetite.

They were such good people, I could hardly believe my luck in falling into their household. The straightforward openness of their style made everything possible, made it possible for me to do simply what I wanted to do without the resentment and conniving I was accustomed to. It took a good deal of adjusting on my part. Once the complaints, especially the complaint about my having the best bedroom, were aired, discussed and understood, there was such a feeling of acceptance and warmth in the house as I had never before encountered or even imagined.

Mr. Hultman was the bottom line. He didn't talk very much. He would sit, traditionally, in the big chair in the living room after dinner, reading the newspaper, smoking his pipe, his glasses slipped down a bit on his nose, his face knobby, his hair sticking up in back, shoulders broad and muscular, as Mrs. Hultman bustled cheerily about and Steve and Sally and I variously played or did homework. If there was any discussion it was Mrs. Hultman and us kids that did the talking, but when Mr. Hultman did speak, it was final. He had heard everything that needed to be heard, had thought about it with justice and kindness, and had decided. And that was that. And his thoughtful gentleness was such that he seemed to always make the right decisions.

Steve and Sally were nice kids. Like Ray had been. They were fine, decent kids, both considerably older than I. All this was discussed in the meetings too. Sally was just going through the universal private chaos of puberty, so she was distant, aloof from the rest of the family in a way, didn't want to do much, didn't want to play. But she was not unkind. She was pleasant. Steve was a little more available to me even though he was so much older. He accepted me as I was.

These people were the backbone of America, quietly, tolerantly religious, cheerfully patriotic, unambitious, no real aspirations, no fanaticism, no burning needs. They were civilized. They knew how to live and they lived that way, honest, upright, happy and comfortable.

Obviously, it was perfectly safe for me to bring all my stuff here, my toys, my magic tricks, my scrapbooks, my radio, my books. I collected them all and arranged them in my room. And I went to work on them, delighting in them each in turn. There were many disturbing gaps in my Dick Tracy scrapbook but I straightened it out as best I could. Since I wasn't stealing I had very little money, but I got all the food I needed from Mrs. Hultman's plump and smiling largesse.

Except by this time I had become emotionally dependent on having my own special treats that I would carry around in my pockets. For years now, my pockets had always bulged with one thing and another — candy, medicine, toys. And although Mrs. Hultman gave me all I needed to eat and more, I needed that extra treat, something I got for myself.

This was hard now to achieve because, as far as I can remember, I never stole while I was at the Hultman's and so I had very little money and didn't steal even a comic book or a candy bar from a store. But there was a little store across the street at the end of the block. It was positioned like the drug store near the Russells' house, the culminating target of my crime career. This store, though, was a tiny grocery store, really a house with the front room made into a store, with shelves piled high with things people might need in a hurry, things like sugar, dog food, crackers, and canned beans stacked up all the way to the ceiling, and a ladder there so that those things too high to reach could be gotten down. An old couple ran it, a nice old couple who were friendly and seemed to like kids, who could climb the ladder with amazing agility to fetch down something that someone would need, would exchange a few pleasantries and a smile with every customer. It was a very comfortable store to have nearby. By the door was a counter with an elaborately decorative cash register and a glass case with a few sundry items, in the middle of which was always the great wonder of this store, a sheet of chocolate in squares, with thin separations between them, like a sheet of stamps and its perforations. It was an exquisitely fascinating thing, that chocolate, each square several scrumptious bites of the best chocolate imaginable in the world. A nickel a square, it was, and whenever I had money after school I'd go there and buy one, they'd break it off and wrap it in tissue, and I'd unwrap it part way, eat half of it walking slowly home, wrap the other half up carefully and put it beside my bed where, since I kept my room always perfectly tidy, no one, not even

Mrs. Hultman, ever went in there but me.

Every evening I went to my room before nine o'clock, put my homework and my other things tidily in their proper places on my bureau, draped my clothes on the chair so they wouldn't wrinkle, placed my shoes under the chair, and draped my socks across them, laid my truss on top of the clothes so I wouldn't forget it, and last of all put my glasses beside the radio as I turned it on in time for *I Love a Mystery*. I listened every night in rapture to the theme song, which was a small section of Rachmaninoff's *Isle of the Dead*. Then I would unwrap the rest of my piece of chocolate and eat it as the day's mystery unfolded, Jack and Reggie struggling bravely down dark tunnels or across treacherous swamps. Many of the other parts were played with the most amazing versatility by Mercedes McCambridge, who was legend for her ability to change her voice and her vocal personality so well that sometimes she would play several roles at once. I would strain my sensibilities to listen and know if it was she playing this role or that.

At quarter after nine the program was over, the chocolate eaten, its tissue crumpled in the wastebasket beside my bed. Then I would put my glasses back on and read awhile. I had some books of my own and some from the library and I liked to be reading several at once so that I could read to fit my mood. I kept them all together in a stack beside the radio. There were Tarzan books and ghost and horror books, Poe, de Maupassant, Jekyll and Hyde, and the animal books of Terhune and London.

Dick Tracy's villain now was a gangster-pianist called 88 Keys. Steve and Sally and I were all reading Dick Tracy avidly and talking about it. 88 Keys had a marvellous death that thrilled us all. He kidnapped a girl and was driving with her down a country road when his car hit a pig and the picture showed a spiral of lines where the car spun, and the X's on the pig's face to show he was dead. When the cops arrived, there was the pig, the car, the girl — hurt but not killed — an old tool shed on the hillside, a few trees, but 88 Keys nowhere in sight. Everyone but Dick Tracy said he must have got away, but Dick Tracy looked at the tool shed. Several frames showed the tool shed from different angles. Dick Tracy looked at it, talked at it, then took his machine gun and shot a big X on the door of the tool shed. Then the body of 88 Keys was dragged out of the shed, and Dick Tracy said, "I told him to come out and he wouldn't do it. So I mowed him down." Something like that. The next villain was called Flattop.

Dick Tracy was the epitome but there were other comics I liked too, with other kinds of characters. There were B. O. Plenty and Gravel Gertie and Vitamin Flintheart. I didn't like parody. The characters had to believe in themselves or I couldn't see any use in reading about them. I didn't like things to be unbelievably bizarre. It was okay if they were deformed or freakish. I never had trouble with Rabelais later on or with Jonathan Swift. They believed. I liked Abbott and Costello, Charlie Chaplin, Buster Keaton, Frankenstein. They all believed. But the movie, *Abbott and Costello Meet Frankenstein* was just awful. It was parody. Nobody believed anything. It destroyed them all for me. And Hollywood at this time got into doing that, sicking monsters on each other. One was *Frankenstein Meets the Wolf Man,* and another had Dracula, Frankenstein and Wolf Man all together. I hoped to God they'd keep the Mummy out of it because the Mummy to me was a very serious thing. My best comic that I made, *Demono,* was modeled after the Mummy and I couldn't stand the thought that he might be desecrated in this way, and as far as I recall, they didn't do so. I had so little money at that time that often I couldn't afford to buy the chocolate piece. I could have made comic strips and sold them, as I did before, but I didn't want to do anything like what I had done in north Denver, even if it was a harmless thing. Wanting, though, to charm Steve and Sally, I made some for them. Sally wasn't interested. Steve liked my comic strips though. He particularly liked Sad Sack, the scrawny little soldier who always did things wrong. Sad Sack was okay, I could make *Sad Sack* comic strips whenever I wanted to please Steve. Though it was a far cry from *Demono*. But I wasn't in the mood anyway to make *Demono* strips.

With Steve so much older and Sally aloof, I still had no special friend in the family. I was still left to my own devices. But the warmth, kindness and fairness, the discussions of problems, the loving, thoughtful rosiness of Mrs. Hultman, the solid stable security of Mr. Hultman, and the cheerful acceptance from Steve and Sally made it impossible for me to be lonely or in any way discontented. It gave me the security to create in my own private room, where no one else ever went, a real living world of my own, to develop in myself those things that I respected and was fascinated by.

Granted, I had by now become a monster of neuroses and weaknesses, a shambles of misdirected hungers. But there were things I had encountered that fascinated me, something in Dick Tracy of character and feeling, something in the radio shows of form and rhythm, something in church of vast forces beyond the everyday and of some mysterious unity of the human spirit, something in my own singing and my abilities to do things that others couldn't do or never thought of which gave me some self-respect. And here, in the care and comfort of this family of good people, in the privacy of my room, I was able to bring together these things, think about them and develop them in an environment where I didn't have to be defensive.

The Hultmans belonged to a Swedish church. Happily, they had a strong belief in religious tolerance because singing at Saint John's was terribly important to me. But sometimes they would go to meetings during the week and I would go along with them. And there in the basement of the church they would gather with the other Swedish people and, around tables, would eat tiny Swedish pancakes and talk in Swedish with each other. The pancakes were wonderful, the atmosphere dark and earthen. Here, in the dimly lit basement, Mr. and Mrs. Hultman again became foreigners, from some place I didn't know and couldn't relate to. I would sit shoveling down those very tasty pancakes and looking around me, big-eyed, at these alien people eating, chattering incomprehensibly with each other. It seemed spooky to me. The closest description I can come to it would be Van Gogh's picture of the potato eaters. It was such a contrast to their home which was exceptionally bright and cheery.

Sometimes there would be meetings at the Hultman's house and then we'd eat in the dining room with special plates and silverware. Some of those church people would come, there would be Swedish meals, the pancakes again perhaps — such pancakes they were — with exotic sauces and sprinkles. At the house, they would speak English. It was brightly lit there in the dining room. The food was delicious, the people happy to be together. It was very jolly. It was ecstatic.

Sometime around Christmas, their church had a big money drive for some good purpose and Sally said she'd go from door to door to solicit money. It was a great chance for me to get to know her so I went with her. Sometimes Steve went along too but we were the most successful when it was just Sally and me. We'd go up to the door, Sally would ring the doorbell, they'd open and she'd begin, giving the basic spiel. Then I'd chime in with a great show of enthusiasm, and between the two of us we were well-nigh irresistible. We offered them something in return, a magazine subscription or a certificate, and most of all, an opportunity to be easily virtuous, to contribute, no matter how little, to a good cause. It was a whole lot of fun. We'd trudge down cold, dark streets together from one door to the next. I knew that Sally was pleased to have me along, that she wouldn't even in those safe days, want to walk dark streets alone, and that she was delighted and relieved also at my ability to talk to strangers. We were both amazed at our success as her pocket filled with money. When we'd get home, Mr. and

Mrs. Hultman were awed at the amount of money we brought.

It was a joyous and important shock to me to see that I could actually be of service to the community, that I, with my own abilities, could contribute to a virtuous cause. The March of Dimes jar was only a few months in the past.

At school, I was getting such good grades, they decided to skip me half a year. I really was good at most everything, especially reading. I could read beautifully aloud, with lots of expression, and I could comprehend what I was reading as well as the teacher. In all the English classes, I was terrific. I had good work habits too and always finished all my homework on time. Even in north Denver, I did that, even in Harmony Hall. Because of my good reading comprehension and good work habits, I was doing very well in history too, but being skipped left gaps in the history so that I didn't know certain things. In geography, I had a problem too because I had been skipped over learning about longitude and latitude. 'When they talked about it I couldn't understand.

But it was in math where the big problem was. I had been holding my own in math before I was skipped. It was hard work and I didn't like it but I was keeping up. Then when I was skipped, instead of getting problems like six divided by three it was 73.62 divided by four and I just went blank. I couldn't do anything. Thank heavens I had memorized the multiplication tables before the big jump. But this divided-by sign and all these decimals and fractions, just dumped on me like that, were too much. Something snapped in my head. There was no way anyone seemed able to teach it to me. No matter what they'd say or how much they'd explain, I was still lost in a fog of incomprehension about it. It crippled me forever about math. Ever since then, I've gone foggy in the head at the sight of decimals or fractions.

I always worked hard at my school work. It was something I could do. I took a long time doing homework, listened carefully to the teacher, got all the papers in on time, did special reports and projects, carried my books — as I had always done — everywhere I went. Keeping up with the schoolwork wasn't an easy thing for me. I didn't have the lazy brilliance of a few of the students who could get straight A's seemingly without effort. It was work, constant and thoughtful, and it took concentration. Skipping half a grade put me in an awful situation. If that had happened without the happy home life of the Hultmans around me, I think it would have destroyed me. But there was much going on to please and distract me.

As part of the war effort, the city devised a paper drive among the schools. There was a special assembly in our school with a movie and speeches. Everyone across the whole country wanted to help however they could with the war effort. It was a real joy to be able to do something that the nation asked us to do.

In groups of two to four, we would go to all the houses and ask for old newspapers. Many people saved their old newspapers in their basements. We were to measure these stacks of newspapers with a ruler and tie them into bundles. Someone would have to sit on each stack so that it could be tied tight — under the sitter's butt. Then there would be a competition among the schools, and whichever school brought in the most papers would get honored, and the results would be in all the papers.

Sally and Steve and I got into that paper drive in a big way. It was the delight of our weekends. We had a little red wagon that we'd take with us, and we'd knock on doors and ask for old newspapers, then we'd go into the basements and stack and measure and tie the papers up in strings and giggle together, then load what we got onto the little red wagon and trundle it home. Then we'd go out to the next house and do it all over again.

Some of the houses were strange, some of the people were weird, and some of the basements we went into were creepy. We never knew what we might find. One thing, of course, that I was eager to find was those Dick Tracy comics that I'd missed in spite of all my efforts, months ago in north Denver, and so I'd slow down the work looking for them and sometimes Sally and Steve would get crabby with me about that. Sometimes they'd find something they knew I wanted and they'd give it to me. Or we'd all stop and look at war pictures and read the articles about the war and I'd cut them out and fold them into my pockets for my scrapbooks.

One time I saw Steve take a screwdriver that was on the floor of one of the basements and put it in his pocket. I was shocked. "You really shouldn't do that," I said. "Oh," he said breezily, "they'll never miss it." This was strange to me, I was the thief, and I had given it up. Why did he steal? He had a home full of security and love; he was big and strong and well-liked at school. He just picked the screwdriver up. And nothing would happen from it. It was so casual. It was strange. It disturbed me, disturbed my image of him and of me too. There had been one time when both Steve and I went with Sally on her money drive for the church and we were getting a lot of money that day and Steve had said, "I think we deserve a chocolate soda," and we had taken some of that money that was for the church and we had spent it together on chocolate sodas, giggling, but feeling a little bad. Steve, being the oldest, was the leader, unquestionable. And there was no way I would say "No" to a chocolate soda.

During the paper drive, collection days were wonderful at school. There was no time for class on those mornings. We'd haul our papers to the school, all neatly bundled, and then have to go back home for more. Sometimes Mr. Hultman would have to drive us and our papers to school. And the whole school would be working, unloading cars and passing bundles to each other and piling the bundles high in front of the schoolhouse. Everyone was jolly and laughing and working hard; spring was coming in; and the stars and stripes waved overhead. Steve liked to help us and there were other big kids there too, carrying immense heaps of newspapers, tossing them high onto the heap. Our school came out about third in the city. We were proud and it was a lot of fun.

It was too bad that this year of all years I was enjoying school so much — except for math, of course. Because somewhere that spring I learned how to convincingly play sick. I found out that biting on the end of the thermometer makes the mercury go up. Instead of using this knowledge to stay home from school as I surely would have earlier, I took the thermometer to school to demonstrate, bit too hard, and there was mercury and broken glass in my mouth, and the teacher said mercury was poison so I spat it out onto the floor and was scared all day that I was poisoned and I felt foolish.

There was a red-haired kid in my class whose father was a fireman and one time for a fire drill the kid's father came with his big beautiful red truck, sirens going and lights flashing, pulled up in front of the schoolhouse, stretched the ladder out to its full height, climbed up to the top of it and waved smiling at all of us gathered in tidy bunches in the school yard. I was so jealous of that red-haired kid, I could hardly stand it. I wanted a father, any father, but most especially I wanted a father just like that. He was so grand and heroic, if he had been my father, I would have been full of joy. I looked enviously at the red-haired kid and I was ready to hate him for being so lucky but when I saw his face glowing unabashed with exactly the joy and pride I thought would have been mine if I'd had such a father, I felt something in me switch over. I felt happy for him, happy in his happiness. The glory in his face as he looked up at his father warmed me and I wasn't envious anymore. It was very satisfying. It was a big moment in my life.

It was spring now and Sally's birthday and she brought home a kitten that some kid at school had given to her. Mr. and Mrs. Hultman, especially Mrs. Hultman, were against having pets. It was a very tense scene. It was supposed to have been a lovely smiling birthday but now it was ruined. Mrs. Hultman wanted absolutely to give the kitten back to whoever had given it to Sally but Mr. Hultman grudgingly said it was all right to keep the kitten and this made Mrs. Hultman very upset. She said the kitten would have to live in the garage, she wasn't having it in the house.

So the kitten was put into the garage but Mr. Hultman didn't like that because every time he took the car out, he had to get out and look to see that he wasn't going to run over the kitten. So Sally tied the kitten to a tree with a string round its neck, and one day when we came home it was hanging dead from a high branch in the tree. It was an awful thing. There was the burial scene behind the garage with everyone very grim and Sally crying and crying. Then Sally went into fits of crying for days after that. She told Steve and me she thought Mrs. Hultman had done it, had killed the kitten in that horrible way. Steve and I tried to talk her out of that but we wondered too. Mrs. Hultman had been so against the kitten. Would she do that? We wondered about the dark depths of her behind that rosy face.

The dinner table was no longer the bubbling open chatter that it had been. Mrs. Hultman must have known that she was accused of murder. She treated Sally with unusual gentleness, even seemed afraid of her, nervous around her. Once she burst out, "I couldn't be expected to watch a kitten all day long!" and another time she said, "It just goes to show we shouldn't have any pets." And Steve and Sally and I would look at each other then and we'd wonder if she felt guilty because she had killed the kitten, actually climbed the tree and hanged it, or only because she was relieved that it was dead.

Then it was nearly the last day of school and we had the radio on at breakfast as usual and we heard over the radio that the allies were invading Normandy and that Hitler's Germany was defeated at last! The joy of victory swept over the land, the whole country was laughing with hope and happiness. In school, everyone was beaming and laughing, even hugging each other, and one girl came up to me and kissed me right on the mouth. She was a very very pretty girl too and she kissed me right on the mouth and I had never been kissed anything like that before and I liked it a whole lot.

21

Summer of '44

THERE WAS A LITTLE GIRL two houses down the alley whose name was Laurie and her eyes bugged out. She was about a year older than I was. She had a real nice doll house with tiny dolls and furniture and rugs and mirrors and pictures on the walls and I was fascinated with it. For a while, I went over there nearly every day to play with her with her doll house. It was really fine and Laurie was a nice girl and it was lovely to be playing with dolls with a girl. Ryda Rue and I had played with hollyhock dolls together in Macomb and it reminded me of that. Sally came too sometimes and we'd all three play happily with the dolls.

But it didn't last very long. Laurie's mother thought it was shocking that a boy would play dolls with girls. She said I should be ashamed of it. She also said I must have worms and she tried to talk Mrs. Hultman into giving me enemas for worms. She was just awful so I had to quit going over there and I built my own doll house and Sally helped me sometimes. We built it out of a cardboard box and we made everything or found things and that was a lot of fun.

Shortly after I quit playing dolls at Laurie's house I was playing in the dirt alone down the alley and I felt an ant crawling in my crotch and I was just opening my pants to get it out of there when it bit me on the end of my foreskin. It really hurt. Then my foreskin got red and swollen but I couldn't show it to anyone. It stayed red and swollen for several days and I worried a lot about it. I wondered if I was being punished for all the ants I had killed in my life. Then eventually the swelling went away.

There were some model airplanes that had been stored at 930 Washington and Steve and I worked together on those. It was wonderful to me how much better I could handle model airplanes now that I was older and Steve was there to make them with me.

When Steve wanted to go to the site of the airplane crash, I went with him and this time I was tolerant when he picked up a few things there. I didn't even mention how I had acted just after the crash.

Shortly after school let out, Steve got a paper route for the Rocky Mountain News and so every morning we'd all wake up at six and Steve would already be up and there'd be papers out in the yard and we'd all go out and help him fold them, roll them, tuck in the corner so they wouldn't unroll, and stuff them, dozens of them, into canvas bags on his bike. It was another one of those lovely scenes of family togetherness that the Hultmans were so good at and that warmed me all over. Steve would thank us then, sheepishly, and he'd give Sally and me a little of the money he was making out of it because we helped him. And at seven, he'd set off with a huge load on his bike, tossing the papers onto porches as he went.

When he went to collect the money, I'd go with him, walking in the afternoons. I always wanted to be with Steve if I could. He knew things I didn't know, things I had no concept of, like that people had hair growing in their crotches when they grew up. I hadn't imagined anything like that.

Sometimes he'd sit in the basement and whittle and I'd go down there with him and we'd talk about things, about how it was going to be after we were grown up and what the world was like.

Everything was so nice at the Hultmans that I actually resented going to choir practice and Mrs. Hultman would have to remind me, clucking and titching, that it was time and I had better go.

Then there was a plan to send me to the mountains again, maybe with the choir or maybe some new scheme Clara dug up. Mr. Hultman felt strongly that I should go and get some exercise. Why did people always want me to go to the mountains? I detested the mountains. I wanted to stay in town. There was much to do in town, nothing in the mountains but horror, neuroses and discomfort. I spoke loud and long against going to the mountains and somehow I got out of going.

I wasn't seeing much of Clara now because for one thing, I really didn't want to leave the Hultmans and, for another, Pete had left her and she was real busy hunting up another man. The only time I'd see her was if there was some doctor's appointment to get a new truss or new glasses.

In the corner of the backyard there was a thicket of bushes and we could go into it and nobody would see what we were doing. Sally and I took a couple of tin cans in there and we started digging a hole, spreading the dirt out among the bushes. Pretty soon Steve got a can and joined us. We dug down and down and then we dug across under the back fence. Under the alley, we dug out a room. We were like miners digging with our cans. We decided that no one at all should know about it but us three. It was a secret among us. It was a wonderful room, big enough for two of us to squat in, with a niche for a candle, and other crannies for other little things. We'd go in there and we'd feel like guerrillas or fugitives or cave men.

It was still early in the summer when Grandmaw sent for me to come and visit Winfield again for a couple of weeks. This wasn't like going to the mountains. There was no denying Grandmaw.

It was my first train trip alone. It was exciting. Clara took me to the train and gave instructions to the porter. I'd been so used to riding on streetcars, the train seemed wonderfully elegant — plush seats, padded and comfortable — the porters and the conductors friendly and helpful.

When I got to Grandmaw's house, there it all was, everything the same as it had been, the front yard with the goldfish pond, and the little black boy in plaster, gaudily dressed, still fishing in it, the old shade trees, the orchard in the side yard, chickens clucking out back, the big wrap-around porch, the familiar furniture in the house and the smell too, that sweet warm smell of Grandmaw's house, chicken fat and cinnamon. Grandmaw was the same as she had been before, full of life and sparkle and doing wonderful things.

Aunt Maryann and Uncle Herbert had divorced and Uncle Herbert had remarried and was living in Wichita so that Aunt Maryann and my cousin Ronnie who had been my childhood playmate, were living there with Grandmaw. Ronnie I surely could recognize. He was a lot bigger, of course, but he was just the same as he had been.

But I was different. I had become sophisticated. I had been going to movies and reading books. I had had adventures and I had been devising my own activities for years. I had lived in the city and had grown accustomed to shops and movie houses, drug stores and dime stores and bright lights while Ronnie had been living here with Grandmaw and her cinnamon rolls and her chickens and her Christmas decorations, with the heat and the dust in the summer and the cold wind in the winter, this whole time.

I told Ronnie tales from Tarzan and from the horror stories I'd read and from the movies I'd seen. Ronnie was amazed at it all. He had had very little interest in books, he said, but he contributed stories of Paul Bunyan. I thought Paul Bunyan was kid stuff, but Grandmaw, when he showed it to her, got disturbed about it, calling it all lies and exaggerations, telling us we shouldn't read stuff like that, because it

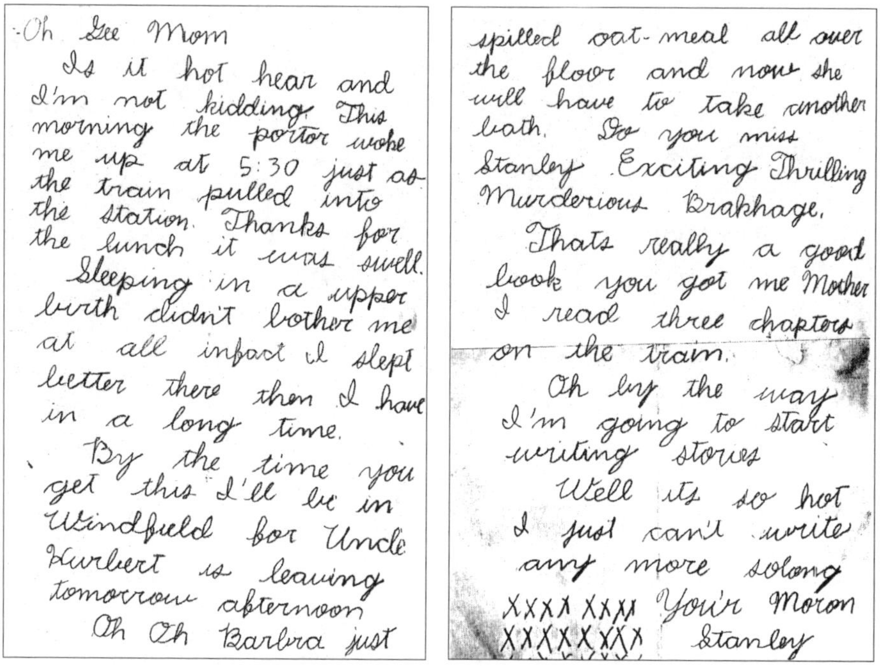

Oh Gee Mom
Is it hot hear and I'm not kidding. This morning the portor woke me up at 5:30 just as the train pulled into the station. Thanks for the lunch it was swell.
Sleeping in a upper birth didn't bother me at all infact I slept better there then I have in a long time.
By the time you get this I'll be in Windfield for Uncle Hurbert is leaving tomorrow afternoon
Oh Oh Barbra just spilled oat-meal all over the floor and now she will have to take another bath. Do you miss Stanley Exciting Thrilling Murderious Brakhage.
Thats really a good book you got me Mother I read three chapters on the train.
Oh by the way I'm going to start writing stories
Well its so hot I just can't write any more solong
XXXX XXXX You'r Moron
XXXXXXXX Stanley

wasn't proper, because our time would be much better spent reading the Bible. Then I realized how sheltered he was. I warned him. I told him the Bible was fabulous too, not that I was ready to exactly question its validity, but I felt he was stifled by her. She wouldn't let him read.

We went out back and we talked about her as we went up the hill to look at the old oil pump that was still pumping away up there, day and night, eeeee — dump, eeeee — dump, still doing it after all these years. I told him about the time I'd seen her wringing the neck of a chicken and then we'd had chicken for supper and how awful that was and how I'd hated chicken ever since. He told me how all the neighbors brought their kittens to Grandmaw to kill and she'd drown them in the fish pond in the front yard. Or if it was winter, she'd put them in a burlap bag and beat the bag with a hammer until it stopped squirming.

But, try as we might, we couldn't hate her. She was so lively and

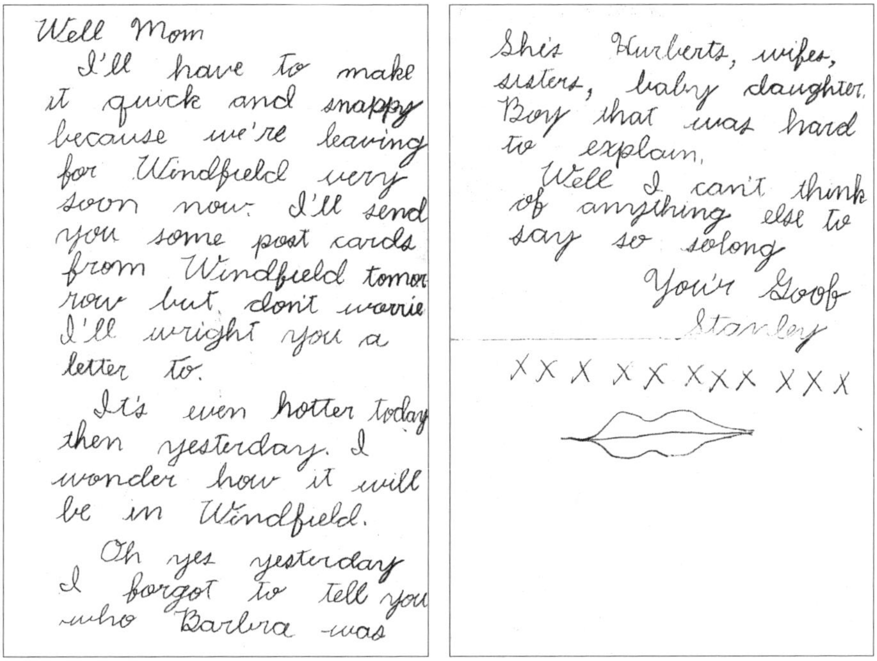

Well Mom
I'll have to make it quick and snappy because we're leaving for Windfield very soon now. I'll send you some post cards from Windfield tomorrow but don't worrie I'll wright you a letter to.

It's even hotter today then yesterday. I wonder how it will be in Windfield.

Oh yes yesterday I forgot to tell you who Barbra was She's Hurberts, wifes, sisters, baby daughter. Boy that was hard to explain.

Well I can't think of anything else to say so solong

You'r Goof
Stanley

XXX XX XXX XXX

was always making delicious things to eat and creating wonderful projects to do. She had a new dog she was teaching tricks to (Mugsy had died) and she put the new dog through all the tricks and she made us some of her cinnamon rolls and she got us involved in helping her with her Christmas decorations — cutting and pasting and putting on sparkles — and it was all warmth and sweetness around her.

Everyone and everything else besides Grandmaw was dismal and depressing. Aunt Maryann seemed to be ailing, Ronnie was still playing little kids' games. The boarder in the front room was a mother with a little toddler. I guess the father was a GI. Two or three times a day when the mother would put the toddler to bed, we'd hear this weird rhythmic creaking after she'd come out of the room. We asked her what that noise was and she said, "That's how he goes to sleep." We went and peeked in the door to see what he was doing. The kid was on his hands and knees, rocking himself forward and back, forward and

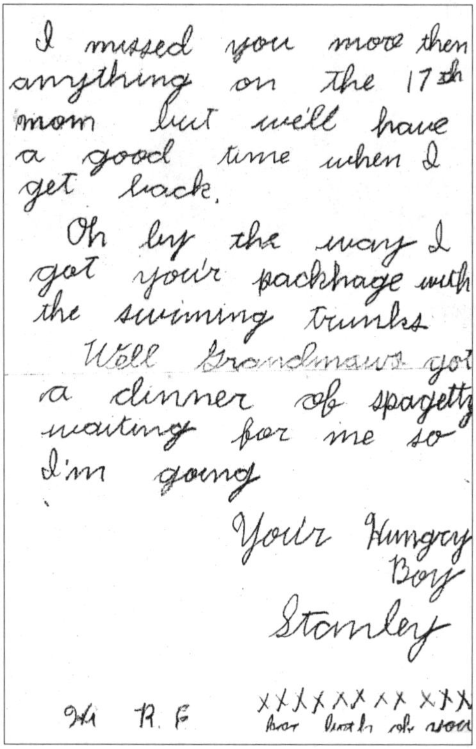
I missed you more then anything on the 17th mom but well have a good time when I get back.
Oh by the way I got your packhage with the swiming trunks
Well Grandmaws got a dinner of spagetty waiting for me so I'm going
Your Hungry Boy
Stanley
Hi R. F
XXXXXXXXXXX for both of you

back and then he collapsed and was asleep.

It was a great pleasure to see fireflies again. It must have been the first or second evening I was there that Ronnie and I went out and filled a jar with them and then we talked late into the night in our bedroom with no light anywhere but that eerie jar crawling with insects.

Grandmaw wasn't happy about us going to movies either but Clara had given me money for movies and Grandmaw let us go to one. Winfield's movie theatre was tiny and old and musty with a ratty old marquee. The movie was a Peter Lorre horror movie, *The Beast With Five Fingers*, all about somebody's chopped-off hand crawling around the house seeking revenge. I can't recall what the serial was but I told Ronnie to write and tell me how it went but he said he could never possibly go to movies without me there.

And there were those hot nights again, the terrible things about Kansas, hot and still with crickets buzzing outside and the oil pump going eeeee — dump, eeeee — dump, while I lay naked sweating into the sheets as Ronnie snored across the room. He showed me what people do sometimes when it's too hot to sleep. You would take the sheets and wet them in cold water, put them back on the bed and lie between them wet. I did that a couple of times. It sure did cool me off but it was so weird I couldn't sleep anyway, so I didn't do it anymore.

I couldn't take the little kid games Ronnie proposed that we play. I felt he was terribly deprived, except for the highly enviable position of being raised by that wonderful old grandmother. But the things he proposed that we do to entertain ourselves were dismal and deadly so I decided we should do plays every afternoon on the front porch and it should be a serial of Batman and Robin. We would write them (or I would write them and he would approve) in the evening, practice them in the morning, and perform in the afternoon.

We made capes out of pillowcases and masks out of scraps. We had to symbolize all kinds of terrible things — for instance, we would knock chairs off the porch to symbolize a car going off a cliff and I would do all the sound effects, the skidding tires and the crash sound when the car landed at the bottom. We made airplanes and cars out of cardboard or furniture. Ronnie would be the villain and I'd be Batman, and we'd tie me up and set dynamite beside me, and I'd hiss like a dynamite fuse behind the gag over my mouth. Or there would have to be an explosion and I would make the sound while Ronnie threw a lot of papers into the air to symbolize it visually.

There was to be another explosion later and we wanted it to be something other than paper and we asked Grandmaw for something we could use that would be fluffy and she gave us the stuffing she was going to use for an angel. Although she admired our ingenuity, she must have felt it was frightfully ungodly. I know she was very troubled about it. She wouldn't let us burn a cardboard box on the porch to symbolize a house burning down. We had to burn the box out by the trash. She was squirming and troubled about it all the time but Maryann must have said something about how good it was for Ronnie, because, although Grandmaw was horrified, she let us do it for some time. But finally, and I think the burning house was the last straw, she said couldn't we play something else now, and so we had to stop.

There were visitors, of course, while I was there. Most of the people

I didn't remember and they'd talk about people who had died since I had been there when I was little and I didn't remember the people who had died either. Most of the visitors saw our afternoon show. We always had an audience of neighbor kids and maybe their parents. Aunt Maryann always watched and Grandmaw too, and any visitors that dropped in. When the Waxman sisters came, I remembered them well and I talked with them about all the sophisticated things I'd been doing, the books I'd been reading and the comic strips I'd made. I sang for them too and they seemed to be terribly impressed with me, which pleased me no end. Uncle Herbert came two or three times too, and whenever he'd come, Aunt Maryann would try not to be there.

I couldn't get over the dowdiness of downtown Winfield. There were more exciting drug stores on every corner of Denver than any store you could find in Winfield. There was, however, Grandmaw, bursting with liveliness and cinnamon rolls and other delights. There was the very gratifying admiration from everyone, kids, neighbors, visitors, and most especially the Waxman sisters. And there was the constant dedicated adulation of Ronnie. I came into Winfield like a clap of thunder. I may have even to some extent eclipsed Grandmaw while I was there. And so, when I left, I was inspired with myself and my abilities, my imagination and my showmanship, and my knowledge of things that other people didn't know about. It was a wonderful vacation.

When I got back, the Hultmans told me about how a telephone truck had fallen into the tunnel that we had made under the alley. They'd all been in the house at the time, even Mr. Hultman had been home, and they had heard this big noise and all looked out the back window and there was the truck, its back end sticking up, and Sally had shrieked something about the tunnel. Mr. and Mrs. Hultman had looked at Steve and Sally with the most terrible faces and then the story had all come pouring out and Mr. Hultman had been furious and had gotten a strap to beat them with and Mrs. Hultman had stood around

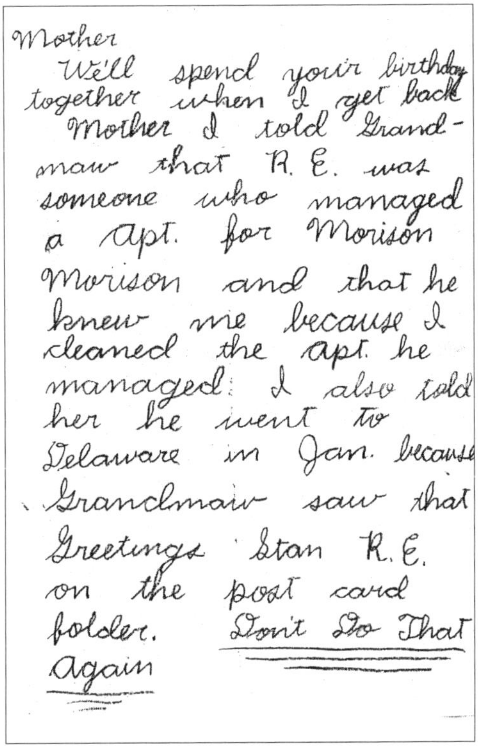

Mother
We'll spend your birthday together when I get back
Mother I told Grand-maw that R. E. was someone who managed a Apt. for Morison Morison and that he knew me because I cleaned the apt. he managed: I also told her he went to Delaware in Jan. because Grandmaw saw that Greetings Stan R. E. on the post card folder. Don't Do That Again

praying and saying, "Thank God the children weren't in there!" over and over again, while Mr. Hultman stood white-faced and furious, with the strap dangling from his hand, which he never did use and finally put away again. Steve and Sally had had to show them, then, the hole hidden in the thicket in the corner of the yard, the dirt spread around under the bushes, the garbage-can-lid-trap-door covering the hole, everything. A wrecker had to come to pull out the telephone truck, a dump truck had to come to fill the hole and another machine had to smooth the dirt across the hole. Mrs. Hultman had asked the kids, "Why didn't you tell us?" and they had answered, "Because it was a secret." But now all the excitement was over and the main thing we felt was sad that we didn't have our tunnel anymore.

It was early July now. I had missed two weeks of choir practice and had to catch up. Mr.Pew wanted me to learn another solo part. He trusted me more and more with solo parts, and my singing, the purity of my voice, and the perfection of my pitch were so exceptional, people were commenting about it all the time. Still, being a cautious and careful man, he kept me down to brief solos, less than a minute long. I was, after all, an eleven-year-old kid. But I knew I was the best thing that had happened to him in a long time. Anyone could hear that with half an ear.

Jon was there, as always, and he and I had much to say to each other. Even though it had been years now since I had drawn that fatal picture of his deformed hand on the blackboard, there was still a certain tension between us, a sort of formality. We didn't confide in each other. But we had much to talk about. We yearned for something to get our minds into that was like the greatness of the Bach cantatas we were singing in choir — but something of words, of theatre, of sweat and anguish.

We had been exchanging Classic Comics with each other for months now, *Dr. Jekyll and Mr. Hyde, The House of the Seven Gables, The Purloined Letter, Gulliver's Travels, Les Misérables,* all cut, squashed, and illustrated into little comic books. Nonetheless, there was still a glimmer in them of something of what we were after and we devoured them and discussed them seriously and at great length.

After my very stimulating theatrical success with Batman and Robin in Winfield, I suggested to Jon that we could try building a puppet theatre to put on some of the Classic Comics. So Jon invited me over to his house one day and we were designing the theatre when Jon's mother came into the room and started talking to us in a way that no adult had ever spoken to me before. She was troubled, she spoke to us mind-to-mind, she frowned, not at us, but in an effort to be articulate, to convey to us a concept that was extremely important to her, something she wanted us both to understand. It was about the Classic Comics. They didn't represent the great books, she said. In the great books, every word was meaningful and important. Any editing was a desecration to a great work of literature and the Classic Comics were a desecration beyond bearing for any sensitive soul who respected the arts.

I wanted to argue with her, to tell her that in the Classic Comics I had been given a sense of something, a recognition of minds that groped like mine was groping, of worlds of the imagination that stimulated me to let my imagination soar. I looked over at Jon. He was hushed and serious so I too kept quiet and listened.

She told us she felt the same way about translation that she did about editing and she cared so much about Dante's *Divine Comedy* that she was studying the Italian language solely for the purpose of reading *The Divine Comedy* as it had been written. We should read books, she said, instead of comics. We should read those great classics themselves, read them word for word. If we didn't understand some of what we were reading, we should read it anyway and go on reading and later we would understand more. She feared, she said, that the easiness of the Classic Comics would keep us from going to the considerable time and effort that reading the book would entail. She recommended the works of Robert Louis Stevenson then as a good author for us to read. Full of adventure, she said. Or, she challenged us, we could use the Classic Comics as recommendations and read the books that most attracted us. But for heaven's sake, she said, don't skip passages, don't skip a single word.

This impassioned speech of Jon's mother was a revelation to me that did more than excite me. It confirmed for me that there were indeed outlets for such minds as Jon's and mine. It gave me a strange and immense feeling of community, the realization that I really might be able to meet with and revel in such minds, even though the people might be dead, because they had made things, like books, that were worthy of such respect as was emanating from Jon's mother, such respect as I had never imagined. Her reverence for great books, for every word being meaningful and essential, made me realize that art was something more than a good show, more than a wandering imagination, it was and could be an intricately balanced complexity of thought and inspiration and feeling, a deep and companionable conversation with the universe.

After she left the room, I didn't feel terribly changed. I wasn't reeling in an ecstasy of revelation. However, her speech, on that sunny summer afternoon in Jon's basement room, opened for me a world I could inhabit for the rest of my life and never feel constricted, a world of whose existence I hadn't until then been at all sure. In all my life since then, I have gone back to her speech as the final test, as touching home, to know if what I've found or what I'm doing has the creative integrity to come up to the position of honor that she presented as the proper place for a great work of art.

Jon and I talked after she left the room. I gave him my argument about how the Classic Comics were okay, were more than okay because they could show to little kids that there were great works of literature in the world. Little kids. But I wasn't one of those any more, not after such a lecture as she had given. Jon and I both decided to pick out a great classic from those whose comics versions we had read, and read it word for word. My favorite of all the Classic Comics was *Les Misérables* and even though it was originally written in French and I had, therefore, to read a translation, I determined to get a copy as soon as I could. And I would also look into Robert Louis Stevenson.

And I realized that by simply telling her feelings and presenting her thoughts, she had put on a better show than all of my dynamics and theatrics to date put together. Well, there was no way then that I could achieve such articulation as she had shown me. But some day I would be able to do that, to do a show that would open up whole worlds out of only talk.

Clara had finally snagged a new boy friend and she called me over to meet him. He was a rather ghastly sight after the handsome and friendly Pete. His name was Scully. He was little and scrawny and swarthy with bulging, shifty eyes in a thin face with thin lips. Slick, oily, quiet, graceful, he would have been perfect to play the part of a pickpocket in a movie or one of those greasy little types who picks locks or embezzles. He supported himself in a quiet way, a room of his own somewhere. He didn't seem to like kids either, wasn't interested, as Pete had been, in finding ways to amuse me.

I took the opportunity of the flush of their new love affair to get out of them the three books I needed, *Kidnapped*, *Treasure Island*, and *Les Misérables*. I installed *Les Misérables* in Clara's apartment and took the two Stevenson books home with me to the Hultmans'.

It wasn't long after that first meeting that Clara proposed that she and Scully and I spend a week in the mountains together and this time there was no getting out of it. At least I had new books to read. I decided to take *Kidnapped* along with me.

It was a one-bedroom cabin in a string of such cabins. Ours was the last cabin in the row and right beside the creek. I slept on the couch against the wall in the living room and the creek was only a few yards away. It was nice going to sleep to the sound of the water hissing and chinkling over the rocks.

There was a gas cook stove in the cabin, but every morning we'd go to the little cafe that was at the other end of the string of cabins and have tomato juice and flapjacks. The only places in all these war years that you could get tomato juice was in restaurants and it had been a long time since I'd been able to drink it. So that cheered me up a lot, that I could have tomato juice, a big glass of it every morning at that cafe. Flapjacks were the specialty of that place and there were all kinds of jellies and syrups in a little rack on each table. Scully told me that the thing to do was to try each kind of jelly and syrup and then stick with the kind I liked best. In my delight over the tomato juice after a good night's sleep, I decided that was a good idea and I tried all the jellies and syrups. It was jolly there in the cafe, the windows still steamed up after a cold night at high altitude, and it seemed that I might make it through the week without too much trauma.

There was a little footbridge by our cabin which frightened me at first because you could see the water rushing by between the planks, but it was the only place where the sun shone for most of the day and it was never really warm there in the mountains. The cabin had only two windows and it was in the shade and quite dark even when the sun was bright. So I took *Kidnapped* out to the footbridge where the sun was warm and I started reading it. I'd stop reading every once in a while and look through the planks at the water rushing by, and as the sunlight moved I moved further out onto the footbridge and sprawled there, staying in the sun, reading, and watching the water rush by.

In the afternoon, Scully came out to the bridge with his fishing pole and sat quietly fishing. At first he made me nervous because Pete would have tried to make me fish too but then Scully didn't. He didn't say anything, just sat there and fished and I read and when Clara called us to the cabin for supper, he said to her that I was the best fishing companion he ever knew. "He doesn't scare the fish," he said. "He just lies there reading and he doesn't scare the fish."

Then after supper, Scully brought out his books and started reading too. He seemed to be studying. I was really curious. I couldn't imagine what sort of books such a man as that would read. He had them spread all over the bed, papers and magazines and a couple of really thick, thick books bound in dark blood-red with thin ribbons of gold across. I tried to go on reading my book but my mind wasn't in it. He was sprawled there among his books and papers and magazines in his undershirt and his undershorts, long baggy shorts that came down nearly to his knees. He had thick legs, narrow shoulders, greasy hair sticking up on one side, and he was going from magazine to book to papers in some sort of concentrated reverie of studying. Finally I couldn't stand it any more and I went over to the bed to see.

The magazines had pictures of horses on the cover and inside. The newspapers were like newspapers on the front page but inside, there were charts and figures. The books were incredible, several inches thick, the type small and in two columns on each page. "Horse racing," he said, "I bet on the horses." He was making notes on a clipboard with a pencil, looking from magazines to papers to the big red books, writing, scribbling intensely on the clipboard, looking back into the books, doing arithmetic. "I have a system," he said shyly, proudly.

The next day as I was lying on the footbridge, I could hear voices in the stream and I listened to them, watched the water through the planks as I listened to the voices. The voices were out of *Kidnapped.* I listened in fascination as they dramatized the tale. The stream could say anything. It spoke to me too. "You can do it too," it said.

Scully came out again to fish in the afternoon and we shared the footbridge companionably, quietly, each concentrating on his own activity, making no demands.

There was a place he had heard about down the stream a couple of miles that was really good fishing so we drove down there and I read there on a rock in the sun while he fished. The second time we went, there were people there, several cars, which disgusted him but he took his pole anyway and went further downstream to fish while I started playing with the four or five kids that were there. There was one incident that haunts me with a good deal of shame. There were two brothers there, one older and one younger than I. And the older one started teasing the little one by talking about toe jam, which upset his brother. I started to get in on it too then saying something about flapjacks, how they're real good with toe jam, getting more and more inventive as the little kid got more and more upset. Soon, he was crying wildly, terribly, as his brother and I teased and laughed and went on relentlessly talking about toe jam. It was a lot like the time I scared that little kid with the cat's eye ring in 930 Washington Street and made him so frightened that he wet his pants. The kids' parents weren't there so he had no one to call upon for help but finally he ran away into the woods and I still remember his back as he ran and how it looked, frantic and anguished, and the shock I felt that I had done that. But I remembered the value of toe jam and used it again and again for years.

The next morning at breakfast in the little cafe, I couldn't stand the sight of apple butter because it looked like toe jam to me and it made me queasy to look at it. It was horrible to me to see Clara eating it with relish. The thought came to my mind that this was a punishment for my being a bully to that little kid. I've had a problem with apple butter ever since then, telling myself it's all right to eat it; the other boy had said that the Eskimos eat toe jam as a delicacy. I invent bullying conversations with that little kid about it, even now.

We went back to Denver on Saturday so that I could go to church. After church, Scully and I went in his car to a tiny little magazine store where he bought the latest racing forms and I saw some newspapers from other cities that had some comics that I'd never seen before. I asked Scully to buy them for me and he did. We did this every Sunday for a long time after that and I saved those comics and made a little theatre out of a shoe box, slits on either side wide enough for the comics to fit through. I had seen the design for it somewhere — you cut slits on the sides of a shoe box, paste the comic strips into a long ribbon, roll it up onto a stick, then pull it through the shoe box onto another stick, and you have something like a movie. I put bits of cloth across the empty spaces of the box by way of curtains and I showed my comic movies of strips that no one had ever seen to all the kids I could find on Washington Street and any adults I could get to look at it too.

From then on, I spent Sunday afternoons after church at Clara's fixing up and showing these out-of-town comics in their movie box to the neighbor kids, and playing cowboys and Indians with them in the vacant lot. I rode with Scully every Sunday after church to the little magazine shop. Sometimes we'd ride in silence and sometimes he'd tell me a little about himself or tell risqué jokes, most of which I didn't understand but I laughed at them anyway.

I was curious about his past but it was hard to get him to talk about it. Evidently he had been in vaudeville for years, playing the horn and dancing, but he kept saying it was inappropriate for children to hear about. He'd make his bet at the little magazine shop and pick up the new racing forms and then he'd spend the rest of the afternoon in his underwear on the bed with his books and papers spread about him. The main thing I liked him for was that he didn't want to change me. He seemed to understand me. And I liked the intensity of his efforts over horse racing. To some extent, I understood him too.

And every Sunday I'd read a little in *Les Misérables*. It took me two or three years to read it to the end. I never did skip, not a single word, and I understood very little in it. There were long descriptions of streets that would go on for pages and the way I was reading would go on for weeks and weeks. But it fascinated me. There was a power in it, a seriousness beyond that of everyday life. In *Les Misérables* I found kindred souls and a state of mind I related to. I was one of them.

As always, I carried books everywhere. At the Hultman's, whenever I'd go outside, I carried *Treasure Island* now and I was determined to read aloud to the neighborhood kids. I'd go out the door with *Treasure Island* under my arm and I'd listen for them and I'd go where they were, put *Treasure Island* down on the nearest porch and play with them until someone would say, "What'll we do now?" and then I'd say, "Let's read *Treasure Island*" and they'd gather 'round me on the porch or under a tree and I'd read to them.

I couldn't read simply, word following word. I knew that from the beginning. They would have been bored halfway through the first paragraph. Anyway, that wasn't what interested me. What interested me was the show. I'd make *Treasure Island* into a comic strip, into a movie. I'd hold their attention as long as I could with my dramatic presentation. I had different voices for the different characters, the little boy,

Long John Silver, the parrot, all of them, and I put in lots of noises — creakings, screams, guns, explosions. I developed my reading skills to a high pitch, transforming each sentence, each paragraph into some high excitement, inventing dialogue, skipping descriptions and big words, doing sound effects on one sentence while I was reading the next paragraph and planning what to do with it. With *Les Misérables*, I stuck strictly to the precepts that Jon's mother gave me, but in *Treasure Island*, I disobeyed them all and used it, changed it, following the advice of the stream under the footbridge, "You can do it too."

I learned early on to keep an eye on my audience, to find a cliff-hanger, or make one up, and stop there before they got too restless and whispered or played or scraped their bare feet on the concrete steps.

I hated that sound, bare feet scraping on concrete. I still hate it, like other people hate the sound of fingernails on a blackboard. I could scratch the blackboard and it wouldn't trouble me. In fact, I had the habit for years, when the teacher wasn't yet in the schoolroom, I would scratch the blackboard when I came in, if only to call attention to myself, to give them all a jolt. "The monster has arrived," something like that, and they'd all shudder. For me, it was bare feet on concrete. Then I'd shudder and I couldn't go on reading, the show would fall apart. And then they'd want to play some stupid game and I'd feel obliged to play with them so that they'd let me read to them again soon.

There was Laurie with the bulging eyes and there was Sidney who lived a couple of doors down, and there were some younger kids, I don't remember them very well. Steve and Sally only played with us occasionally. They had older friends and didn't play like children much anymore. Sidney was in my grade in school, smart, game, friendly and handsome.

Then one morning I was reading to everyone from the crotch of a spreading apple tree and a couple of the kids had climbed higher up into it. Sidney was hanging by his knees from a lower branch, shorts, no shirt, his face red, and his penis and his balls had slipped out from under cover and were showing. It fascinated me. Of course, I had seen boys naked endlessly in the shower at gym class, but at those times I was always so involved in my own ugliness, my too-little penis, my truss, my fat, that it was just a horror. Here in the apple tree, I could look at it privately, his private parts. I thought about it a lot afterwards, about how peculiar one's private parts were, hidden treasures buried under the clothes like the treasure buried in the cave on Treasure Island.

There was a time about a year later when I saw a little girl's private parts. Scully and Clara and I went to Cheesman Park and they put me in the wading pool while they lounged on the grass, he with his racing forms and books and she catching a tan. The little girl had got wet to her waist and was sitting on the edge of the pool, her skirt up, her underpants to the side, legs apart, and I sat in the water looking and looking at the double fold of skin, the slit in the middle. It was thrilling. We sat that way a long time, she ignoring me and I sitting in the water gazing in endless fascination at her private parts.

There was a kid down the alley who had rheumatic fever and his mother tried to get us to visit him all the time. She was always ready with cookies and Kool-Aid. The kid was thin and pale and blond and had a hank of hair that hung over one eye so we all called him Veronica Lake after the movie star who always wore her hair that way. He'd sit and couldn't play anything and didn't have much to say so in spite of the cookies and Kool-Aid it was a bore to visit him. I suggested to his mother that some of us could put on a play in his yard and she thought that was a great idea.

It was a long play, all about Demono, and I played Demono, my hair hanging over my eyes, lower teeth jutting forward, the lurching walk, the outreaching all-powerful hand of death ready to strangle everyone in his path. I never wrote it down, just told the kids what to say and do, and we practiced it all several times. Of course, Demono had to be done to death at the end. He was always headed toward death, but also he was already dead so that made it difficult. And people were always mistreating him, making him madder. One time they put me into the woodshed and I thought about 88 Keys, the bad guy Dick Tracy had shot in a woodshed, but I broke out again. In the end, it was a couple of very sweet young children who finally did him in, little innocents, they each gave him a kiss and he died in agony.

It was a beautiful sunny day when we put it on. We had passed around tickets to the neighbors and the sick kid's mother brought out chairs and ice cream and cookies and Kool-Aid. A lot of parents came and other kids. We had sheets up on the line to enclose the stage. The woodshed was great for dramatic entrances. Veronica Lake was brought out and he sat on one of the chairs. The Hultmans were there, and Sally helped with the chairs and the Kool-Aid and stuff, though she wasn't in the play. The sick kid had to go in early, it was too much excitement for him. He couldn't eat that stuff anyway. But it was a great success, everyone was very impressed with it and praised us and sat around afterwards saying nice things while they ate their ice cream and they really did seem to have enjoyed it. That day is a charming and wonderful memory.

I tried to get another play going then but the kids were tired of doing it so I had to content myself for the rest of the summer with reading to them from *Treasure Island*.

22

Glimmers of Power

ABOUT A BLOCK AWAY from the real estate company where Clara worked was an apartment building that needed someone to vacuum the hallways once a week and Clara volunteered me. This was shortly after the beginning of school. So every Saturday morning I'd go there on the streetcar, or sometimes I'd spend Friday night at Clara's and she'd drive me when she went to work. She worked Saturday mornings, most people did in those days.

It was a hard job. The hallways were long and dark and dusty and there were three floors and three vacuum cleaners, big heavy things with lights in the front of them. I'd start with the third floor at the far end and I'd vacuum as far as the cord could reach, pushing the cord out of the way, then I'd unplug it and plug it in farther on and go again. It didn't help having three vacuum cleaners because I had to do the stairs. So when I finished the third floor, I went down and had to carry the second floor vacuum cleaner up to the top of the stairs and vacuum down the stairs. The vacuums weren't built for stairs, they didn't go easily into the crannies, they were heavy and ungainly and the cord was always in the way. Then I'd do the long, long hallways of the second floor, plugging and unplugging and pushing the cord and then I'd have to carry the first floor vacuum up to do the lower flight of stairs and finish up with the endless hallways of the first floor.

At best, it took a couple of hours but there were a lot of difficulties. Sometimes one of the vacuum cleaners would go wrong and I'd have to go and find the manager and get him to fix it. Or the bag would have to be emptied and I'd have to drag the vacuum down the stairs and out to the trash barrel in the back alley and empty it. Or it was the end of the month and I was expected at the end of every month to scrub all the wainscoting along all that length of hallways. I dreaded the end of the month because of that wainscoting. I had to scrape crud out of the cracks of it with my fingernails and I'd be scolded that I must scrub along the line of the grain of the wood. I had to walk along slowly, the length of the hallway, bent over and scrubbing, then had to go back the other side, bent over and scrubbing, and then vacuum the whole length of the rug and then do it all over again twice more for the other floors. I felt very strongly that the scrubbing of the wainscoting shouldn't be part of that job but what I felt had nothing to do with what I had to do.

It was dismal, solitary and immense, that job. It was not a happy thing for an eleven-year-old kid to be doing. Sometimes it was eerily silent in the hallways and sometimes I could hear noises from the apartments, people talking or radios going. Sometimes someone would walk down the hallway past me and maybe they'd nod or say hello but I wouldn't look at them, wouldn't answer, didn't hear. My eyes were puffy slits behind black-rimmed glasses. I did what I was made to do. I emanated dark and silent resentment. I was Demono, dormant. Saturday mornings had suddenly become a bleak time, a time to get through without being there, a time to kill by working as fast as I could, Demono raging across the desert toward the city.

I might have been reading *Treasure Island* to the kids, I might have been working with Sally on the doll house or with Steve on model airplanes and talking about life, I might have been doing plays or making comic strip movies for my shoebox theatre or talking about literature with Jon. But I wasn't. I was vacuuming endless ill-lit hallways and picking dirt out of wainscoting with my fingernails, crouched, glowering, a sullen shadowy monster, misplaced, misunderstood, mistreated, and yearning to attack.

When I finished work, Clara would pick me up and take me to the Blue Parrot for lunch, and after that I could go to the movie at the Mayan Theatre, halfway on the streetcar to the Hultmans. There were a couple of problems with this, however.

It had been a long time since I had seen movies regularly and I had a hunger for them that I find difficult to explain. Movies were and are my solace and the deepest connection I know that relates me to humanity. In movies, I can feel the heartbeat of the culture, the warmth of it entering my spirit, feeding me, soothing me, guiding me. Movies would show paths, styles, mythologies, identities, lives to live, attitudes to look through like a lens or wear like a mask, to wear so closely as to almost become one with. In a good movie, I became a fetus, my eyes the umbilical connection to the rhythmic flow of the lifeblood of the society as mother, as mother with me inside, perennially as yet unborn. So that, no matter how silly or light or inconsequential the movie might have seemed to others, it was deeply, urgently, seriously important to me to go to it, to connect again with the source, the rhythm of the culture, for me, the rhythm of life.

When I had to clean the wainscoting, there was no time to eat at the Blue Parrot. Much as I loved to eat, much as I enjoyed the Blue Parrot, I would have much preferred to go without food than to miss the beginning of a movie. But Clara couldn't understand that. She dawdled, pointed out the merits of the cinnamon rolls or the charm of the real live parrot squawking and chattering in the cage by the window.

Then she went on an enormous binge of trying to fix me up, getting my glasses adjusted and my truss and my teeth fixed, taking me to doctors who put me on diets or subjected me to other hideous tortures, all of them there in the Republic Building just down the street from the Mayan theatre, all of the appointments scheduled for Saturday afternoon when I was raging to be in the movie house with its strange, swirly Mayan-type decorations, its vast darkened auditorium with an audience spread out behind me as I sat in front of them, hearing the amiable rustle of them as I absorbed the movie through my eyes.

Perhaps Clara was jealous of the passion I had for the movies, or maybe she simply enjoyed manipulating me against my will. In any case, some Saturday afternoons I could go to the movies and other Saturday afternoons I was taken to some doctor and put through some stupidity, some restriction, some appalling routine of idiotic torture. The worst of it was that I knew that doctors had saved Clara's life that time, had saved my life several times already and would do so again and again. So I was submissive to them, letting them do as they would, missed the movies time and time again so they could measure and poke at my hernia or make me read the eye chart once again or talk to me about my eating.

One day at school, just inside the door of the schoolroom, I was talking with a kid and suddenly he was punching me hard and fast in the belly, joking and laughing while he was doing it. I wish I could remember the conversation we were having but I don't. We were talking, maybe I was insulting him or something, just normal talk it seemed to me, and then suddenly he was assaulting me with the utmost contempt, with no sense of me as being worthy of respect. I didn't know what to do. And then he went laughing away down the hall and there was nothing to do. But I was shaken. I had thought I was past being beaten on.

The auto body shop where Mr. Hultman worked was a block or two from Saint John's Cathedral where I sang in the choir. So often I would go there after choir practice on Wednesday evenings and he and Steve would be working. Steve was learning the trade from his father. There was one Wednesday evening I arrived and they went on working. But I wanted to go home. I didn't want to miss *I Love a Mystery*. So I got in the driver's seat of a car and I started honking and laughing and honking and wouldn't stop. Mr. Hultman yelled at me and hauled me out of the car and whacked me on the bottom. I was furious. What right had he to bully me? He wasn't my father. I had no father. My real father had deserted me before I was born. Lou had deserted me too and Lou had killed Ritzy. Nobody was my father. Nobody had the right to spank me when I did something wrong, nobody. I was special that way. I was rejected and adopted and rejected again. Clara couldn't handle me. Nobody could handle me. Not like that. I suffered enough. I didn't need to be punished too. Even if I did do something wrong. I was a monster, I was Demono. People better be nice to me, they better be nice to me or get out of my way. Or they'd be real sorry. I stormed out of there, I picked up my books and left the shop and started walking to the bus stop.

Pretty soon, his car came along and stopped beside me. He got out of the car and came around and he started talking to me. The motor was running and the sound of it was a rhythmic drone behind his voice. The lights of the car lit up the street in front of us. Wind was whipping autumn leaves from the trees, whirling them fluttering and dancing across lawns and into the car's lights. I stood, stiff and indignant, my books clutched at my side. I was shivering.

He said he felt I needed a father, a man to guide me, to show me what paths to take and what paths not to take, to discuss things with. A father is the one who should, by praise, by example, by talking and by punishment, show a boy what is right and what is wrong. And when a kid does something wrong, he should be punished by his father. The Hultmans had taken me into their home as more than a boarder, more than a guest, they had taken me in as part of the family, as a kid with the same position that Steve and Sally had, the position of a child growing up in a family.

I was deeply touched. I was more than persuaded that he was within his rights. Suddenly, from what Mr. Hultman said, I realized that a place in society that I had long ago given up even dreaming of was there for the taking. I got into the car, the family car, and we drove home.

But there was an unspoken sacrifice I felt the loss of but couldn't articulate. While this occasion clearly offered me a place as a child in a real home, an acceptance by a real man, a father, to be my father, while it warmed me and shattered and swept away the barrier I had built around me — as the glass in Kai's eye and heart were shattered and swept away in the Snow Queen's palace when Gerda found him and wept over him — while it opened in me the possibility of happy blossoming, it did not provide a theatre for what was now my real self. Fixing cars was a dirty and uninteresting thing to do. I couldn't join Mr. Hultman as Steve was doing. The church and Jon too and his mother and movies and books and other such things had hinted at possibilities I found much more attractive. Even though that moment on the chilly windswept autumn street did not provide such possibilities, it did make it possible for me to relax and become myself. If such a man as Mr. Hultman could open his fatherly arms to such a kid as I was, surely it really was true that nothing was impossible.

It wasn't long after that that Steve found a pistol in the glove compartment of a neighbor's car, and just as he had done with an old rusty screwdriver in the corner of a basement full of newspapers, or with a dime in the gutter, he slipped it into his pocket and took it home to his basement room. I didn't hear about it until one day Sally, in very uncharacteristic intimacy, whispered in my ear, "Steve has a gun! Don't tell anyone!" We tried to think what we should do about it but we couldn't think of anything we could do. I very much wanted to see it but

I didn't know how I could. And then one evening as I was sitting in bed reading, I heard a loud bang from the basement and Sally screaming, and I sat spellbound listening to Mr. Hultman's voice roaring, Steve's crying, and then it was over. The hole in the wall was plastered up. The pistol was gone and I would never see it. And Steve was downcast for weeks after. It was such a dire business that no one ever mentioned it after that night.

The Hultmans, like everyone else, were intensely interested in the war. They saved bacon grease like everyone else did, read about the war in the papers, listened to all the speeches, kept track of all the movements of the armies in Europe and in the Pacific, and discussed it all at the dinner table. It was a constant source of conversation. Mr. Hultman studied it carefully and talked about the geography and the terrain. There were times during the war again and again when one otherwise inconsequential hill or island would make all the difference and he would explain that to us over dinner. It was wonderful how he talked with us kids just like with adults and we were eager to hear and to understand his point of view.

This was the year of the presidential election and Mr. Hultman talked a good deal about that at the dinner table too. I was totally shocked when he spoke against Franklin Delano Roosevelt. All my life, I had heard Roosevelt referred to as the great and brilliant savior of this great country of ours, the pillar and keystone of America. I had always loved Roosevelt with complete trust and without question. So when Mr. Hultman said it was time to get Roosevelt out of office, I was as horrified as if he was proposing that we let the Germans win the war. But then he explained why he felt that way. "Mr. Roosevelt has been President for twelve years now," he said, "for your entire life." Democracy, he said, was supposed to be government by the people, not by one man. There should be turnover in presidents. New people should always be able to take the presidential position. Roosevelt had too much power. There should be a new hand on the tiller, a new eye to the horizon. Thomas E. Dewey had brains and energy for the job and he had good ideas. He should be president now.

I was convinced. I was even very excited about it. Even though I still admired Roosevelt, I could see Mr. Hultman's point of view. It was time for a change. I got a Thomas E. Dewey button and wore it everywhere I went for several weeks.

23

Ending in Beginnings

CHRISTMAS VACATION CAME and with it, very deep snows that kept cars off the streets. Steve and Sally and I took sleds and trekked through the glittering stuff for miles, looking at tree branches weighted with it, at tunnels shoveled out through it, at cars buried in it. It was magical.

After Christmas, Mr. Pew felt I was stable enough now to be a real soloist in the church. He raised my monthly pay to three dollars, and from that time on regularly gave me solos to sing.

The light in the church, beaming through the tall arched stained glass windows picturing the passionate inspirations of the apostles, colored and glinted onto everything with rainbow hues. The congregation, subdued and respectful, bowed or knelt in prayer, stood to sing, sat hushed and listening as Dean Elbert preached to them about Good and Evil and about the life of Jesus. In the movies I absorbed, but in church there were things to do. I could pray. I could actually talk with God. I listened to Dean Elbert's sermons and to the prayers he led the people in. When he led the prayers, there were all of us sending up the same thought to God, the same message. When the choir sang and Mr. Pew played the organ, it was prayer beyond prayer. I could hear, I could feel the music opening passages between God and Man. Singing in the choir, I felt the message going both ways. We were talking to God and He was talking to us in the same breath. When I sang solos, the passage was through me. The more exquisite the song and the more beautifully I sang, the more I felt myself to be something more than a messenger, I became the voice of God. I would listen as I was singing and the incredible beauty and power of what I was doing was so contrary to the wretched self-image I had as a boy that I knew the singing didn't come from me, it came from God. The better my singing was and the more solos I did, the more I separated my singing from my self. Fat, trussed, bespectacled and wheezing, I let that sweet, pure voice dance in the air of the vaulted church with the colors that were dancing from the stained-glass windows and the dust motes that swirled through their beams.

I was singing for God. God was singing through me. I was His instrument. I sang reverently, passionately, love of God in my heart and God's love in my voice. My singing was an act of love between God and humanity and I was devoted. I was honored to have been chosen as an instrument of His love. It was a weighty responsibility and I was very intense in my care of it. During choir practice and most particularly in the church service, I went into a state of concentration that was very like a frenzy. My mind was flying with the music, my body formed and ready for the cue to sing and when the cue came and I sang, I was aflame with the purity and passion of doing work for God.

It was a state of grace in which the sweat, and shuffling and murmurs of the other members of the choir and of the congregation at best faded away and at worst invaded, pierced my concentration, and when that happened I would be enraged, feeling that they and their distraction, weakening the perfection of my concentration, were, must be, the voice and actions, the embodiment, of the Enemy of God, they must be the Devil. I had found a way to serve God. I had found a calling. And with that calling, I found the Devil and the Devil hounded me and poked me and when that happened, I had no patience. When that happened, I would rage. As, some years before, I had discovered that if I flailed my arms like a windmill, the bullies couldn't break through that, couldn't touch me or my books, so now I replaced that windmill defense with a verbal one. The techniques I had learned in singing, techniques of vocal projection and rhythm I discovered could be used in defense.

Some of the boys in the choir were disturbed by my specialness, by my tension, and by the way I separated myself from them to sing the solo parts. I had taken a step which took me outside their harmony into a forefront, a place in the spotlight where they couldn't go. They could only listen to my voice, which everyone knew and acknowledged was the best voice in the whole choir, perhaps the best in all of Denver. But they had known that before and had accepted it. What they found difficult to accept was that by my entering this state of grace, this strange frenzy of singing as an instrument of God, as the voice of God, I acquired a meaningfulness that left them discontented with their lack of it — not their lack of the frenzy, that repulsed them and appalled them, horrified them. And when they heard me, with that very attitude of separateness, of craziness, sing so beautifully, I seemed to be opposing and denying what they had thought was the first law of the church and of society, the law of harmony, of unity, of being a member of that unity, the choir.

Then Clara started coming to Saint John's to hear me sing and to fuss over me with possessive pride. I hated to see her there. She wasn't there to join us in prayer. She fussed and burbled at Dean Elbert and at Mr. Pew. It made me ashamed and it distracted me, infuriated me. Once she came into the choir room where we rehearsed and she made a fuss and I told her — I raged at her — never to do that again and she never did. But she fussed all the more with Dean Elbert and Mr. Pew.

She took my monthly three dollars now and told everyone it was for my education, she would save it for my music education. She took my pay from my job too and said it was to send me to college. She burbled with Mr. Pew about how I'd grow up to be another Enrico Caruso and make her rich. I remembered how she'd made me sing "You Are My Sunshine" over and over again to help her in her romance with Adam the taxi driver, and I remembered the records she had cut of my singing when I was little. Pete had some records of Enrico Caruso singing and some other operatic things and I didn't find operatic music very interesting. The thought of being another Caruso seemed boring to me, singing all that stuff. I wanted to sing only for God and I wished she'd quit coming to my church. It was my church, not hers. She should go back to her own church and leave me alone to sing for God.

And after church every Sunday, Scully and I would go to the magazine shop and Scully would lay some money on the horses and pick up the new racing form and I would get a newspaper from some other city to cut out the comic strips so that I could put them into movies I was making in my shoebox theatre.

Scully told me stories sometimes as we drove to the shop, stories of his vaudeville days as hoofer and horn player. The troupe would go from town to town and do its show, much like the carnivals were doing. There was never very much money, but then it was the 30's, nobody had much and some had none. The traveling vaudeville shows that Scully was in sometimes had money and then they would stay in a nice hotel and ride in the Pullman sleeping car of the train. Maybe a week later they'd have no money, their booking agent would have taken what little there was to pay for his own ticket back to the city and left them stranded some place like Wahoo, Nebraska, climbing out the hotel window to avoid being asked to pay for their rooms.

There was one member of the troupe who wore a toupee and was extremely secretive about it, causing the others to snigger behind his back. Once, in the sleeping car, he was snoring loudly and a Fuller Brush salesman who was trying to sleep on the bunk above him was becoming enraged. Finally the salesman said he'd haul the man out of his bunk if he didn't stop snoring but the man did go on snoring so the Fuller Brush salesman grabbed him by the hair to yank him out of bed and the hair came off in a mass in his hand. The poor salesman screamed and fled and was never seen again. The whole car was awake and saw their companion's bald pate, and he saw that they saw it, and after that things were easier because he didn't have to hide it.

There was another fellow who was always playing pranks. He'd go up to a woman on the street, a total stranger, slap her on the butt and bellow, "Woman! I thought I told you to stay home!" One time he went to a movie with another guy and when the two lovers on the screen were kissing and there was a hushed silence, he let an enormous fart that resounded through the auditorium. He stood up and roared at his companion, "That was really disgusting! I'm never going to a movie with you again!" Then he swept out of the movie theatre, leaving the other guy to creep out after him in shame and fury.

There was the joke too about the zebra that Farmer Brown bought and the zebra was going about the farm asking all the animals what they do for Farmer Brown. He asked the hen and she said, "I lay eggs for Farmer Brown," and he asked the cow, who said, "I give milk to Farmer Brown." The horse said, "I pull the plow for Farmer Brown." Then he came to the bull and he asked the bull what he did for Farmer Brown and the bull said, "Honey! Take off them stripy pajamas and I'll show you what I do!"

In January, I started at Grant Junior High School and suddenly instead of walking a couple of blocks to the nearby grade school I had to take the streetcar with Steve and Sally and ride it half an hour. It was a bright crisp winter's day, a big old red brick schoolhouse like the others, the same musty smell, the same rippled glass in the windows. I must have gone into this one, though, with a smile because the classrooms seemed bright, my classmates cheery, the teachers friendly. There were some kids there I knew from last year. It was strange and confusing to go from one classroom with one teacher to another classroom with another teacher for the next subject. The science room had a skeleton in the corner and frogs in jars on a shelf. The whole setup seemed to be a real forward step in the direction of college, the thought of which was beginning to excite me a great deal.

Nobody, I thought, would go to college except the bright and serious kids, the kids who really wanted to learn, to work hard to get somewhere, to be someone. That's what I wanted. I wanted to be someone. I didn't mind working, not at all. When I was working, even at the vacuuming job, I knew I was doing something useful. And as I was useful to, or noticed by, others, just so much did I seem to exist. Then I was part of the world. The problem with the vacuuming job was that there I wasn't being the person I wanted to be. Grant Junior High seemed to provide a lot of possibilities — even more than there were at the Hultmans' — of doing things that I wanted to do, where I might be myself more than I'd ever had a chance to before.

I began by getting totally out of gym class forever. Here's where those doctors that ruined my Saturdays the previous semester more than justified my loss of the Saturday afternoon movies. I easily got a doctor's excuse saying I shouldn't do any heavy exercise because of my asthma, and with this precious thing I accosted the coach. Grumbling, he allowed me to sit on the bleachers during the energetic games and exercises, and I sat in my gym shorts reading a book while the thumps and shouts of the kids echoed around me. He did seem to hate having me sitting there and tried to get me to do things in the games that didn't take much exertion. Then I would wheeze sometimes. One day, I wheezed all the rest of the day in the classrooms and the teachers were appalled and they talked to the principal and he gave me a note that said I didn't have to go to gym class anymore. After that, I sat alone for an hour every day in an empty classroom and read my book. But soon, either because they needed the classroom or because they didn't like leaving me alone, they decided I should spend that hour in the library.

Shelves and shelves of books, walls covered with them, cases full of them on both sides, big books and little books, picture books and story books, books of every color and size and shape, filled with dreams and thoughts and adventures and lives. I wanted to read them all, all of them. I put down the book I was carrying and browsed through the shelves. That's how I first found what books to read, by walking down the aisles, looking for a book that intrigued me and taking it. Taking it off the shelf and to a chair and opening it and reading it. The librarian tried to teach me the Dewey Decimal System but I wasn't interested in learning it. I would read everything.

I didn't check them out. I read them in the hour I was there. *Silver Chief, Dog of the North* I read there, and a lot of Albert Payson Terhune, and *Black Beauty*, a lot of animal books. I had the book I was reading now at the library and the book I was carrying. There was the one I was reading to the kids. That was going really slow now. And the stack of books by my bed, of which I was in the middle of all of them, and read from different ones according to my mood. And there was *Les Misérables* at Clara's house.

Junior high was the great time of field trips. I think the first was to a dairy. It was amazing and wonderful to see the big machines working, see the milk coming through. Machinery is always exciting. The bottles moved along a conveyor belt and then each one stopped at a place to be filled. Then they moved on a ways and each one stopped again to get its lid put on and sealed by the machine. There was the cottage cheese machine, a big vat with a huge wooden paddle slowly moving around and around in it. We all gathered around and peeked over the edge of the vat. We could see the curds forming in the vat and someone told us all about it and how it was made. I was looking at all the kids standing over the vat of cottage cheese and thinking about hairs and germs dribbling into it. There was a Dick Tracy character named the Brow who was terribly picky about germs. If he ever got a cracked cup in a restaurant, he'd smash it because you can't wash the germs out of the crack. Then some kid sneezed into the vat and I was appalled. The teacher was appalled too. We each got a dish of cottage cheese to eat after that and I guess we ate it but on the way back to school on the streetcar the teacher talked indignantly about the germs. Ever since that time, if I find a hair or anything in my food, I think of all those kids dribbling germs into the cottage cheese vat.

Then there was a field trip on which we were to go to the Denver Mint. I was pretty excited to go there and see how money was made. The teacher said there was a hunk or a bar of gold in the lobby that wasn't very big. If it was a rock anyone could pic it up. There was a sign in front of it that said anyone who could pick it up could have it but nobody could. It weighed about half a ton.

But we never went into the Mint because there was a terrible accident on the way.

We went to all our field trips by streetcar. The streetcars were really very nice. They were wonderful things. I liked the pale purple sparks they made where their arms touched the cables over the street. I liked the rackety movement of them and the spaciousness inside them, the wide seats of woven basketry. The difference in the faces between people who rode in buses and those in the streetcars was immense. In the bus, people looked hypnotized and more than a little sick. But the people in streetcars always looked like they were going on an adventure. Buses, of course, had fumes. But the streetcars didn't have any fumes because they ran by electricity. They had a quiet rumble and their wheels rattled along their tracks and they were always going *thun-*

kety-thunk and ringing their little bells. They were jolly.

The first streetcar already had quite a few people in it and when about half the class got in there was no more room. The rest of us, including me, waited for the next one, about fifteen minutes. When we got to the Mint, the rest of the class was standing around there on the lawn and they looked awful. Some of the girls were crying and all the faces were kind of green and very grim. Eyes looked pained and haunted.

What had happened was that a little three-year-old kid had toddled out into the street, into the track of the streetcar. One problem with streetcars was that they couldn't swerve because they were on tracks. The driver put on his brakes but the little kid's foot was across the one track and it got cut off. Some of the class had seen him running out and then there was screaming and the squealing of brakes and a lot of blood and someone tied a tourniquet around his leg and some of the girls fainted and an ambulance came and took the kid away and then the streetcar went on its way. There were big headlines about it in the newspapers the next day. I have a distinct image in my mind, a picture in black and white of the little shoe and sock with the foot still in it lying in the sawdust between the tracks. I know I didn't see it in reality and I don't think that the newspaper would print such a picture but there it is, every detail sharp in my memory.

Then our English class took a field trip to the Denver Post and we got to see how newspapers were made. We went into the room where page one of that day's paper was just then being pressed. And there was page one flipping through again and again, hundreds of them, thousands, several every second, and the machines were roaring. Then we went and saw the reporters all in a big room hunched over their separate typewriters, smoking, disheveled, and typing madly, and phones were ringing, it was very intense, and in some way very romantic. As we were leaving, they gave us each a section of a newspaper page in pressed cardboard. I asked if they had *Dick Tracy* for me but they didn't. The print stuck out and I could feel it with my fingertips like Braille.

When the class met the next day, we were so excited about newspapers that we decided to make one ourselves just for our English class, and I was voted to be the editor. There was already a school newspaper, the *Live Wire,* but this one would be only for our class. Since I was the editor, I gave it its name, the *Bookworm News,* and we made three or four issues, one each month to the end of the school year. It was a great deal of work for all of us — writing articles, getting them together and into the newspaper format. The teacher mimeographed it then. It was a very popular paper. It seemed as though everyone in the whole school read every word and we were very excited and proud. The teachers were excited about it too and felt it should be encouraged. We decided early on that we'd keep putting out the *Bookworm News* for all the years we would be in Grant Junior High and I was extremely excited about it. It seemed like something I could do. I could do journalism. Those reporters in that big room, I could work like that, fast and frantic, making a form out of confusion. I liked the disheveled look of them.

Scully was a scrawny homely little fellow but he could really dance. On the dance floor, he was king. On the dance floor, all those other men who had other virtues like beauty, power, or brains, had to stand back and stare at him in wonder. And so, every chance they could, Clara and Scully danced.

There were expenses. Clara had to have dresses, dancing dresses, she had to have shoes to match and purses to match the shoes. She had to have dancing lessons too. And nylon stockings which cost a lot of money during the war years. The number of shoes she had was amazing. I looked in her closet and saw dozens of pairs of shoes, many dozens of them.

Clara was in a lot of hysterics these days because she had taken

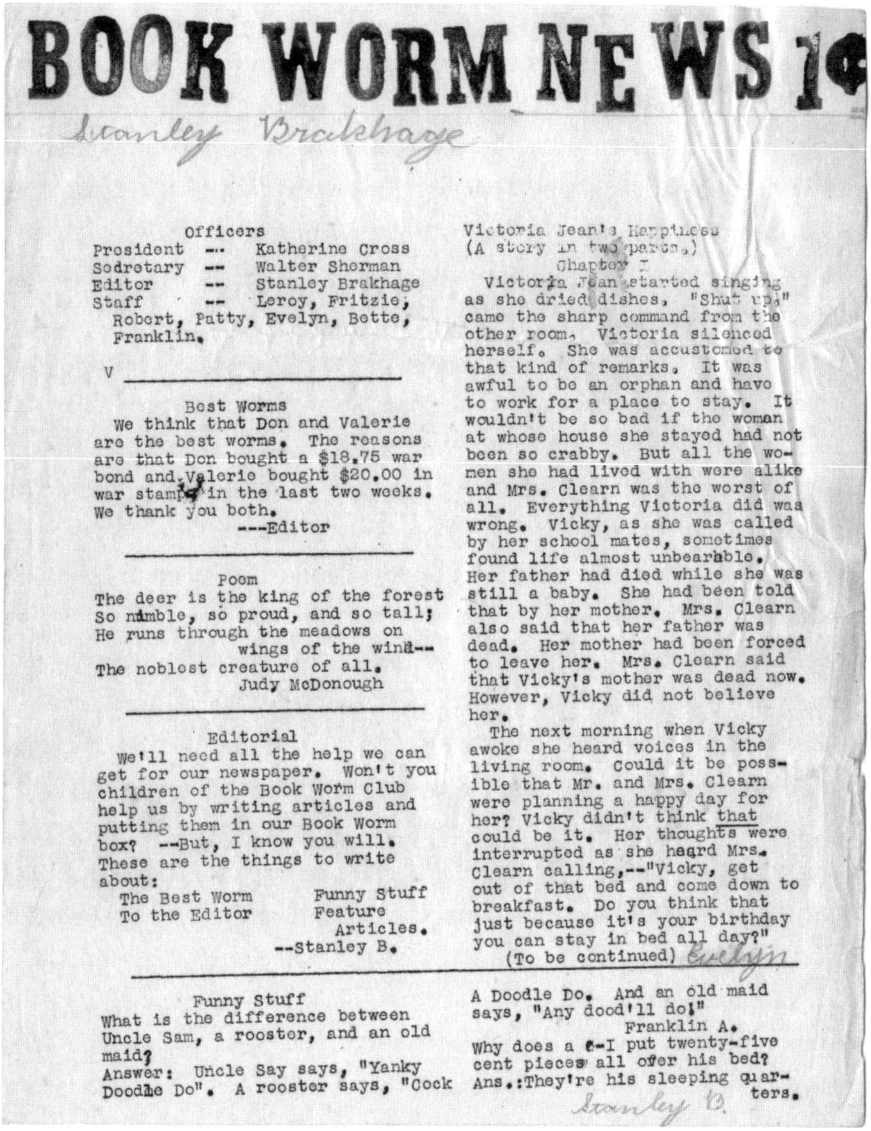

BOOK WORM NEWS 1¢

Stanley Brakhage

Officers
President -- Katherine Cross
Sedretary -- Walter Sherman
Editor -- Stanley Brakhage
Staff -- Leroy, Fritzie, Robert, Patty, Evelyn, Bette, Franklin.

V

Best Worms
We think that Don and Valerie are the best worms. The reasons are that Don bought a $18.75 war bond and Valerie bought $20.00 in war stamps in the last two weeks. We thank you both.
---Editor

Poem
The deer is the king of the forest
So nimble, so proud, and so tall;
He runs through the meadows on
wings of the wind--
The noblest creature of all.
Judy McDonough

Editorial
We'll need all the help we can get for our newspaper. Won't you children of the Book Worm Club help us by writing articles and putting them in our Book Worm box? --But, I know you will. These are the things to write about:
The Best Worm — Funny Stuff
To the Editor — Feature Articles.
--Stanley B.

Victoria Jean's Happiness
(A story in two parts.)
Chapter I
Victoria Jean started singing as she dried dishes. "Shut up," came the sharp command from the other room. Victoria silenced herself. She was accustomed to that kind of remarks. It was awful to be an orphan and have to work for a place to stay. It wouldn't be so bad if the woman at whose house she stayed had not been so crabby. But all the women she had lived with were alike and Mrs. Clearn was the worst of all. Everything Victoria did was wrong. Vicky, as she was called by her school mates, sometimes found life almost unbearable. Her father had died while she was still a baby. She had been told that by her mother. Mrs. Clearn also said that her father was dead. Her mother had been forced to leave her. Mrs. Clearn said that Vicky's mother was dead now. However, Vicky did not believe her.
The next morning when Vicky awoke she heard voices in the living room. Could it be possible that Mr. and Mrs. Clearn were planning a happy day for her? Vicky didn't think that could be it. Her thoughts were interrupted as she heard Mrs. Clearn calling,--"Vicky, get out of that bed and come down to breakfast. Do you think that just because it's your birthday you can stay in bed all day?"
(To be continued) Evelyn

Funny Stuff
What is the difference between Uncle Sam, a rooster, and an old maid?
Answer: Uncle Say says, "Yanky Doodle Do". A rooster says, "Cock A Doodle Do. And an old maid says, "Any dood'll do!"
Franklin A.
Why does a G-I put twenty-five cent pieces all over his bed?
Ans.: They're his sleeping quarters.
Stanley B.

money from her real estate company with the intention of paying it back before the end of the fiscal year but she hadn't been able to pay it back. I was completely in sympathy with her and I brooded and worried about it a lot. I felt she was a victim of circumstances. She said that if she were caught, they might send her to jail for embezzling. She asked me to pray that she wouldn't get caught and I did pray, fervently. And she didn't get caught.

Somehow, I never made the connection between the shoes and the embezzling and the money I was working hard to make so I could go to college, never allowed the realization to enter my head. I kept everything separate, everything separate and in its place as Grandmaw had taught me to do when I was very young.

Spring was in the air. The little buds were beginning to burst open on the trees. One evening I was sitting around the supper table with the Hultmans and there was no dessert. So I said, "If I had a nickel, I'd go across the street and buy a piece of that chocolate." And Mr. Hultman said, "You're too fat." And Mrs. Hultman who was at least as fat as I was, said, "He's a growing boy!" and Mr. Hultman said, "He should get more exercise. He just sits around and reads." I hated that. It scared me. Then Mr. Hultman turned to me and said, "I'll give you a nickel if you can run around the block in five minutes." Steve and Sally both said they knew I couldn't do that. I said indignantly that of course I could do it. Excitement bubbled up around the table and pretty soon I said to Mr. Hultman, "I'm ready," and he pulled his stopwatch out of his pocket and there was the hush and then he said, "Go!" and I ran out the door and off around the block. When I got back, I was wheezing and had an awful side ache and sweat was drenching my clothes but I had done it. Sally came in from the backyard where she had been watching to see that I didn't take a short cut. I was offended. "You should have known I wouldn't cheat!" I said. Then Mr. Hultman gave me a nickel and I took it and went across the street and bought myself a piece of chocolate and ate half on the way home and wrapped up and saved the other half for when I was reading in bed. That was the ritual and I loved it. If I had my rituals, the world could fall in chaos around me and I could still be happy enough. I was more dependent on my rituals than on people or anything.

On April twelfth, President Roosevelt died. It was a Thursday. School was let out, people all went home from work, and I found myself at Clara's apartment. Clara was crying. I didn't know what to do or how to feel. I had heard so much against him the past year, from Mr. Hultman and on the radio and everywhere, people calling him warmonger and tyrant. I turned on the radio and voices that had spoken against him were now praising him to the skies, calling him a great man. I felt disconnected. He had written a speech for the next day in which he had planned to say, "The only limit to our realization of tomorrow will be our doubts of today." Then, as a formal moment of national grieving, they played Samuel Barber's "Adagio for Strings" with Toscanini conducting and I listened with intense wonder as that strange and beautiful music played. It was very moving.

Two weeks later, Mussolini was killed and pictures were published of his body hung by the heels in a market square. This picture haunted me. Then, less than a week after that, Hitler was burned to death in a bunker in the invasion of Berlin. Of course, no one was quite sure that it was Hitler's body they found and there was such a prevalent feeling in everyone that he couldn't be killed. So many assassination attempts had been made on him and no matter how well carried out, they had all failed. Stories went around immediately that he had escaped to South America.

It was only a week after Hitler died that V-E Day was declared, Victory in Europe. But there were still those Japs killing our soldiers in the South Pacific. And since I didn't believe that Hitler was dead, there was no sense of achievement for me. It was all very confusing.

That's about when I started working for the Abstract Company after school, to save money for college. I was hired by a very tall, stout man with black hair parted in the middle and slicked down to each side. He had a nice smile and a mild manner. They didn't know quite what to do with me at first. I started out collating papers, then binding them into a heavy bright red Christmassy-looking folder with heavy staples at the fold. The paper was smooth and silky and on it, page after page, very official-looking, was the whole legal history of a building, and on the bright red cover was the name of the Abstract Company and "Title Guarantee" in florid letters. There was a certain definite charm to me in those abstracts. And then they were rolled up in a big thick rubber band and sent by messenger on foot to real estate companies or banks around town.

This filled my time until well after five o'clock and I would get home to the Hultman's after supper was over and Mrs. Hultman would have saved out a plateful of food for me and I would eat it alone in the breakfast nook and I would listen to the news on the radio while I was eating it. Then, on Wednesdays I'd go to choir practice, and on other days I'd do homework till time for the radio serials which I would listen to in bed in my room. Saturdays were completely full now with vacuuming in the morning, a movie in the afternoon, choir practice in the evening. Sunday was church in the morning and either Jon or Scully and Clara in the afternoon. I had very little time anymore to be with the Hultmans. I was sorry to miss the dinner table conversations and the various other family delights. But I rather liked being so busy. There's something wonderful in working long and hard. It was the first time in my life I was able to do it and in doing it, in working, I could feel strength growing in me. For the first time in my life I was contributing in a recognizable way to my own care and my own future. How I could have thought that Clara was saving my money intact when she was embezzling from her real estate company is hard to encompass. I was, however, blithely confident without question that the money I made in choir and in my jobs was being saved by her in "a special place" as she repeatedly told me. And I joyed in that assurance. I was working now to create for myself a golden future. I was going to college and in college,

I'd meet great minds, I would find serious people I could really relate to, I would find my true family, something greater beyond compare to this manipulating, rejecting and frustrating woman who was all I had for a mother, something more rewarding than this warm, kindly, salt-of-the-earth contentment that was the Hultman family. Ambition flamed in me as I worked to create my future and felt my energy opening out, going home to the accepting warmth of the Hultmans, finding excitement now in Clara's plans and projects for me to work, finding in my singing inspiration and a basic understanding of the internal effort and shaping of the self that is the endless struggle for mastery of a craft.

Why, Grandmaw could go to church on Sunday morning and hear a sermon on "Thou shalt not kill" and be a pillar of the church, then go home and strangle a hen for Sunday dinner, a hen she had raised from the egg and had fed and taught to come when she called, taught to be tame and easy to catch. That was the way it was done.

In my case, I had to not know. It had to never enter my head that if Clara was threatened with jail for embezzling from her real estate company, my little nest egg for college that I was working so long and hard for was not really for college at all — that all those shoes in her closet should have told me where my hours of labor were going. The shoes and the nylons. Flimsy, filmy things they were. You could see through them like glass. And like a balloon, the slightest touch with a rough surface and they were destroyed. Clara would shriek as startlingly as a balloon popping. Keep the nylons in the dresser drawer, the shoes in the closet, the embezzling at the real estate company, the nest egg for my future in its secret place that Clara would never show me. I never thought that it might not even exist, that it simply might be there in the dresser drawer, in the closet, with nylon stockings and lacy undies and shoes and purses and dresses.

I was working to go to college. I worked hard and well and conscientiously. Thus I learned how to work. Blocking out the connections, I learned to concentrate, to pour myself either into what I was doing or into fantasies. I was happy for the first time in years. Somewhere I had acquired a self-assurance, undoubtedly from the acceptance of the Hultman family. It was like a startling discovery that perhaps I could exercise my energies in ways that would be accepted and praised by the adults, by society, and that people would actually go out of their way to help me develop toward my goal. I wanted to write, to write for the newspaper, to go to college, to be with others who took life seriously, who were striving for something. I was going to show them now, I'd show them all that I was something grand and wonderful.

In the meantime, however, Clara wanted me to learn to dance. There was nothing I dreaded more. But at her church someone had started dancing lessons for children. Some little girl asked me to go with her to the church social that started it off. The Hultmans gave no support to my reluctance to dance. It was time I started going out with girls, they said. Steve and Sally were both dating. And dancing was very much in fashion now. There were many steps to learn, waltz, fox trot, rumba, tango, etc., etc., and Arthur Murray Dance Studio was everywhere, mostly upstairs above shops, and music tinkled out of them and you could see people dancing, or their shadows, through the windows.

So I had to go to the church social. There were all those little girls and boys and the teacher teaching us how to dance and the phonograph playing in the corner. "Left, right, together, right, left, together, left, right, together, right, left, together." Kool-Aid in little cups and little girls asking me to dance. It was just awful. And it was most infuriating because it was on a Saturday afternoon and I was missing a really attractive double bill at the Mayan. I went to Clara afterwards and I carried on passionately about how I didn't want to go on with that. They were going to be doing it every Saturday afternoon and the thought of facing that church basement every Saturday afternoon, passing right by the Mayan on the streetcar, well, it couldn't be borne and I made a big scene to get out of it.

The result was that I had to go with Clara on a weekday afternoon after working at the Abstract Company, wear a suit to school all day and then to work, then after work go to the Arthur Murray Dance Studio with the neon sign on the window and stand up with a patiently disgusted woman while Clara sashayed about the floor with an advanced partner. The window went to the floor and we were visible from the street. I was embarrassed and horrified. One evening after dancing class it was snowing and very cold and Clara's car wouldn't start. She called Scully to bring us some help and he said he would but we waited for it seemed like hours and he never showed up. When we were really getting cold, she tried to start the car again and it started right up and then began a nightmare drive through town, skidding and slithering from one bar to the next looking for Scully. Finally, giving up, she drove home to 930 Washington Street. On the tricky, inclined, narrow driveway, she spun the tires, she crying, I screaming when I smelled and saw smoke coming out of one of the tires, screaming louder when it blew out with a bang. I had suffered this way many times from this driving-in-snow trauma when she had taken me home from movies.

It was a five-week introductory dance course and I was counting the weeks until it was over and then Clara signed us up for five more. I put my foot down. "It's a special deal!" she wailed, but I wouldn't do it. I would dance no more.

Before school even finished, I was put into the delivery department at the Abstract Company and met the man who would be my boss for the next several years. He was a little man with white hair, warts and a big nose. He always wore dark plaid jackets and he always wore a cap with a bill. He was fussy, officious and had a grandiose idea of his own importance. His name was Winston. We liked each other from the beginning. I suppose this was partly because I could quickly and naturally get involved in his fussiness and in his love of the grandiose but also I think because we had both been nearly destroyed by bullies. To him, the delivery of these abstracts was the one thing that could keep his nose above the water. To me, it was an important step toward a great future. So we both treated the work with respect.

There were two other delivery boys under Winston's domination but they were both college students. Normally, I should have been the bottom dog, but since Winston and I hit it off so well I was given equality with them, even a higher position.

But during the school year — if only because it was already late in the afternoon when I arrived — I was sent to deliver those abstracts that belonged nearby. It was nice to be carrying something terribly important to someone who wanted it very much, nice to walk along the business streets of a city with real business to do, nice to be carrying a fine leather satchel down the street — like a man. I must never lose the abstracts, never set down my satchel. There were thousands of dollars involved. The Abstract Company was placing its trust in me. They were depending on me to protect and deliver these abstracts, to get the proper signature on a certain piece of paper. In all the years I worked for that company, I never did lose an abstract, always got the right signature on the right piece of paper and brought that back.

The company took up two floors of a building that spread over a quarter of a city block to the alley. Delivery was downstairs, and the lunchroom too. There was an elevator to the upstairs. I seldom went there but it rather fascinated me. There was a big walk-in vault full of abstracts and a massive door guarding it. And the door was usually open so I could look inside. The door itself was much more interesting than anything in the vault. There were three wondrous things in this vast room: that door, the enormous ledger on a pedestal that clerks would write in, and the huge camera with bellows suspended vertically from the ceiling over a table. There was a busy atmosphere

here that I liked. They all knew what they were doing and they did it with concentration.

When summer came, I worked full-time. I worked the same hours that everyone else worked, all those adults, and I was one of them. It was about a fifty-hour week. I was twelve years old. I gave up the vacuuming job and worked Saturday mornings at the Abstract Company instead.

I'd get up early and have breakfast in the breakfast nook with the Hultmans. Mr. Hultman and Steve worked a fifty-hour week too, maybe more. Mrs. Hultman would be bustling about serving everyone and the rest of us ate the cereal or pancakes or whatever she gave us. We never ate in silence. Sometimes Mr. Hultman would talk about politics or about the weather, sometimes Steve and Sally would get going on teasing each other or, rarely, they would tease me. But Mrs. Hultman would soon stop that and I'd giggle. Sometimes Mr. Hultman would entertain us with rough tales, tales of what it was like to be tough and manly. Mr. Hultman's hands were gnarled and calloused, he could never quite get all the grease out of them so there were black lines at his knuckles and in the corners of his nails. Often he would have sores on his hands that looked terribly painful but he would brush off the thought of them, proudly casual. He was tough; he could take anything like a man. One time he found a fly in his cereal and he pointed it out to everyone and then he said, "Extra protein," and, laughing, he ate it. Sally ran hysterically from the table, Mr. Hultman, Steve and I all laughed, and Mrs. Hultman scolded.

Steve at that time was stocky with soft pudgy hands, soft skin with freckles, and the faintest beginning of a golden down growing on his face. He was very protective of Sally, and he was gentle, a sweet guy. He seemed to me to be trying to be tough without being dangerous. He seemed sad a lot, though.

When breakfast was over, Mr. Hultman and Steve would go off to their body shop in the car and I would take the streetcar downtown to my work. It irritated Mr. Hultman that Sally wasn't working. "What're you going to do all day?" he'd hurl at her as we men were all leaving, "curl your hair?"

Well, I wasn't curling my hair. Mr. Hultman couldn't say I wasn't working. I wasn't fixing cars, but I had a real job with a real salary and long hours. I very much wanted Mr. Hultman's approval and I was willing to work fifty hours a week across each summer for it — for his approval and for my education and for my future. I was hitting my stride now. I was of an age now when all the vague confusions of childhood have firmed up into ideals, and the Hultmans had come to me just at the time I needed them for that. Now I was gathering assurances, working on heroic stances. No more would I be at the mercy of whatever people were up to around me, of the foggy, frightening emptiness of meaningless days. Someday I would meet great minds and when I did, among them was where I would find my community. But before that could be achieved, there was much to do. I must work hard, save money for college, read as many books as I could get hold of, and search everywhere for what interested me, for food for my imagination, some inkling of what direction I would go, what great things I would do when I found my future, when I "grew up." What I wanted to do now was to develop my power. I wanted to learn how to be powerful in my own way. But everything I would do would stem from this childhood. I was "under childhood" and in many ways would be always.

Afterword

The Child in the Man

BY TONY PIPOLO

We live by memory ... and not by truth, says Stravinsky somewhere.
— Stan Brakhage [I]

"You know, the more I think of the shows I put on and the way I acted at such a young age, the more I am reminded of Mugsy, the very smart little Boston Bull that Grandmaw trained. Maybe I saw the honors he got for his act and I wanted such honors, too. Maybe it was as simple as that. Maybe I wanted to be smiled upon by my grandmother as she smiled upon him. But although I have always vociferously defended Sigmund Freud as a discoverer of truth which his followers have been trying to obscure, nonetheless, I am as fiercely defensive as anyone, as Freud himself was, of my neuroses and my illusions and my delusions. Ezra Pound was called insane with the epithet, 'delusions of grandeur' but he was grand! He was accused because, or so say the rumors, he called himself the greatest poet alive — and he was that! And I too am great, I am very great, it's not a delusion, it's the simple truth. I'm great and I have a destiny and anyone who gets in my way must be working for the evil one!"

THIS IS STAN BRAKHAGE, "speaking" as the first-person protagonist of *Brakhage's Childhood*, a text composed by his (first) wife Jane (Brakhage) Wodening, in accordance with the memories he recounted to her in 1982 and 1983. The book, partly excerpted as *The Autobiography of Stan Brakhage* in 1987 [2] (in one letter Brakhage muses it might have been called *The Confessions of Stan Brakhage*) — now eschews any claim as autobiography. Nevertheless, it is the same text, written in the first person, and reads quite convincingly as any work so labeled. If anything, its "autobiographical" tenor has been strengthened by its author's choice to restore the real names of the original, which had been temporarily replaced by fictional names after she and Stan divorced.

In almost all of Wodening's stories, one discerns her ability to nearly efface herself, even when she is the first person narrator. Here, she creates Brakhage's point of view, keeping the tone, for the most part — as she says in her Preface — closer to that of the child, although frequently she conjures that distinct voice he adopted in lectures and introductions to screenings, and discernible in letters and critical texts. The shift can be heard in the long quotation cited at the beginning of this Afterword — which moves from the gentle, folksy tone of the first four sentences, characteristic of Wodening's prose, to the swelling bluster of the last five sentences typical of Brakhage at his most egoistic.

In letters to friends and colleagues Brakhage declared that Jane was doing a better job of writing his life story than he ever could. In one, he mentions that the manuscript is "close to 200 pages" and that despite the nightmares he had after she read back what she had written, he "sees that it holds up as a truth of me I could never have evolved by myself." [3] Elsewhere, he speaks of "telling Jane all I could remember of my childhood between ages 7 and 8, giving her 'three-months work' on the autobiography ... (this interlude fraught with pain and anguish, but well worth it — not at all psychoanalytical, just rather an emptying of the mind of the known)." [4]

Since the book is ostensibly a reconstruction of Brakhage's childhood memories — many of which are corroborated by material in the Stan Brakhage Papers / Archive of the University of Colorado at Boulder — it's worth considering, given his prolific talent for writing letters and books rife with self-appraisals, why he agreed to have his wife compose this "autobiographical" text. What purpose did it serve and what can we make of the mediation established between his memories and the written form they now assume? To say that it was inspired by Gertrude Stein's *The Autobiography of Alice B. Toklas* is not quite the whole story.

Brakhage, who was adopted, made tentative efforts as an adult to find his real mother, but did not pursue the investigation very far. He publicly fantasized that his father may have been the novelist Thomas Wolfe.[5] When he learned he was adopted, he says he was actually relieved because he felt — at age four? — that his parents were "stupid and insensitive." Prompted perhaps by a desire to appropriate control, if not invent an alternative history, retroactively, over the apparently miserable one he had, he seized the opportunity presented by Jane's offer to write up his childhood. Very likely, the memories he recounted are compromises between the facts as he knew or believed them and embellishments he could not resist. Having Jane write the text meant he could always disown it in the future as a distortion of what he intended, although her devotion to the project no doubt also provided the encouragement he needed to carry it out. The mediation, therefore, acted as both shield and facilitator: He could assume a certain distance from the material while feeling free to confess embarrassing "truths." He could admit exaggerations, channeling them through his willing collaborator, letting her, the fantasized "good mother" he never had, take responsibility for placing them into a credible context. Agreeing to the project may also have been a way to affect, even hijack his wife's muse, inspiring her to compose a saga, which, had it continued, might eclipse the legends that inspired her own work and emulate the mythic reach he had broached with his film *Dog Star Man* (1962–63).

But we should not discount a genuine longing that may have underwritten this collaboration: that through the careful selection of facts, memories, and even their embellishments, Brakhage could help shape the course of his childhood as a story of triumph over misfortune — something which may have had a special urgency at a time when all of his children were gone and he and Jane faced a marital crisis. The tenor and sensitivity of her achievement makes clear that she intuited this need and understood the psychodynamics and ramifications of this oddly affecting collusion of two people whose marriage was slowly unraveling. In the end, she created a masterly fiction about a fiction that reveals undeniable truths, assuming an autobiographical posture at once commanding and equivocal, a chronicle of semi-Dickensian misery offset by plainspoken observations about an American childhood bearing the mark of its author's writing style, demonstrated in books written during and after her life with Stan Brakhage.

Readers familiar with the Brakhage persona, with his penchant for mythmaking, his seductive speaking style, his brilliant, prolific output over nearly half a century, of films, theoretical texts, and correspondence, will probably have no difficulty extrapolating the persona of Stan Brakhage from that of the author of this book. As for the larger question of trying to distinguish fiction from truth, this is no more difficult to determine in the book than it is throughout the writings, letters, and public declarations of Brakhage himself.

Clara

Any act of displacement invites psychoanalytic speculation, as does the very urge to record childhood memories. Brakhage avoided personal analysis perhaps for the same reason many artists do: fear that uncovering the sources of his anxieties and conflicts would neutralize his creative impulses. If no serious attempt to examine his work or his life from a psychoanalytic perspective has been attempted, it may be because his admirers wrestle with a similar conflict, alleging that psychoanalyzing the man would be disrespectful to the artist, but, in fact, fearing that knowing more about the man might compromise their admiration for his art. Yet, as the opening quotation admits, Brakhage had no difficulty embracing the paradox, fiercely defending his neuroses and delusions while passionately admiring Freud's "truth." At the time he began reading Freud, he had a dream of "being welcomed into his office" and lounging "upon the famous couch ... [where he] talked and talked ... blam[ing] the World, or others, for something." In the dream Freud only interrupts once with a "questioning sound, as if to indicate he had not quite heard and/or couldn't quite believe what he'd heard me say." Then, he is ushered to the door with "some indication that this would be quite regular." [6]

Even if he only invented this dream, it encapsulates his mixed feelings: a wish to be analyzed, but only by the — unavailable — best, and even then wondering if his complaints would be tolerated and understood. Nevertheless, many of Brakhage's letters read as if they were, in fact, guided by the principle of free association, replete with digressions, accusations, confessions, fragments, slips of the pen, and word play. And, given the voluminous body of these letters, it is fair to say that he used the form as freely and revealingly as a patient would the format of an orthodox analysis, "talking and talking" about whatever passed through him — effusive celebrations of his wife, his children, friends, books, art, and movies, changing course midway through a sentence, lashing out at perceived wrongs, both private and public, acknowledging unattractive character traits, then backtracking to defend them, vowing all kinds of sweeping promises he couldn't keep, and so on. Indeed, it is because this correspondence is such a rich, invaluable source that I have used it in this essay to complement, corroborate, or contradict the statements and implications of Wodening's book.

While it would require more information than we have — from the letters and from the childhood book — to construct an adequate profile of Brakhage's earliest years, some speculation is reasonable. From the tenor of many letters, for example, as well as his own acknowledgment and Wodening's recollections, rage seems to have been an ongoing characteristic of his life — at least up until the collaboration on this book. As rooted in infantile personality structure, rage implies a sweeping indifference to rational assessment of a state of affairs, driven by an insatiable demand to override all inhibitions against getting what one needs or wants. Although the word is used occasionally in the book, there is no fully described episode that appears to capture the fury it implies.

Wodening, for example, witnessed countless expressions of it in their life together, but could not recall Brakhage expressing rage while recounting his memories, other than when speaking of his mother. In his allusion to the latter's "innocent monstrosity," he says that he "knows full well" that "my own instincts ... were warped by age 4 or 5 probably,"[7] an indication of how closely he links the miseries of his childhood to his mother and an admission of how she and they twisted his judgment for all future relationships. His frustrations with her no doubt surfaced early, given Clara's letters to Stan in the 1950s, in which she would caution him, following her transmission of some bad news, "no rages now," all three words underlined. Freud posited the oral stage of the child's development as "oral or cannibalistic ... as the first stage of sexual life ... in which the object is closely associated with that of the ingestion of food; the aim is incorporation ... in childhood phantasies this mode is not attached solely to oral activity but ... may be transposed on to other functions (respiration, sight)." [8]

Apart from the potential relevance of this view to young Stanley's asthma and vision problems, there is certainly sufficient evidence in the book to suggest that it directly relates to his omnivorous appetite for candy and junk food, often stolen and hoarded in defiance, suggesting that whatever else this consumption represented, it was an expression of conflicted rage against Clara that he could not express in any other way, and that may well have evolved from inadequate oral gratification and interpersonal bonding during infancy. Hence, while "incorporating" her, as any dependent infant or child is forced to do, he simultaneously "destroyed" her, which Freud suggests is the real aim of the "biting and devouring" typical of the oral-sadism that accompanies this stage. While in Freud's writings, and later Melanie Klein's, these activities are associated with the infant's relationship to the mother's breast, their ramifications for psychic development are not eliminated in the absence of breast feeding, which I take to have been the case with Brakhage. Klein makes this clear when she posits that "the lost prenatal unity with the mother and the feeling of security that goes with it ... largely depends on the infant's capacity to cathect sufficiently the breast or its symbolic representative, the bottle." [9] This capacity, of course, was complicated in Brakhage's case; we know nothing of the "prenatal unity" with his biological mother or whether it produced a "feeling of security," and even supposing that those conditions were optimal, whether they were continued and reinforced by Clara's bottle-feeding or disrupted and contravened.

Given what we do know of the early childhood circumstances and the role played by unknown constitutional factors inherent to Brakhage, it's more than likely that his infant and pre-Oedipal years did not, as

Klein supposes they should, "turn his mother into a loved object" or induce the concomitant "feeling that there exists outside him something that will give him all he needs and desires." [10] On the contrary, this earliest connection more likely induced those "primitive, pathological internalized object relations ... [later] activated in their transferences" to others.[11] The man who could say "that every fragment of my childhood saw [sic] teeth on my nervous system" [12] could hardly have formed a trusting personality grounded in early maternal love. That he was able to form any durable relationships in his adult life was clearly owing to the more salutary aspects of his character.

The more young Stanley indulged his food addiction, the more he increased the overweight body of which he was ashamed, thus punishing himself for acting on his repressed rage. Only much later did he publicly admit the extent of his rage toward his mother when he claimed that the inspiration behind his film *Murder Psalm* (1980) was a dream in which he had murdered her. As his letters confirm, this rage extended over his lifetime and to those he loved, as if, driven mad by cabin fever — like Grady, the former caretaker in Stanley Kubrick's *The Shining* (also 1980) — or by the gods, like Seneca's Heracles — he could feel so threatened by his children's efforts to "NORMALIZE" him that he is compelled to "split" from them, feeling "as if I had taken a hatchet to my children (as I did in a dream to Clara 3 years ago)." [13]

As an adult, he seemed driven to explore the nature of his rages. "A list of signs, heard over the radio, indicating possible sexual child abuse caused hair to stand on end, cold sweat from me, because 3/4ths of them are symptoms of my childhood; but I've no memory of such, thus it'll probably not get into the autobiography)." [14] Elsewhere, he leaves out the word "sexual": he's "an orphan ... 4 times fucked over (1) adoption, (2) for selfish/hopeless reasons (to save that hopeless marriage), (3) abused (out of 15 signs of child abuse, I heard on late talk radio, 12 of them apply directly to me — tho' I have no memory of any actual such), and (4) divorce ... and, oh, yes, (5) bereft even of the alone-mother-son-relationship inasmuch as Clara always jobbed me OUT to one nightmare situation after another (only the final, the Hultmans, an exception)."[15] But the Hultmans were not the only exception. The book recounts the time he spent with the Spaulding family and their son Ray, of whom he has only good memories and whom he was reluctant to leave, especially since what followed was the hellish summer at Harmony Hall, run, if we take him at his word, like a boot camp by two sadistic female disciplinarians. Although there is no reason to doubt that Brakhage had no recollection of actual sexual abuse, neither — given the physical reactions he describes upon hearing about it — is there reason to rule it out as having occurred. We should note, however, that excluding it from the book was also a way of strengthening his credibility — i.e., since he would not want Jane to include anything he could not recall, everything in the book should therefore be trusted.

Sexual abuse aside, there is plenty to corroborate events in the book and to support his complaints. Not only did Clara not bond with him after she left her husband Lou (Ludwig), and "job" him off, as he puts it, but she often did so because she was involved with other men and Stanley was in the way. This meant not only frequent moves from one unstable situation to another, one erratic sleeping arrangement after another, but also having to adjust to the various personalities of Clara's paramours. For every Pete, an upstanding serviceman who treated him well, there was an Adam who beat him when inebriated. For a while whenever money ran out, Clara appealed to Lou. It's no surprise that young Stanley resorted to all sorts of mischief in revenge — e.g., stealing regularly from her purse; setting fire to the drapes in one house, and the dumbwaiter in another — often resulting in their having to move.

If there was one constant amid these dislocations, it was, ironically, Hollywood movies. Wherever they moved, one of the first things he learned was where the local movie theater was in relation to his new "home." Movies were his salvation; they were always there in endless supply, something he could depend on and enjoy enthusiastically, without restriction, a frequent and lovingly-embraced balm to his soul. His interests and tastes ranged widely: the latest horror or crime thrillers, major attractions like *The Wizard of Oz* and *Gone With the Wind* (both 1939), or, what he seems to have cherished most, serials he could follow chapter by chapter every Saturday. Even newsreels seized his attention, especially if they featured FDR or Hitler or developments that led to World War II. Whole days were spent at the movies, particularly Saturdays, when Clara would drop him off and pick him up hours later. It would be worth examining just how movie experiences played a role, beyond the obvious one, in his life, filling in for absent parents, and stimulating a love of adventure, fantasy, showmanship, and an ideal world. Certain films had an especially strong hold on him. The Boris Karloff character in *The Mummy* (1932), which he must have seen in re-release, induced fear, as, wrapped in bandages that concealed his decayed flesh, the creature may have connoted a seductive fusion for a boy with aggressive instincts inside a body he loathed to display.[16]

Signs of real affection between Clara and Stanley are virtually absent from the book, even though letters between them in the 1950s abound in declarations of love. Admittedly, Clara's are often insecure efforts to reassure herself of his love for her, as if she had good reasons to doubt it. Nonetheless, in one letter, Brakhage wrote, "I realize now just how dear you are to me. We both have much to forgive each other for ... I beg pardon for all the hurt I may have given you in cutting myself off from you and denying my love for you ... I thought that by denying my love I would cut from myself all those weaknesses which come from the unsatisfied childhood. And for my weaknesses of the present, I sought to lay blame on you for them, as though you could be the blame, as though you also weren't a prey to life."[17]

The sentiments and seemingly balanced view here are in direct contrast to his unremitting rage against Clara at the time he was recounting his memories, which is probably why Wodening toned it all down as incompatible with the years covered in the book. Apparently, in the 1980s Clara finagled several credit card transactions that involved two of Brakhage's children, fueling his anger and arousing his memories of similar acts of vicious irresponsibility in his childhood and after he married Jane. In the last chapter of the book, when he is age twelve, we learn that Clara asked him, quite earnestly, to pray that she wouldn't be caught and sentenced to jail after having embezzled from the real-estate company where she worked; and that she spent all the money he earned from his first full-time job on nylons and shoes, while telling him she hid the money in a secret place for his college education. Later, she "borrowed" a substantial amount of money from Jane's parents which she never returned, and which he and Jane knew nothing about until years after.

When she was too old to live alone, Brakhage told one of his mother's caretakers that he "hasn't been able to bring [himself] to visit Clara — she just finally took me too close to some dangerous edge of being."[18] "I don't believe she's senile AT ALL, but merely using that, just as when ... [she] rehears[ed] me, small child all the way from Denver to Kansas as to what to say to my Grandmother, her mother, about how she'd go to jail if she weren't lent some more money ... leaving me, feeling dirty all the time, to tell my well rehearsed story — thus complicit in conning my beloved Grandmother, whom I never afterward could feel close to again.... I wasn't ever going to be able to talk to Clara again, or look at her dead or alive ever again."[19]

Given Clara's labile nature, bad judgment, frequent neglect, fiscal irresponsibility, and dependency on men, she most likely felt saddled with a burden she was too weak to bear, especially after she left Lou. We might think Brakhage unfair when, in the last chapter of the book, he concludes that she was a "manipulating, rejecting, and frustrating woman who was all I had for a mother." But although there is evidence she behaved like a doting mother at first, recording, in a traditional infant log, statistical details of his early development, walking, talking and so forth, much can be gleaned from the often daily letters she wrote to him in the 1950s — while he was at Dartmouth, or making fledgling efforts at filmmaking in Chicago, San Francisco, and New York — which paint a picture of an insecure, grasping, neurotic woman who required constant attention and reassurance. The content ranged from recounting daily activities and movie going, to jealous suspicions about poets and filmmakers who became important to him (e.g., Robert Duncan and Lawrence Jordan), and comments on films and art that revealed a middle-brow sensibility that must have irritated him. She would hint at debts and money shortages, just enough to make him anxious without divulging the details, and, even worse, would burden him with the ups and downs of her love life and desperate need for male attention — in one stating bluntly, "I need someone, Stan, so I don't swallow you alive." [20]

A typical, allegedly complimentary letter is all too revealing of her maternal style: "Your fat, little, hernia-crippled, asthmatic, goggle-eyed body, has turned into a long, lank, lean, handsome, lithe, beautiful young man's body." [21] The flattering part, a clueless, inappropriate appraisal of her son's mature body, is preceded by a detailed, even grotesque description of his earlier self. The latter not only confirms Brakhage's account of the physical infirmities that plagued his childhood, but suggests that his pre-occupation with them owes a great deal to the insensitive view Clara must have had at the time, to which her choice of words written years after the fact, strongly attests. They intimate, however unintentionally, that this was how she felt and talked about his body when he was a child, adding to the shame he felt at school around other boys rather than helping him to cope with it.

Given the evidence of such a letter, the implications of the shame that pervades the childhood book may even be understated, in that it clearly distorted his perspective, justifying his anger and resentments against boys who he believed not only had real homes where they were loved, but who were loved *because* they were physically fit and attractive. This went further, when at age eleven, during the war, with everyone preoccupied with food stamps and rations, his overeating was deemed "unpatriotic" because it was taking food away from the soldiers fighting and dying for the country. Young Stanley admits both sadistic pleasure and guilt when he learns that one of these normal, loved, and privileged grown-up boys has been killed. At the same time, he wanted desperately to be a soldier like them, and would act out war scenarios, much like other boys, going so far as to steal a Purple Heart from a car, which he says was "the worst thing he had ever done."

And so, Brakhage's complaint that he was even denied the close mother-son relationship following divorce, may have been partly rooted in a repugnance he sensed that Clara could not conceal. It would appear that her addiction to men, as documented in the book, complemented this in that it underlined his unattractiveness. At the same time her remarks about his "beautiful young's man's body" lend an unsavory edge to her petulant whining over physical and sexual needs in letters to him where she speaks of trying not to suffocate him, while nevertheless leaning on him during lonely intervals. It's possible that since Lou was homosexual and eventually lived with a man for many years until he died that his and Clara's sex life was less than ideal, perhaps even largely non-existent for the few years they were together. If so, Clara's acting out with men might well have been a reaction to years of rejection and insecurity about her attractiveness, which would partly explain one aspect of her behavior.

All of this suggests that the conditions for the emergence of a classical Oedipus complex are hard to determine: neither an unambiguous enough maternal attachment nor an adequate male rival seemed present. Brakhage tells us, in fact, that, given the instability of his life, especially after Clara left Lou and took up with other men, "by far the strongest and most constant adult male influence in my entire childhood [was Adolf Hitler]. He was always there in newsreels until my teens. I saw more of him than of any other man." Young Stanley yearns to be accepted by a strong male figure, but feels he was a big disappointment to Lou for not being a "regular" kid good at sports. Throughout the book, his strongest expressions of affection are towards other boys, and an occasional man like Pete, because they embodied everything he was not: handsome, athletic, brave, strong, and of upstanding moral character — the epitome of Jack Armstrong, the All-American Boy.

But if conditions precluded a recognizable Oedipus complex at the appropriate age, and therefore no resolution of such, evidence of Oedipally-tinged rivalries in his adult life can be discerned in relationships with men, especially in connection to Jane. For, if she came to be not only his wife but the image of the primal mother he never had — an image forever enshrined in *Window Water Baby Moving* (1959), a film that registers, beyond paternal pride, an exhilaration that may also reflect a vicarious imagining of his own birth — then every strong, idealized male figure that entered their lives thereafter was a potential threat. Jane's brother, the poet Jack Collum, was one, but also Bearthm, their first son. In one communication with me, Jane recalled Brakhage, looking distressed as they walked side by side and he observed her looking down and cooing lovingly at the infant in her arms, asking her curtly what transpired between them. "He's saying, 'Me Oedipus, you Jocasta,'" quipped Jane.

This might be amusing were it not that, according to Jane, Brakhage remained jealous of his first son, a point elaborated elsewhere [22] and one that shows up in the correspondence. "Last Sat., showing a mixture of films to George Kuchar and 'friends,' one after another excused themselves (all perfectly sound pretexts) until I was left in the dark alone viewing my work. Bear, as usual, led the exodus, with his usual pained expression (as if he'd die if he had to watch one more Brakhage film, but also with that gleam of Oedipal pride in his eye that, by God he DIDN'T have to put up with this anymore, etc.) ..."[23] It's a toss-up whose gleam flares the brighter here. As we shall see, however, Brakhage's wounded pride tied to Oedipal feelings was not limited to familial relations.

The Lonely Monster

From a psychoanalytic point of view, the importance of the childhood book, however mediated or incomplete as a record of the past, is that it reveals a great deal about Brakhage at the time he recounted the memories — for despite the psychological baggage the process undoubtedly tapped, it's unlikely he was fully aware of its ramifications for the present. His recollections are less about filling in, or reconstructing the past, than they are, unconsciously, about deflecting, confessing to, or providing defensive rationalizations for, troublesome feelings around circumstances in the present. But if this essay discovers within the book rich material for suggesting just how Brakhage's past resonates with the present, it is owing to the eloquent and restrained prose of Jane Wodening, which strikes a perfect balance, never allowing her knowledge of the man — as well as the child in the man — to interfere with her respect for the subtle evocations of literary form.

As the long quotation at the beginning suggests, Brakhage's experience at age four was directly tied to the convictions he formed about himself throughout his adult life, and the behavior that ensued. To deny his convictions would be hypocritical, he avowed. "False modesty erodes integrity and integrity is what my destiny is made of and without my destiny, I die.... This I proved in pre-school and have been proving ever since."

To read such an assessment of one's character as the "simple truth" is naïve. Brakhage, here, superimposes a blanket retroactive value on the memories he is recalling, as if everything throughout his childhood, good and bad, were not only part of his "destiny," but driven by an unwavering commitment to truth. Yet underlying the bravado and righteousness, there is a desperate need to assert a superior self-image and disavow the fragile structure that sustains it. The "truth" of the assertion, "false modesty erodes integrity" is apparent, but the next phrase, "integrity is what my destiny is made of," can only be a self-aggrandizing wish; while the phrase, "without my destiny, I die," as banal as it is redundant, says nothing about Brakhage that isn't true of everyone. Taken out of context, though, every key word undoubtedly carried significance — even sincerity — for the man who made the statement. The truth, therefore, lies not in the perverse form of syllogistic logic which the sentence adopts, but in what it reveals of the ego that needs to insist upon the virtuousness of its character. People usually do that because the qualities of virtue to which they repeatedly lay claim are not readily apparent in their actions and behavior toward others. Brakhage's desperate need to cling to this virtue demonstrated just how vulnerable he would be if, in fact, he was ever forced to concede it as a delusion.

Consider, for example, his "admission" in the opening quotation that he clings to his neuroses, itself an example of false modesty. He justifies his inflated sense of self-importance and his "fierce defense" of his neuroses by claiming that such behavior is consistent with Freud's. His naïve dismissal of Freud's followers is no surprise since none quite fit the heroic stature of the "founding" figure, whose original achievements against the norms were based on his pioneer investigations of his own psyche, much like the way Brakhage's achievements in the art of film originally sprang from explorations of his own life. Thus, he could align himself with another genius devoted to the "truth," as he was. Nevertheless, his self-description virtually encapsulates the clinical profile of pathological narcissism, as delineated by Otto Kernberg, a "follower" of Freud hardly bent on "obscuring" the truth.

Pathological narcissism (as opposed to the ordinary kind we all bear) is by no means incompatible with artistic genius. It is characterized by a grandiose sense of self-importance, "an unusual degree of self-reference," an "inordinate need for tribute from others," and "pathological forms of self-love and ... object love."[24] All of these traits are in evidence in Brakhage's public declarations and in his dealings with others throughout his adult life, the "models" of which are discernible in the memories recounted in the book. Indeed, while Brakhage did not undergo orthodox psychoanalysis, he fit to a "t" in many relationships the kind of patient described by Kernberg who is so full of narcissistic rage that his transference would seesaw wildly between "ruthless demandingness and depreciatory attacks on the therapist."[25] So, to Brakhage's implicit dismissal of psychoanalytic investigation, in the neat, deceptively innocent phrase, "maybe it's as simple as that," let us say "yes" — except for the terrible consequences.

Recognizing and dealing with this condition is, of course, complicated, if not compounded, when the individual who fits the profile also happens to possess enormous artistic and intellectual gifts, with talent in multiple areas, indefatigable energies toward creating works of unquestioned originality and merit — works admired by a community of artists, filmmakers, writers, and scholars. Add to this, lecturing and teaching abilities that, however they fed his ego, also affected and inspired numerous individuals over decades. So, when Brakhage characterized himself as "the world's greatest living visionary,"[26] he was doing two things: describing something that illuminati of the film and literary worlds fully acknowledged as true, *and* manifesting a character disorder that from early on bedeviled his personal life and relationships. This was the paradox and the misfortune of those areas of his life most affected by the disorder.

While we presume that Brakhage managed to live, love, raise a family, and experience joy, despite the crippling effects he himself acknowledged of his earliest years, this essay confines itself to the unfortunate effects of the latter, leaving to a more comprehensive biographical study the complex interaction of the positive and negative aspects in relation to the seemingly paradoxical nature of his underlying psychology. The paradox I speak of has to do with the co-existence of two, seemingly contradictory traits: on the one hand, a strong enough ego, facilitating the intellectual confidence to apply his considerable gifts toward great creative achievements; and on the other hand, the lack of stable internal emotional and psychological structures to cope with narcissistic injury and make it possible to love and admire others *as others*.

This is the dilemma faced by the pathological narcissist, whose constant need to be fed by others is like a stomach that, without food, forces insidious acids to bubble up and attack the organ's protective linings. As Heinz Kohut, the founder of self psychology, asserts, the tendency to idealize others is driven by the belief, indeed the desperate hope, that these "others" can repair the deficits in personality development, providing the validation and love of which they were deprived as children and continue to crave. This idealization phase is inevitably followed by the deprecation and expulsion of these very suppliers, once they no longer provide such sustenance. Kohut labeled these suppliers "self-objects" because their identities as individuals are overshadowed by the adjunctive role they play for the narcissist.[27] One sees this dynamic played out throughout Brakhage's correspondence, as one friendship after another, at first fulsomely embraced and celebrated, eventually went sour. Typical of the narcissist, Brakhage rationalized his own role in the eventual breakdown of such relationships, assuming the victim's posture even while repudiating that as a weakness. Often he would adopt a pleading, abject tone — "I seem to keep losing friends. I must be a terrible person to know" [28] — only to switch gears a moment later.

In one letter, a paragraph that begins, "I have very few friends these days," moves to sweeping self-pity, then to child-like retaliation, then to rationalization and a stab at self-analysis, and then back to pleading: "I have been much used by almost everyone I know and much abused (publically rejected, for whatever surge of ego it gives P. Adams, Hollis Frampton, Kenneth Anger, Jonas Mekas, Ken Jacobs now this summer, etcetera, etcetera) and I am damn sick of that — had the pleasing notion this morning that I should take out a small ad in The Village Voice and announce to all those who've stopped speaking to ME that now I've finally decided to stop speaking to THEM.... I have somehow given the impression to my friends that I was an infinite pin-cushion/push-over for their egocentricities (perhaps because I was so constantly bullied as a little fat boy?) ... and thus can hardly blame them for taking beseemingly endless advantage of that: truth is I've come to the natural end of my tolerance of all such. I want my friends to know that I, too, hurt, am easily hurt, have often been hurt in our exchanges.... I am NOT the god-damn rock-o-gibraltar many have taken me to be." [29]

This is a typical example of the free-wheeling style of Brakhage's letters that so resembles a lively psychoanalytic session. As the reference to being "bullied as a little fat boy" indicates, he traced — and justified — much of his behavior to circumstances in his childhood. These memories were haunting enough for Brakhage to relate, even when they were unflattering to his ego, but in this instance it seemed a way to characterize those "friends" he lists as just another group of bullies he had to fight, while pretending he hardly blames them for taking advantage. On the evidence of many letters like this and the sentiments they perpetuated, his life — its achievements, joys, and rewards notwithstanding — seems to have been an endless cycle of misery looking for company from which genuine relief was always out of reach. As

Wodening's book has it, and many letters attest, he identified with the Ugly Duckling not primarily because it eventually became a beautiful swan, but because he thought of himself as a "clearly designated monster ... the ONE who ISN'T 'innocent,'"[30] doomed to be misunderstood and misappreciated. Of all the comics he created and drew, his favorite was *Demono*, a creature like himself, in touch with dark forces. At age eleven, angry that his mother found him a job vacuuming an office building on Saturdays, which meant no movies, he says, "I emanated dark and silent resentment. I was Demono, dormant."

Such fantasized identities must have comforted his loneliness, but the book also registers painful yearnings for a real home and family, and a desire for companionship. The description of his time with the Hultmans — whose two adopted children no doubt helped him feel less of an outsider — glows with joy and relief. He is so impressed by how orderly the home was run and how everything was openly discussed with the children that it may well be that that experience was the inspiration behind his and Jane's efforts to create a similar community spirit with their five children by having family meetings to air grievances. Even the end of the unhappy summer at Harmony Hall shows this craving. Stanley and the boys constructed a miniature village from rocks, sticks, and assorted scraps, inspired by such a fantasy:

> "Remembering the village makes me feel disturbed and bitter. It was an exquisite thing.... an amazingly wondrous thing, an enchanted village, a jewel of human expression. It was an ideal civilization. Among the ten of us there was kindness and warmth, camaraderie and shared obsession. We were making incomparable loveliness out of trash. Everything in the village was there because of a natural need, either for the safety and comfort of the village or as a personal expression. Yet no individual kid was terribly important. The important thing was the village itself and the feeling of community

> we all had. What makes me bitter is the fact that this has never happened to me again. It seems to me that such a spirit of togetherness should be the norm, that people should naturally work together to make, in concert, the most wonderful community possible with what means are available, that the splendor, the attraction of such an endeavor should keep people from self-indulgence and destructiveness. Yet it's never happened to me again, I've never even seen it again."

It's impossible not to detect Wodening's voice in the congenial tenor of this description. But it's equally difficult not to link the accent on camaraderie and obsession, on making lovely things out of meager means, on personal expression and the feeling of community, with the extended "family" of avant-garde filmmakers and their champions to which Brakhage belonged — leading the pack, of course, just as he was elected mayor of the village — several of whose leading lights he cites in the above letter to Carolee Schneemann. He claims elsewhere that he tried "to reconcile, unsuccessfully" the rejection he felt from Jacobs, and accuses Frampton of having "pretended to friendliness to set me up for future hurt."[31] So angry did he remain with the latter that on hearing of Frampton's death shortly after, he writes to a fellow filmmaker, "Hollis' death came as a confused grief (as abt [sic] the last act of his toward me was one of the meanest I've ever sustained in a mean time; but then earlier memories mixed with that ... dunno really what to say ... about the general drift of affections)."[32]

It's hard not to sense in his emphasizing that such a communal experience never happened again that he had in mind the breakdown of such feelings among those whose friendships he cherished and lost. The board meetings at Anthology Film Archives were "among the most painful of my entire life" — "I nearly lost ALL those friends thru the terrible encounters of those meetings.... P. Adams certainly was lost to me from those meetings on."[33] While Brakhage admits he "caused most of the pain," he attributes this to his constant state of anxiety and to "spasms of nervous reaction." It is noteworthy that in the description of the village, he links, almost by cause and effect, falling into "self-indulgence and destructiveness" to the collapse of an imagined, mutually supportive community, which, while a clear example of displaced responsibility — a masked cry of "you made me do it" — nevertheless reveals the utter loneliness which he felt was his fate. Clearly, these losses had their effect: "NOTHING," he tells Bruce Baillie, in "my pretty rough childhood and fairly terrible teens ... match[es] the hatred from left AND right the last 5 years, the hate mail and public and private nastinesses of MUCH of the film community, young AND old, the 'rejections' of 'old friends,' so called."[34] This pattern weaves in and out of Brakhage's correspondence, and surfaces, thinly disguised in the childhood book.

No doubt his grandiosity had much to do with his sabotaging of relationships. It was safer to court allegiances with those who couldn't reject him — distant, great leaders of every stripe, all of whom were probably as fiercely attached to their narcissism and equally convinced that it was inseparable from their genius. While Brakhage, the artist, identified with Freud, Pound, Stein, and their like, young, adopted Stanley felt an affinity with Moses, a foundling who became the leader of his people, Franklin Delano Roosevelt (who was President during the entire period covered by the childhood book), and Adolf Hitler whose rousing speeches in newsreels and on the radio in the late thirties/early forties utterly entranced him. Erik Erikson once described Hitler as an adolescent gang leader, which may suggest his appeal as a model for how Stanley ran "gangs" for a time, and how he, the brains of the operations, would make his minions do the dirty work of executing ever more ingenious thefts.

A more benign version of the power he felt Hitler embodied, conveyed in the book, is reflected in his desire to be the savior of the world, the enlightener, the one with the answer to every mystery of life, who wanted to be invited every Sunday to the local Protestant church to show films and speak eloquently to a congregation that would welcome, love and understand what he had to say and go away enriched. Anyone who has attended Brakhage's film showings and lectures should have no difficulty grasping how closely he approximated this wish in his adult life. No doubt the *idée fixe* that his films — like the angelic singing voice with perfect pitch with which he was apparently blessed — were "given" to him, that he was the chosen vessel to channel their unique visions, was the most hubristic expression of this conviction.

It appears that young Stanley was more impressed by the commanding style of his idols than by their moral characters or the truth of what they said, for whatever notion he had of "truth," it became the justification beyond reproach for behavior that was anything but. Over and over in his interactions, cruel or insensitive treatment of others is rationalized as serving the truth at all costs. As any psychoanalyst knows, a patient who persistently clings to a particular virtue has conveniently appropriated that virtue as a defense. Insisting on one's truthfulness is the most suspect of all since "truth" is often relative, can be bent to one's will, fused with insidious behavior, and made to serve the ends of a defensive ego.

"Friends Hurt / The Most"

— Archilochos[35]

Arguably, the most extended and most poignant account of Stan's friendships in Wodening's book is the one with a slightly older boy named Jon Stark. It is so convincing and revealing — perhaps, in part, because it is also the least flattering — that it can serve as a paradigm of how Brakhage became both wielder of, and victim to, the pernicious effects of pathological narcissism. His "champion in gym class," defending Stan against those who called him "Fatty" and mocked his inability to perform activities, Jon had a deformity of his own — a hand with only a pinky and a thumb with a mass of formless flesh between — so he knew what it was to be humiliated. He and Stan became fast friends, went to movies together, played after school and on weekends, and talked about many serious subjects. Only when Stan is invited to Jon's home does he realize that he belonged to a wealthy family. He dines well and is driven home by the chauffeur.

On the first class of third grade, following summer vacation, "the teacher conceived a game to introduce the kids to each other. We would each draw one of the other children on the blackboard and the rest of the class would guess who it was." The one whose sketch is readily guessed would win the praise and admiration of the teacher, something Stan repeatedly sought and received throughout elementary school. He begins to draw Jon, but is torn about whether to include the deformed hand, which, of course, would be a dead giveaway to his identity, and thereby insure Stan's winning the contest. He ponders for a while, rationalizes that, after all, he would only be drawing what is true, and decides to include the hand in the picture. "Everyone recognized him immediately. It was lovely. I shone." Stan then looks over at Jon who, head lowered over his desk, is humiliated, "hurt and angry." In the playground at recess, Jon accuses him of being "very, very cruel" and says he doesn't want to be his friend any more.

Stan defends himself, expresses surprise that Jon is hurt, minimizes what he himself did, claims innocence, and denies being cruel. None of this is necessarily unusual for a young child; apology, not to mention genuine remorse, requires fairly sophisticated development. But in the account as written, he becomes angry about "los[ing] what I needed. Why was the center of my happiness always taken away?" Rather than acknowledge that it was his action that humiliated Jon and destroyed the friendship, young Stanley sees it as just another example of life's injustice, that every time he found something good or someone to love, it is taken away. And, of course, there is some truth to this, given the revolving door of Clara's paramours, and of those short-lived situations with families where he was happy. Even though he and Jon made up somewhat the following year, the friendship was never the same. It would seem that for Brakhage, hurting others, self-pity, and the cost of telling the truth all went hand in hand.

Though Brakhage apparently could not overcome similar psychodynamics in the future, Wodening remembers him conveying remorse while relating this story. If so, it's more than likely because such feelings were triggered, however unconsciously, by a re-enactment in the present. This suggests that the sources of at least some of the childhood memories were not only results of excavations prompted by conversations between Brakhage and his wife, but that the strongest ones were more palpably prompted by specific circumstances in the present. And in fact, the fallout with the writer Guy Davenport, a long-standing friend of both Stan and Jane, occurred during the very period that Brakhage was recounting his memories to Jane. In his letter to James Ottis (March 6, 1983) quoted above, we learn that he told Jane "all that he could recall of his childhood memories between ages 7 and 8" — which would include the third grade experience and the Jon Stark episode — giving her "three-months work." In the letter to Charles Boultenhouse later that year [36] he states that her manuscript has now reached 200 pages, which means it was well past that episode.

Like the full, rich friendship between Stan and Jon described in the book — "what excited us was a developing similarity of minds" — the friendship with Davenport was stimulating for both men. Jane told me they "lived between the lines" and could finish each other's sentences. The friendship went back to when the Brakhage children were still very young. Stan shares intimate details of his daughter Neowyn's delivery of his and Jane's first grandchild [37] and speaks of the children "scattered" in different parts of the country, as he and Jane are getting used to living alone, all because Davenport is "one of the very few of my found family — if you don't mind my thus imagining you, telling you of the birth of our grandchild as best my trembling fingers can tap out." Some shop talk follows, then he mentions that Jane was so inspired by a letter from Davenport that she "finished three pieces, two chapters of [her] Wolf and Coyote book [and] a story about a mad Professor in the neighborhood" — which impressed Stan because it assumed a detachment necessary to write "about a man she absolutely detests." "Your encouragement," he tells Davenport, "was, I feel, the midwife of that writ." In another letter, he mentions reading aloud Davenport's "57 Views of Fujiyama," to which Jane "clapped her hands and said, 'I love him.'" Though Brakhage immediately interprets her outburst to "mean, on examination, both you and Basho," that appended remark suggests a not entirely unconscious rearing of a dormant Oedipal twitch. He continues with extensive talk of Gertrude Stein and Marguerite Young (who, contrary to Brakhage's enthusiasm, left Davenport cold) and effusive praise of Davenport's own writing, calling him a "wonder."[38]

Then, on December 9, 1982, Brakhage is asked to provide a reference letter for Davenport, who has been nominated for a John D. and Catherine T. MacArthur Foundation prize. He writes the reference letter, dated November 18, 1982 (a mistake, corrected in pencil by the archivist to suggest the far more likely date, December 18). To anyone not privy to the MacArthur's guidelines, Brakhage's letter, on the surface, would seem laudatory. He assumes (underlined) that the Foundation already knows Davenport to be "one of our greatest living writers," and goes on to praise Davenport for being one of the "very few artists who can find the time and energy to both maintain personal creativity and to devote themselves to helping others, and, therefore the Arts in general." In other words, the letter speaks of Davenport's teaching, mentoring, and inspirational skills rather than his talents as a creative writer — the thrust, in fact, of the Foundation's seeking "evidence of originality, dedication to creative pursuits, and capacity for self-direction. The awards are given to these individuals over five years so that they may have the time and freedom to fulfill their promise by devoting themselves to their own creative endeavors."[39]

Brakhage surely understood that he was not focusing on what the foundation wanted to know. Against the rules — as Jane recalls and Davenport later acknowledges — he sent a copy of the reference letter to Davenport. Although there is no document to indicate exactly when, Jane thinks it must have been soon after he had written it. In any case, in another letter, written eleven days after he sent the reference letter off, Brakhage makes no mention of having done so, and does not hint in any way that he has sent a copy of it to Davenport. He details, as always, the adventures of his grown children, mentions that he and Jane have "celebrated [their] 25th anniversary with a bit of turbot, cooked broccoli, eggnog laced with cognac, pumpkin bread with whipped cream, candles and much quiet cheer (the ONLY anniversary, but one, we can remember ever having without a quarrel)." Because of arthritic pains, he says, he "can't work more than two hours a day ... but DO work steadily and am slowly piecing together a very strange and unique 'Tortured Dust' — a little over 40 min completed now." Turning "50 in a couple of weeks (have lived half my life with Jane)," he feels he is "finally adjusting to the wear and tear of earthn [sic] tumble — maybe just worn out ... maybe just inheritor of some well-earned peace awhile now."[40]

There certainly does not appear to be anything untoward in this letter, nothing to suggest Brakhage had second thoughts about the reference letter. The next communication available in the Archive is a letter from Brakhage to Davenport, dated July 24, 1983, responding to a phone call from Davenport (perhaps following his having received a copy of the reference letter?) in which Davenport had "rejected"

Brakhage, leaving him "very hurt." After "months" of thinking about it, Brakhage concludes that a "misunderstanding" is at fault, that he (Brakhage) "has no sense of honor appropro [sic] grants, prizes, and the like," mocks the politics and the "slot-machine" luck of the draw, and justifies his emphasis on Davenport's "influence as a teacher...because I've heard this aspect interests the MacArthur Foundation most." He "cannot imagine [that] sending [Davenport a copy of] the letter in itself could have caused such anger." [41] For his part, Davenport who, like Brakhage, would have learned about the MacArthur Foundation Awards announced the previous February, understandably reacts with a note [42] worth quoting in its terse entirety:

"Stan:
You abuse the confidence of the MacArthur Foundation,
you see to it — gratuitously, irresponsibly, and with vicious
insensitivity — that I know I have been considered and passed
over for the most generous and prestigious of grants, and you
are hurt! Jesus."

The succinctness of Davenport's reply — bordered by double black lines typical of death announcements — is the perfect foil to the web of pleading rhetoric woven by Brakhage: the same lack of remorse, the same surprise at the other's reaction, the same failure to acknowledge the wound he has inflicted, the same insistence that he is innocent of any error or malice, all laced with the same hurt at having been wounded and having lost yet another person important to him through some fickle turn of fate rather than any behavior of his.

Taken together, both the earlier incident and the later testify to the enduring nature of the psychodynamics in question. For if the Stark incident in the book is a mediated description of Brakhage recalling an unhappy memory without imposing adult feelings onto the seven or eight-year old Stanley, the Davenport case presents us with the virtually identical set of reactions — this time unmediated — from the words of Brakhage himself in the "present." A child's inability to empathize is one thing; an adult who continues to exhibit "little empathy for the feelings of others" is ruled by a narcissistic disorder.[43] If Davenport read between the lines of Brakhage's letter to the Foundation — as he was purportedly able to do in their conversations — he might have sensed that beyond "vicious insensitivity," Brakhage was acting out in the crudest terms yet another Oedipal conflict, fueled by pathological narcissism. Far from "gratuitous," therefore, sending Davenport a copy of the reference letter amounted to rubbing his rival's face in defeat.[44]

Given these consequences and the parallels that support them, it seems that the Jon Stark story of *Brakhage's Childhood* is not merely being echoed in the Brakhage/Davenport relationship. It is far more likely that the acute tone, the emotional thrust, and the psychological dynamics of the former are actually a veiled account of the fallout from the latter — i.e., Brakhage's treatment of Davenport — which would have been fresh and raw at the time, riddled with the empty, queasy feeling of misperceived Oedipal victory. Given the price one pays for that victory, it is both easier and safer to displace narcissistic injury and pathological defense onto a distant memory than it is to face it in the present. The pain of the loss of Davenport's friendship was no doubt shared by Jane, which may be why its significance and its resonance within the book was once marked by a small clue: among the fictional names once used, the name Garth, given Jon Stark, had a wonderful sonorous evocation of the first two Brakhage sons, Bearthm and Rarc. But it is difficult not to wonder now if the G, in fact, was a nod — however unconscious and regardless of who chose it — to Guy Davenport.

Rage and Pain

From the psychoanalytic perspective, any obsessional pattern of destructive behavior toward others is accompanied by imagined psychological gain. Unless we concede the existence of pure evil or unadulterated masochism — both counter, in principle, to psychoanalytic thinking — we must wonder what unconsciously motivates the enactor, how he or she can give free reign to malicious instincts without realizing the toll it takes on oneself. In Brakhage's case, the pathology of hurting others and disowning responsibility after the fact seems indisputable and persistent — even if we concede that its most damaging form only emerged during acute crises. Whether or not it sustained his image of the perennially suffering, misunderstood monster, no behavior so deeply-ingrained can fail to make one's self as miserable as it makes others. And, judging from his own words and the testimony of others, Brakhage's torments must have been something he faced every day in order to work and survive. The image of him struggling up the mountain in *Dog Star Man* is not unfitting. But just as the oral rage he vented against his adoptive mother increased as he got older, he apparently could not subdue his envies and jealousies against others, nor avoid taking revenge against those "working for the evil one," who disappointed him or let him down — even relatively inconsequential encounters as with the publisher of Turtle Island Press, against whom Brakhage vowed, for some perceived wrong, to get revenge "from the black bottom of my heart ... to destroying your reputation (assuming you still have one)." [45]

Like the rubber ball at the end of *Murder Psalm* hurled into the fountain and splashing a young girl softly blowing a petal across the water, leaving her perplexed (and perhaps inducing an epileptic fit) at the lighthearted malice of the boy who hurled it; or like the snowball that kills in Cocteau's *Blood of a Poet* (1930), narcissistic injury can be inflicted by the slightest, most "innocent" of gestures. Notwithstanding his egoistic self-image, Brakhage was, as he himself confesses in the letter to Schneemann, easily wounded. Indeed, the narcissistic personality can harbor both "haughty grandiosity ... and feelings of inferiority ... without [the one] affecting [the] other." [46] To the pathological narcissist, the right looks or words, flawlessly aimed and timed, do kill; the only way to survive and triumph is to deflect them, to turn them against those whose opprobrium we fear, or, more perversely, those whose esteem we crave but cannot trust long enough to prevent putting it to the ultimate test and poisoning its source. "How can one blame 'innocent monstrosity'?" he had asked in regard to a discussion of parents, "well, I have one clear answer here, which is simply that you'll blame yourSELF if you don't, i.e., guilt binds the relationship SOMEhow ... almost as if it were ALL that were left to most people ... in familial relationship ... it is my own instincts I'm talking abt [sic], knowing full well that MINE are warped (by age 4 or 5 probably) in this respect." [47]

His rage — whether expressed or suppressed — must have been so powerful, so primal that it could never be adequately assuaged through vitriolic attacks on others. This is tantamount to saying that eventually others were no longer the primary targets. As an adult, disappointment in others was, consistent with the mindset of a *conflicted* narcissist, increasingly outmatched by disappointment in himself — that he was not the ideal husband and father he imagined himself to be, which implied that he had failed to expunge in himself the "evil" and selfishness he believed was embodied by his mother. Clearly, he was incapable of achieving sufficient distance from her to rid himself of inheriting her bad traits — as he had imagined he could in the 1957 letter. That suggests that he had internalized them too deeply as a child and they had resurfaced with a vengeance in the 1980s, such that every feeling of disgust and rage towards her had now, inevitably, induced unbearable disgust and rage towards himself. And given who she was and the middle-brow sensibility she could hardly overcome, it must have infuriated him, a man of enormous artistic and intellectual gifts, that he was unable to free himself of such clinging, pathetic character traits inherited from a woman who was not even blood-related. The only defense would be to project every character deformity on to her, while magnifying and clinging to those things that allowed him to transcend such mendacious origins: his enormous talents, his visions, and his "God-given" art.

However we imagine we can conceal the ugliness in ourselves by projecting it outward, those around us perceive more than we suspect. Around the time of the release of *Tortured Dust* (1984), Brakhage, writing of a visit from his son Bearthm, mentions that the latter was learning "how to look into people's eyes and imagine a third eye, or inner eye ... he'd tried this on Jane ... but couldn't get past some very solid 'wall.'" He is afraid to look into his father's eyes, but just as he is about to leave and hugs Stan "stiffly," his father "gripped his shoulders with [his] wrists and ... held him and let him look directly into my eyes ... I was so much letting him INTO my eyes that I have NO memory of his expression — had to ask later of Jane what happened." To his father, Bearthm only said, "Crazy, man," but to Jane he confided that he saw what he expected: "a beautiful explosion of excruciating pain." [48]

An indication of how, despite his efforts, Brakhage's behavior continued to mirror his mother's so late in his life, even her propensity for collecting lovers, can be glimpsed in the pitiable letters he wrote to Jane before they actually divorced in 1986. Like Clara's to him in the 1950s, they were written almost daily for a time and filled with flattery, pleas to forgive his rages, promises to repair the damages, and resolves to do everything to restore her love and trust in him. But, also like Clara's, they reveal a deep, resentful insecurity that undermines genuine feeling, resembling that same unconscious mechanism that we discern in his failed friendships — in which incipient remorse is strangled by narcissistic self-pity — every mea culpa overruled by an *Et tu, Brute?*

This leads back to the question of what gain one "perceives" from acting out against others. Strangely enough, in *Brakhage's Childhood,* however much Stanley is beaten or spanked by Clara or one of her boyfriends, he almost never uses the word "hurt." And if he does, it has a flat, hollow ring, somewhat like his use of it on an occasion I recall in the late 1970s, following a screening at the Museum of Modern Art. It was a response to a perceived insult from a spectator who questioned the very basis of Brakhage's art because he couldn't follow his film — not an unreasonable reaction for anyone unfamiliar with his work. Notwithstanding Brakhage's claim that he is easily hurt — in the letter to Carolee Schneemann — his statement, "you hurt me," in response to the spectator, seemed strained and unconvincing. Having now gone through the papers and letters in the Archive, it seems clearer to me why. Over and over the word seems reserved primarily in response to an idealized or respected person, one who would have the power to inflict real narcissistic injury. While I have no idea who the man in the audience was, he did not fit this description, which is perhaps why Brakhage's "hurt" response came across as feigned, a play for sympathy, an effort to turn the tables, or some form of insincere flattery towards the man.

Yet, even when the word is used in relation to those whom he respects, it seems inadequate, as if its monosyllabic bluntness belies the wound it purports to inflict, cutting off any deep feeling before it can completely emerge. One would have to examine archival evidence more extensively to be certain, but my sense is that its use by Brakhage reflected a deep-seated defense against the full force of perceived injury — in tandem with what I suggested above about his efforts toward remorse being choked off before it had a chance to surface. The clockwork mechanism of such a pattern is a strong indication of its hold over his unconscious, in which its original function as a defense became a lifetime behavioral feature — possibly the only way he felt he could ward off a mortal blow.

In "normal" character development, the individual moves from primary narcissism, "characterized by the total absence of any relationship to the outside world," to a secondary narcissism, which derives from the individual's ability to identify with others, allowing such identifications to flow back and enrich the individual's ego.[49] But in the case of a narcissistically disordered personality, as Kohut has it, the ability to identify with the other is skewed since the "other" is not recognized as such. It only exists to serve and sustain the self's deficient state; as soon as the "other's" needs surface, it not only loses its use value as a self-object, but is in fact a threat to the integrity one imagines one has achieved as a result of believing one has internalized a good object. If, instead of steadily supplying sustenance to the deficient ego of the pathological narcissist, the "other" turns toward its own needs, it is automatically rendered imperfect, thereby devaluing it as an idealized self-object.

Behaviorally, what this suggests in the case of Brakhage is that he could only sustain — or, more precisely, *imagined* on some deep unconscious level that he could only sustain — idealized relationships for as long, *and only as long*, as they fed his hunger and elevated his sense of self-esteem. As soon as it became clear that such figures were imperfect objects themselves, he would rear back in defense and reclaim those libidinal energies he had extended toward the now rejected self-object, projecting in their stead "cool indifference or feelings of rage, humiliation, or emptiness as a response to criticism, indifference, or defeat."[50] It may even be that his first marriage — and to some extent his first family — fell victim to this very pattern.

Few things are sadder and more unsettling than sensing the power of this unconscious phenomenon over an adult whose considerable intellectual and artistic gifts seem helpless to overcome such a pernicious, energy-depleting pattern. Such a person seems unable to free himself from the relentless search for idealized self-objects, along with the concomitant rejection of those who no longer satisfy that need

— a vicious cycle that can only generate misery for all parties. Was the "excruciating pain" that Bearthm "saw" integral to the "beauty" of his father's work? Such sentiments may seem clichéd, but we cannot dismiss the connection in Brakhage's case without looking more closely at the films in light of new insights. My guess is that, far from diminishing his art, it would increase our appreciation of his daunting achievement in the light of the emotional and psychological deficits with which he had to contend. In fact, I believe that the visual density of his films, his use of rapid editing, superimpositions, repeated and layered imagery, were techniques designed, in part, to seize and expose the deepest, least accessible aspects of his psyche that he could not otherwise fathom. This is particularly true of the autobiographical work, from the psychodramas to *Scenes from Under Childhood* (1967–69), and later, the *Sincerity* (1973, 1975, 1978) and *Duplicity* (1978–1980) series, all of which resonate with emotional and psychological revelations yet to be exhausted.

For his unfailing and prompt assistance while researching and writing this essay, I wish to thank Brad Arnold of the Stan Brakhage Papers / Archive in Boulder, Colorado. For their encouragement, generosity, patience, and astute observations, I am grateful to Jane (Brakhage) Wodening, P. Adams Sitney, and Carole Pipolo.

Notes

1 Letter to Chris McCabe and Mimi Brav, December 24, 1983.

2 In *Motion Picture*, Winter/Spring, 1987.

3 Letter to Charles Boultenhouse, October 26, 1983. The final manuscript, as Jane recalls, was about 300 typewritten pages, which suggests that the collaboration on the book continued for perhaps another year and ended about two years before the official divorce.

4 Letter to James Ottis, March (or May) 6, 1983.

5 There are more than a few "explanations" for this. One is that a teacher planted the idea in his head, having found Stan's writing style similar to Wolfe's. P. Adams Sitney, however, recalls Brakhage telling him that an older friend who knew Wolfe insisted on it. Tracking this down, he discovered that Wolfe had visited the town where his real mother lived. But according to the official registry card recording his birth at the Willows Maternity Home, which does not use names, the baby, born January 24, 1933, is identified as Robert; his mother is a 22-year old high school graduate of English extraction studying to be a nurse; and his father a 23-year old bookkeeper of English/German extraction. In a letter to Clara from Willows — a home that declares on its stationery as offering "superior children," she is told that her and Ludwig's appeal to adopt a baby was delayed because "Robert's" mother had every intention of keeping the child until she received news that made it impossible for her to do so. Clara is informed that the baby the Home has in mind for her is normal and healthy in every way.

6 Letter to Mimi Brav, June 12, 1984; Brakhage frequently expressed admiration for Freud, including to me as we drove from New York to Princeton, and back, in the spring of 1990, on the occasion of my inviting him to show films and lecture.

7 Letter to Mimi Brav, August 22, 1984.

8 Sigmund Freud [1915], quoted in J. Laplanche and J. B. Pontalis, *The Language of Psychoanalysis*, trans. Donald Nicholson-Smith, New York: W. W. Norton, 1967, p. 288.

9 Melanie Klein, "Envy and Gratitude," in *Envy and Gratitude and Other Works, 1946–1963*, London: The Hogarth Press, 1980, p. 179.

10 Klein, p. 179.

11 Otto Kernberg, *Borderline Conditions and Pathological Narcissism*, Northvale, New Jersey: Jason Aronson, Inc., 1975, 1985, p. 342.

12 Letter to Christopher McCabe and Mimi Brav, July 20, 1983.

13 Letter to Mimi Brav, May 15, 1984.

14 Letter to James Ottis, March (or May) 6, 1983.

15 Letter to Christopher McCabe and Mimi Brav, August 2, 1984.

16 His passion for Hollywood movies may be why, in the mid-fifties, Brakhage

made several efforts to work in Hollywood, first with Alfred Hitchcock, then with Charles Laughton.

17 Letter to Clara Brakhage, New Year's Day, 1957.

18 Letter to Le Vern [no last name provided], August 21, 1985.

19 Letter to Christopher McCabe and Mimi Brav, August 7, 1984.

20 Letter from Clara Brakhage to Stan Brakhage, no month or day, 1953.

21 Letter from Clara Brakhage to Stan Brakhage, March 7, 1956.

22 Tony Pipolo, "Family Business: on Tortured Dust," *Artforum*, March 2014.

23 Letter to Chris McCabe and Mimi Brav, June 17, 1983.

24 Kernberg, op. cit., pp. 228–230.

25 Ibid., p. 267.

26 Letter to Mimi Brav, July 31, 1984.

27 Heinz Kohut, *The Analysis of the Self*, New York: International Universities Press, Inc., 1971.

28 Letter to Charles Boultenhouse, Oct 26, 1983.

29 Letter to Carolee Schneemann, August 20, 1982.

30 Letter to Mimi Brav, May 26, 1984.

31 Letter to Chris McCabe, August 2, 1983.

32 Letter to Andrew Noren, April 30, 1984.

33 Letter to Tom Mapp, Early June, 1971.

34 Letter to Bruce Baillie, September 18, 1985.

35 In 7 *Greeks*, trans., Guy Davenport, New York: New Directions, 1995, p. 32.

36 October 26, 1983.

37 Letter to Guy Davenport, Thanksgiving Day, 1981.

38 Letter to Guy Davenport, February 17, 1982.

39 Guidelines for the Prize Fellows Program, MacArthur Foundation, enclosed with the letter sent to Brakhage.

40 Letter to Guy Davenport, December 29, 1982.

41 Letter to Guy Davenport, July 24, 1983.

42 Letter from Guy Davenport to Stan Brakhage, July 28, 1983.

43 Kernberg, op. cit., p. 227.

44 Davenport did win a MacArthur Foundation Grant in 1990.

45 Letter to Bob Callahan, Feburary 26, 1986. Turtle Island Press published Brakhage's *Film Biographies* (Berkeley: 1977).

46 Kernberg, op.cit., pp. 331–32.

47 Letter to Mimi Brav, August 22, 1984.

48 Letter to Christopher McCabe and Mimi Brav, May 30, 1984.

49 Freud, *Five Lectures on Psychoanalysis* (1910), excerpted in Laplanche and Pontalis, *The Language of Psychoanalysis*, p. 256.

50 *APA Dictionary of Psychology*, Editor in Chief Gary R. VandenBos, Washington, DC: American Psychological Association, 2007, p. 608.

Acknowledgments

THERE WERE SEVERAL PEOPLE who helped me tremendously in the final bringing out of this book after nearly thirty years of dormancy and I'd like to mention them here.

Brad Arnold at the Stan Brakhage Archive, University of Colorado, who knows me in some respects better than I do myself, knows what's in that archive, cares to fill out the interstices with understanding, and can, as I've heard repeatedly from scholars, bring out relevant items that the scholars didn't even know they wanted. His help was tremendous. The work he did with my own photographs as a friend as well as the comprehensive collection of pictorial and documentary items submitted from the archive to the project makes a huge difference in this book.

I met Tony Pipolo in 2013 when he was in Colorado researching for his article about one of Stan's films for Artforum magazine. When I read the article, I realized that I had found the combination film buff/psychoanalyst that I had been hopelessly dreaming of for decades — so I asked if he'd introduce *Brakhage's Childhood,* and I handed him the last paper copy I had, 100,000 words typed on my typewriter. From that gesture, he understood that he was my last hope, so he phoned me every few weeks to make sure that I was doing the work of getting the book in order. I had originally asked for an introduction, but when I saw the power and depth of his writing from reading this book four times through, I asked that it be an afterword. Tony's writing seemed more explanatory than introductory. I highly recommend thinking with him about the person that Stan was as a child and what he grew up to be and to achieve.

I've known P. Adams Sitney since he was in his teens just out of high school with a red beard and he has always been dear. Since I realized that he was quietly goading the work along, I made him do the honors and briefly introduce the book. I was so pleased with his introduction that I told him I bet he'd be good at writing stories, but he graciously said he was happy writing scholarly works.

Paul Wallace Thompson, Lucy Stroock, and Julie Harrison, all three of whose incredible precision and loving care have humbled me and brought me to realize what a wonderful creature a human being can be. Smart, perceptive, sensitive, gracefully orderly, they polished the book, letter by letter, and I bow to them in thanks.

Steve Clay of Granary Books, my old friend, who, in a world surrounded by famous writers, likes my writing, always has, since the *Rolling Stock* days. He kept my hopes up, so that one day I came for lunch and he said he'd worked out a way to publish this book himself, which was what I had wanted all along.

Author Biographies

JANE (BRAKHAGE) WODENING was born in Chicago in 1936. She was married to Stan Brakhage 1957–1987. After the divorce Jane traveled extensively before settling into a cabin in the Rocky Mountains. She now lives in Denver and is the author of several prose collections including *Lump Gulch Tales, From the Book of Legends, Mountain Woman Tales, Moon Songs,* and *Living Up There.*

P. ADAMS SITNEY edited Brakhage's *Metaphors on Vision.* He has written on him in his books *Visionary Film, Modernist Montage, Eyes Upside Down,* and *The Cinema of Poetry.* He is a professor at Princeton University.

TONY PIPOLO is a psychoanalyst in private practice in New York. He is the author of *Robert Bresson: A Passion for Film* and writes regularly on film for *Artforum, Cineaste, Film Comment,* and *The Psychoanlytic Review.*